CRITICAL ACCLAIM FOR *MISS*
BESS MYERSON AND THE YEAR THAT C

"Susan Dworkin has written skillfully about the complex moment in time when Ms. Myerson won the title. Her book is a human and social portrait of immediate postwar days seen from many different angles, each as American as cheesecake. It is a story of women, of Jews, of the Miss America Pageant, and of Bess Myerson herself. . . .

"Ms. Dworkin, an accomplished novelist, admirably portrays Ms. Myerson as a Jewish Miss America facing anti-Semitism and as an intelligent Miss America trying to overcome the empty role of beauty queen. She describes how Ms. Myerson overcame both conflicts during her reign, signing on as a spokeswoman for the Anti-Defamation League. . . .

"Ms. Dworkin's interviews offer some fascinating glimpses into the recent past. The most intriguing character is Lenora Slaughter, the steely woman who raised the Miss America Pageant out of disrespute by trying to 'out-woman' the women's clubs that had attacked it as 'an obscene and disgusting degradation of American girlhood.' It was also Miss Slaughter who asked Bess Myerson to change her name to something less Jewish."
—Ellen Goodman, *The New York Times Book Review*

"A richly detailed personal story of Myerson's life from her childhood in the Bronx through her years as Miss America told under the skillful hand of writer Susan Dworkin. . . . The book re-creates the era with all its corny optimism and its vicious anti-Semitism."
—*Cleveland Plain Dealer*

"Tells
eration
War II,
and—c
—R
Gates

"Th
source:
Myerso
portrait
—*T*

"*Miss America, 1945*, reads with all the suspense not of a whodunnit but of a who-won-it. It hits with a kaleidoscope of moods and impressions: joy, a time of innocence, the warmth and hilarity of family life, the surprise of victory followed soon by shock and ultimate rage."
—James Kirkwood, Pulitzer Prize–winning coauthor of *A Chorus Line*

"Presented is a vivid picture of America in the 1940s with a focus on Myerson's turbulent year as Miss America. But there are humorous parts, too. This is the most palatable format I've encountered in a book penned by a duo. Background and third-person portions are delivered in a smooth narrative manner."
—*Evening Star-Telegram*, Fort Worth, Texas

"Beautifully crafted and highly entertaining . . . it is an important addition to our understanding of the continuing confrontation between the values of Judaism and the American dream."
—*Long Island Jewish World*

"A fascinating inside look at the politics that surrounded the making of the first Jewish Miss America, who, unbeknownst to her public, took it on the chin from anti-Semites everywhere until finally going on a speaking tour for the Anti-Defamation League that would have knocked off anybody's socks."
—*San Francisco Chronicle*

"The book has much to say about who we were in America in the good old, bad old days of World War II. . . . The story of how Bess became the first Jewish 'Miss America,' the racial prejudice and unnerving hatred she endured, the struggle to 'become,' is especially heartrending."
—Liz Smith

"Susan Dworkin's study of Myerson's victory, presented in the context of Myerson's life and times, is a contribution to the study of social and cultural history in twentieth-century America. . . . Dworkin presents the triumph and trauma of the 1945 victory, and a superb study of the Miss America Pageant."
—*New York History*, the quarterly journal of the New York State Historical Association

Miss AMERICA, 1945

Miss AMERICA, 1945

BESS MYERSON AND THE YEAR THAT CHANGED OUR LIVES

———

SUSAN DWORKIN

———

NEWMARKET PRESS
New York

To the memory of
Bella and Louis Myerson

*The author and publisher wish to gratefully acknowledge the following persons for the
use of photographs from their personal collections: Jeni Freeland Berry, Frank Havens,
Gloria Bair Kienle, Vicki Gold Levi, and Ruth Singer. All other photographs that appear
inside this book are from the personal collection of Bess Myerson. We also thank the
Miss America Pageant Office in Atlantic City for their help in obtaining photographs.*

1   3   5   7   9   10   8   6   4   2   (pb)

Originally published by Newmarket Press in hardcover in 1987 as
Miss America, 1945: Bess Myerson's Own Story.
First paperback edition published in the year 2000.

Library of Congress Cataloging-in-Publication Data

Dworkin, Susan.
Miss America, 1945: Bess Myerson and the Year That Changed Our Lives /
by Susan Dworkin.
cm.
1. Myerson, Bess. 2. Beauty contestants—United States—Biography.
3. Miss America Pageant, Atlantic City, N.J.
I. Title.
HQ1220.U5M953 1998
305.4'092'4—dc19
[B]   98-18445
                                CIP

ISBN 1-55704-000-1 (hc)
ISBN 1-55704-381-7 (pb)

QUANTITY PURCHASES
Companies, professional groups, clubs, and other organizations may qualify for
special terms when ordering quantities of this title. For information, write Special
Sales Department, Newmarket Press, 18 East 48th Street, New York, NY 10017;
call (212) 832-3575; fax (212) 832-3629; or email newmktprs@aol.com.

www.newmarketpress.com

Designed by Ruth Kolbert

Manufactured in the United States of America

Acknowledgments

The interviews that make up so large a part of this book were conducted during an eighteen-month period between February 1986 and July 1987. Some of the most important do not appear in print. However, they served as vital background and provided me with ways of understanding and listening I would not have been able to discover otherwise. Some other individuals who saw my publisher's advertisements took the trouble to write and contribute important facts. I am grateful to all of these people for generously offering their time and recollections:

Karen Aarons, Lib Aldredge, Veronica Anderson, Jeni Freeland Berry, Billie Biederman, Marcella Cisney, Maureen Connelly, Mary Corey, John Gilbert Craig, Jr., Richard Figueroa, Arnold Forster, Harold Glasser, Martha Glazer, Ginger Gomprecht, Sylvia Grace, Barra Grant, Lucille Harteveldt, Jimmy Hatcher, Frank Havens, Bill Henderson, Jean Hogue, Byron Janis, Candy Jones, Nat Kameny, Gilbert Katz, Gloria Kienle, Zelma Kornheiser, Gabe Kosakoff, Vicki Gold Levi, Arlene Anderson Low, Al Marks, Lola Martin Castigan, Ruth McCandliss, Lenore Miller Baker, Donald Oresman, Murray Panitz, Ruth Patterson, Adrian Phillips, Denis Piermont, Marilyn Rogers, Miriam Freund Rosenthal, Ted Rubin, Harold Sachs, Ernest Sardo, May Satchell, Norman Shamberg, Ruth Singer, Murray Sklaroff, Lenora Slaughter Frapert, Sophie Smith, Brant Snavely,

Gloria Steinem, Dr. Calvin Terwilliger, Charles Turner, Lester Waldman, Margie Wallis, Helen Weiss, David Wheeler, James Wilson, Gloria Winter.

My thanks as well to Karen Aarons of the Miss America Pageant; Fred Taraba of the Society of Illustrators; Al Mann of the Veterans Administration; and Vicki Gold Levi, who unlocked whole archives of memories. I am deeply grateful to Suzanne Goldstein, Theresa Burns, and Esther Margolis for their tireless work on the manuscript; to Nancy Rose of Levine, Thall & Plotkin; and to Barra Grant.

For her unswerving commitment to this project and her boundless energy in rediscovering the past, I thank Bess Myerson.

Susan Dworkin

CONTENTS

*Does this mean
that it was not really me whom you loved,
but only what I pretended to be?*

—ALICE MILLER,
in *The Drama of the Gifted Child*

CHAPTER 1

The Title and the Moment

It was the spring of 1945.

I was just graduating from Hunter College, which was a free tuition city school in those days. It was unheard of in our circle for a single girl to take her own apartment. So I was still living at home with my parents and my younger sister Helen in our crowded one-bedroom place in the Bronx. I would have liked to get married. Most of my girlfriends had already done so. We barely had a date for four years. Now suddenly the men came home from the war and everyone was tying the knot. I was one of the last single girls in our group.

What I wanted most of all was to go on for a graduate degree in music at Juilliard or Columbia and study conducting—that was my dream, to be a conductor. Unfortunately, I didn't have the means.

A retiring piano teacher had bequeathed me seven or eight students to add to the half dozen I had already acquired on my own. They paid me fifty cents an hour for the lessons I gave them, and that was barely enough to cover the cost of carfare and lunch and my own piano lessons.

My father couldn't help me. He was a house painter. He would laugh and say, "We're not poor, Besseleh, it's just that we don't have any money. . . ." What I needed was a scholarship. However, all the free money for education that year had been allocated to the returning GIs, who deserved every assistance to pull their lives back together.

Nobody was thinking about what girls needed in 1945. Nobody except this beauty pageant in Atlantic City.

———

IF THEY HAD BUBBLE GUM CARDS FOR MISS AMERICAS LIKE they do for baseball and now football players, maybe somebody would collect the cards—little kids, maybe, in school yards and at balloon-studded conventions—and the beautiful girls would not be forgotten.

The cards could have all the vital statistics. "She endorsed Divine Aura Soap, she had a thirty-six-inch bust, she came from Outback, Kansas, she had thirty-seven-inch hips, she raised two million dollars in War Bonds, she measured forty-two inches from crotch to toe. She tried to be a singer. She worked as a model." She tried very hard.

The truth is that after the measurements, there are very few statistics any little kid would want to trade. The extraordinary achievements of a Miss America (that stuff about the War Bonds) are buried by the perfect relativity of those hips and that bust—and her dreams and aspirations (that stuff about wanting to be a singer) linger only if they come true and take her to stardom. Usually they don't.

Most likely the vital statistics for the beautiful girl would end up on her husband's card, which could read something like this:

"Joe 'Buck' Sinew, nose tackle for the Santa Monica Bombers, intercepted six passes in one game against the Nogales Mammoths before going into the insurance business and becoming a millionaire and giving generously to major charities through the medium of his particularly lovely wife. (Rumor has it she was once Miss America . . .)"

Clearly they don't have bubble gum cards for Miss Americas because nose tackles are more important in our country than beautiful girls, and everybody knows that, most of all the public who watched the Miss America Pageant on TV and for a moment in time made the beautiful girl very famous.

Unlike a good football game, the Pageant lacks memorability because it lacks process. Eleven men against eleven men—now, that's a competition, fair and thrilling. But one girl against forty-nine others is just odd, and to a citizen with a consciousness even slightly raised, rather chilling. So the public—which can hardly be said to have a raised consciousness—even the sexist public gets no afterkick from the Pageant, except maybe a few moments of fun disputing the judges' decisions. No excitement worthy of replay survives. The wit and strength and courage needed to complete every play are hidden. The girls don't sweat or grimace; they seem perfectly calm. They smile and stroll and sing (or whatever they do) and parade what we all know is a given beauty that no one not especially endowed by God and nature can expect to possess in the first place.

No, the Miss America Pageant is no sporting event. It's more like a meal. You eat it; it's terrific; you go to sleep.

Given all that, it is truly amazing when the fame of being Miss America adheres and endures through a lifetime. The beauty queens don't expect it to—not anymore, at least. They're wised up nowadays. The records of their moment of glory lie in a dank storehouse in Atlantic City.

Their scrapbooks are full and fun for grandchildren to leaf through, but time may make them seem a little ridiculous, and if the lady is smart, they gather the dust of self-effacement.

So what do you do when the fame that was supposed to pass lingers on?

What do you make of your life when every victory, every catastrophe, every mundane little event—the giving of a speech, the getting of a job, the birth of a granddaughter—is parenthesized by this former glory?

If everyone thinks it's so little to be Miss America, why does it still almost always adjoin the name of Bess Myerson?

In the 1950s and '60s, when she was famous as a television personality on shows like "I've Got a Secret" and "The Big Pay-off" ... in the 1970s and '80s, when she was famous as New York's Commissioner of Consumer Affairs and then Cultural Affairs, she was still invariably identified as "the former Miss America ..."

This variegated career, braided with the strains of stardom and politics and a tumultuous private life, had its inception in one root year, 1945–46, the year that Bess Myerson served her term as Miss America. She took the crown off her own head in September 1946 and thought, "Well that's it, it's over." But it wasn't over.

Part of the adhesive that glued Bess Myerson to her Miss America title was the extraordinary complexity of the moment in history in which she won it.

In September 1945, America had just accepted the surrender of its enemies in the Second World War. The atomic bomb had just been dropped on Japan. The Nazi death camps had just been liberated. Joy reigned. But a knowledge of evil, a certitude of extinction never before experienced by people, was becoming part of the world's personality.

No country in history had ever seemed stronger than our country at that moment. We set out to build the American century with confidence and verve. Confetti poured like a shower of gold over dancing soldiers and their ecstatic girls in Times Square. Hundreds of thousands of New Yorkers turned out to cheer the returning conqueror of the Nazi empire, General Dwight D. Eisenhower.

It is shocking to see Ike in the news photos, waving to the crowds as he stands unguarded in an open car; no Secret Service men; no fear.

In Italy, UNRRA took over Mussolini's love nest. In Germany, GIs from the 101st Airborne put their feet up on the long oak tables at Hitler's captured mountain retreat. Guys from the American 20th Armored Division took joy rides in Hermann Goering's Mercedes-Benz.

There are still people in this country who won't drive that make of car.

The hot movie of the year was *Incendiary Blonde* with Betty Hutton. The best-selling book was *Brave Men* by Ernie Pyle. The top hit record was "Atchison, Topeka, and Santa Fe" with Bing Crosby and Johnny Mercer. Girls learned from their beauty magazines that the most glamorous thing to be in the summer of 1945 was tan tan tan. They donned their new two-piece bathing suits. They whipped out their reflectors.

Who knew from skin cancer in those days?

In August, after Hiroshima and Nagasaki had been destroyed by the American bombs, American forces were still trying to "flush out" Japanese soldiers who continued fighting and hiding in the caves and pillboxes of Pacific islands. They used a weapon then known as a "jellied flamethrower." Grisly pictures of Japanese soldiers roasting to death appeared in *Life* magazine.

No one objected to the use of this forerunner of napalm. No one boycotted the manufacturer.

Eisenhower, in his wisdom, invited delegations of congressmen and news reporters and photographers into the concentration camps that American forces had liberated in the spring of 1945. The reports of these horrified visitors boggled the minds of most Americans. *Movietone News*, which always preceded the feature films in the movie theaters, brought home footage of the mass graves, the emaciated cadavers, the horror-bombed faces of insane survivors. People gasped and covered the eyes of their children. Soon their senses shut down. It was too much to absorb, too painful to imagine. "Thank God the mad dog Hitler has been defeated," they thought. "Thank God this will never happen again. Now let's get on with the main feature . . . let's get on with the best years of our lives . . . let's get on with the American century."

Historians of the period say it was a time of maximum naïveté, unbridled hopefulness, and by hindsight, an almost pathological insensitivity to misfortune. Geoffrey Perrett wrote, "The ruling passions of the postwar era were security and identity."[1] The American dream, wrote John Morton Blum, was "a little white house in the suburbs where a young wife wearing a pretty blue dress and an anniversary bracelet would greet her veteran husband every evening with slippers to change into from his Johnston and Murphy shoes, with a Scotch whiskey highball and a sirloin steak. . . ."[2]

No one made a judgment as to whether this young nation was actually ready to lead the world. Too exhausted from the war, too eager to go home and be safe and dry again, we accepted unsophisticated reasons for our victory. We thought we had won because we were *right*, and with the sins of Europe and Asia still setting the standard for evil, we did not look closely at our own society.

"Racism was a national disgrace, only just being recognized as such," wrote William L. O'Neill. "Poverty, though widespread, was largely ignored. Sexism flourished. Today nothing about the postwar era seems more peculiar than the universal indifference to women's rights."[3]

"Most people weren't thinking of the war's cost then," Bess Myerson said. "They were just glad the war was over, that the boys were coming home, that red meat and nylon stockings and gas for the car would no longer be rationed. We heard that soon we would have antibiotics to cure every disease and splendid plastics and air conditioning and jet planes to travel by and television in the living room of every house. It was the happiest time I ever remember . . . all the people were happy . . . except for the people who had lost their sons in the war . . . except for the Jews, who had lost everything. . . ."

There it was, the thing that made being Miss America different for Bessie Myerson of the Bronx. As the first and only Jewish Miss America, she shared her victory with five million American Jews who had just lost six million of their coreli-

[1] Geoffrey Perrett, *A Dream of Greatness: The American People, 1945–1963* (New York: Coward, McCann & Geoghegan, 1979), p. 69.
[2] John Morton Blum, *V Was for Victory: Politics and American Culture During World War II* (New York: Harcourt Brace Jovanovich, 1976), p. 104.
[3] William L. O'Neill, *American High: The Years of Confidence,1945–1960* (New York, The Free Press, 1986), p. 39.

gionists in Europe. For them she was a symbol. They saw *themselves* in the piles of bodies on *Movietone News,* they saw their own children, and a beauty queen like Bess or a great baseball player like Hank Greenberg somehow jolted them from the nightmare and proved to them that they were still alive.

In the Jewish community she was the most famous pretty girl since Queen Esther in ancient Persia. A man who had escaped the gas chambers recalled that he had first heard her name in a displaced-persons camp in Czechoslovakia. Girls from Brooklyn put her picture on the bathroom mirror and tried to do their hair the way she did hers. "If you were in high school at the time of her victory," said a New York Jewish doctor who graduated from DeWitt Clinton in 1947, "Bess Myerson was the most important female image in your life. We didn't just know about her. We *felt* her."

After forty-two years, many of us have begun to study that moment in 1945 when, like Bess Myerson in Atlantic City, we feasted on victory and expected the best. The year 1945 was supposed to be the birthday of a new world. We are still trying to figure out what the hell happened.

Miss America 1945 is one of our best witnesses, as full of contradictions as the moment itself. She was the wrong girl with the right stuff. A concert pianist parading in a bathing suit before audiences of legmen; a Jewish liberal made queen-for-a-year in a nation of bigots. The masks of the moment were her masks, too. Like many a Bronx native, she left her regional accent uptown. Like many a child of the Depression, she felt poor long after she was rich. Like many of her countrywomen in those days before the second feminist awakening, she submerged her own obvious strengths beneath the comportment of dependency.

Forty-two years have passed, so she is old enough to have grown up but not old enough to have grown old.

Still tingling with the memory of the applause, she tells how she knocked 'em dead.

Wagging her finger like a Jewish mother, she warns of the pitfalls of vanity and celebrity.

7

Blend her voice with those of scores of others who were there when she was Miss America, when it was thought that fascism would never rise again and no one would ever need another bomb, and you get oral history, you get a mixed chorus singing a faintly funny, slightly bitter, often self-mocking song that might as well be called "The Joke's on Us."

Time has blunted the rage of these voices and exacerbated their regrets. They won't name names; they underplay, euphemize, insist on editing their memories. The style of their recollections tends to bear out the recent claim that "the more psychodynamically important a memory is, the more prone it is to warping or forgetting altogether."[4] So they protect the reputations of people who might have been their worst enemies when they were younger, because experience has brought them a sense of shared vulnerability to the judgments of history.

Odd details surface. The orange hue of wartime stockings. The white fingers of a beloved teacher. The funny title of a dead song. The metallic glint of a steel hook where a young man once wore his own hand.

Forty years after the Second World War, Ernie Sardo, a veteran who met Bess in Atlantic City in 1945, went back to the SS hospital at Heppenheim where he lay dying as a young soldier, and he wondered why he had been spared.

Lenora Slaughter, shaper of the Miss America Pageant, the lady who gave Bess its first scholarship, enjoyed the respect of journalists who treated her (irony of ironies!) as though she were a foremother of women's liberation.

Arnold Forster of the Anti-Defamation League of B'nai B'rith, who worked with Bess on the great brotherhood campaigns of the late 1940s, looked back through his files and contemplated the days when Jews and blacks met for lunch to plot how they might wean the American public from the poisoned wine of racism.

Days long gone. Results never imagined.

---

[4] Theodore Shapiro quoted in Daniel Goleman, "In Memory, People Recreate Their Lives to Suit Their Images of the Present," *The New York Times* (June 23, 1987), p. C1 *et passim*.

The Title and the Moment

Bess Myerson opened her scrapbooks and said: "This was it. This was me forty-two years ago. This was when I was an unspoiled beauty, a provincial from the Bronx, a babe in the woods, a virgin, catapulted into a world I understood nothing about. Do you think I knew anything then? I knew absolutely nothing."

CHAPTER 2

The
Myersons
of the Bronx

My father's name was Louis. He had golden hands. He could build anything. Fix anything. His drive for perfection made him a genius among house painters, but it also prevented him from earning good money. The efforts of his assistants never satisfied him. He would pay them and then go back and do their work all over again.

Dad arrived in this country from Russia in 1907 at the age of eighteen. He worked to bring over the other members of his family. He always insisted that he fell in love with my mother from the moment they met. They married in 1915 when she was twenty-three and he was twenty-six, and for the next sixty-five years the two of them were united in a sort of Kafkaesque dance, perpetual devotion alternating with undying hostility.

They argued constantly.

Although now that I think about it, they didn't argue. My mother argued. My father surrendered.

We were three sisters in our family. I am the middle one, born in 1924. Sylvia is seven years older than I am; Helen is two years younger. We grew up during the Depression, in the Sholom Aleichem Cooperative Houses in the Bronx.

Mom and Dad had originally set up housekeeping in Harlem. Their next move was to Prospect Avenue in the South Bronx. Then they joined the original owners of the Sholom Aleichem, where Dad bought a five-room apartment for one thousand dollars. The apartment was large but unfortunately turned out to be quite dark, with windows facing the courtyard. Mom decided that we needed a sunnier place for my sister Helen, who had asthma. We found one—but it had only one bedroom.

Mom and Dad slept on a sofa-bed in the living room. We girls shared the bedroom, which looked out on Fort Independence Park and Reservoir. Each of use lived there until she was married.

My older sister, Sylvia, became my mentor. She was five-seven and the most voluptuous among us, a fine swimmer—a life-saving instructor, in fact. She knew how to seize opportunities: how to get A's, take subways to Brooklyn, make money, tell hilarious stories. I looked to her as an authority figure and often a surrogate mother as well, because Mom somehow lacked the tender, nuturing skills.

For example, Sylvia helped me decide what to wear.

My mother never told me what to wear. Somehow she didn't believe in the importance of looking nice. It was not a lack of money that deterred her from buying clothes for us. It was the value of clothing that eluded her. In our household, we wore hand-me-downs until we could work and earn money and buy our own.

Helen appeared to be the most delicate one among us because she had a slight frame, and her asthma gave her a certain pallor.

I was built like a boy—a tall, skinny boy, all gangly legs and dangling long arms. To give myself "hips" I sometimes put my summer shorts on under my school skirts.

As is so often the case, our family stereotypes proved misleading. Sylvia, "the strong one," married the first man she met who could stand up to the scrutiny and criticism that Mom turned on all our boyfriends. Helen, "the delicate one," flew away on planes to Europe, traveled cross country with friends, and experienced a freedom that Sylvia and I never dreamed of. And me, "the awkward one," I grew up to be Miss America.

Of course, Helen may tell you I was the tough one; Sylvia may tell you I was the weak one; and we're all right about each other, and we're all wrong. What really mattered was that when we were needy or hurting, we were there for each other.

THE SHOLOM ALEICHEM COOPERATIVE HOUSES WHERE LOUIS and Bella Myerson raised their daughters was a multibuilding complex built in 1926–27. It housed about 250 families, all of them working-class, Jewish, and, at least nominally, politically liberal. They were part of the massive pre-Depression exodus from what would now be called inner-city neighborhoods, which caused the Jewish population of Manhattan to decline from 706,000 in 1923 to 297,000 in 1930. Of this number, two thirds went north to the Bronx. These people chose the Bronx partly for its natural beauty. They wanted a neighborhood with trees and parks and abundant fresh air, where they could raise their American-born children. They also chose it because other neighborhoods outside Manhattan wouldn't let them in. Jackson Heights openly advertised that it was "restricted," with "no Catholics, Jews, or dogs" allowed.[1] The Queensboro Corporation went to court to fight for the right to restrict home sales to Gentiles and won.[2]

In general, the Jews of that era showed marked disinterest in challenging the status quo of ethnic restrictiveness. They had recent European memories of violence and race hatred. More they didn't need.

"My father told me a story about when he was a little boy in Russia," Bess said. "Around Eastertime, when the church service was particularly anti-Semitic, the local gangs would often get drunk and launch a *pogrom* on the Jewish part of town. If the military needed recruits that year, the hooligans would be told to grab the Jewish boys and turn them over for lifetime service. The boys would then be converted to Russian Orthodoxy. Their families would never see them again.

"During one of these attacks, my father's father hid him and

<hr/>

[1] *Building a Borough: Architecture and Planning in the Bronx, 1890–1940* (New York: Bronx Museum of the Arts, 1986), p. 60.
[2] Ibid.

his cousin under the floorboards of the kitchen. When the *pogrom* ended and the Jewish families were picking up the pieces, they opened the trapdoor in the kitchen floor and brought up the two young boys.

"My father had passed out from lack of air. His cousin was dead, suffocated.

"My father kept saying that Americans were different, better, less filled with hate; good people, he said. However, he still didn't take any chances. He lived among his own kind."

Nobody in the New York area enjoyed apartment living as much as the Jews. For reasons historical and cultural, physical privacy meant less to them than to other groups. They appreciated the security of having folks who were just like them all around and close by. It didn't last long, this love affair with the apartment. Eventually the Jewish people accepted the single-family suburban house ideal like other Americans. But in the mid-1920s, the clustered, symbiotic units of the Sholom Aleichem reminded the inhabitants subliminally of the close-knit European *shtetls*, the small Jewish towns where they had been raised.

Equally important, those who like Bella and Louis Myerson subscribed to socialist values distrusted private property and land-owning in principle. In describing the relationship between the ornate, castlelike Sholom Aleichem buildings that architect George Springsteen had designed and the hardworking, unpretentious people within, the art historians of the Bronx Museum pointed out: "Their ideal was the opposite of a private cottage surrounded by green grass. It was closer to a people's palace, involving the achievement of a monumentality of expression not possible through individualism."[3]

The Sholom Aleichem buildings (they stand to this day) were four-story walk-ups identical to each other and divided into sections from "A" to "O." They cascaded down a very steep hill between Sedgwick Avenue on the top side past 238th Street to Cannon Place on the bottom. The Myerson apartment was on the third floor of one of the buildings whose actual address read

[3] Ibid., p. 65.

"Giles Place." Its stairway carried the daughters past neighbors chatting on the landings, past flirtations and arguments, through the heart of a warm, busy community buzzing with gossip. The roof was a "tar beach" where people gathered to hang laundry and socialize and sun themselves in the summer.

It was a common thing in those days for several branches of one family to move into the same development, a European tradition of closeness that would evaporate in subsequent American generations. Bella Myerson's sister Ethel and her brothers Pete and Jack as well as Louis's brothers Sam and Alter lived nearby. Bella's sister Fanny and Louis's two sisters, Yetta and Lena, all lived in other apartments within the same project. If Bess wanted to go over to her Aunt Fanny's apartment and play the piano accompaniment while her Cousin Harold sang operatic arias in his beautiful baritone, she could save time by walking across the rooftops that connected the building sections.

Across the street, Fort Independence Park fairly burst with activity, its many programs reflecting the genius of the then parks commissioner, Robert Moses. Children from the Sholom Aleichem could enjoy afterschool baseball games, punchball, formalized jacks tournaments, and classes in weaving and painting that were free to all. Bess and her friends played marbles on the concrete walkways, collecting "immies" and "steelies." On summer evenings after dinner, neighbors would settle on the benches to talk, or gather around to kibitz a chess game at one of the tables provided for that purpose. Friends from the other large Bronx cooperatives—the Amalgamated and the Coops— might come by for a cup of tea and a piece of cake. A cricket hum of conversation filled the night air. No one who was there then remembers any muggers. No one remembers feeling any sense of danger.

The Sholom Aleichem went bankrupt in the Depression. The bank took over and in 1931 sold the buildings to a private landlord. As the tenants (like so many others in America) lost their jobs, their fellow coop members set up a rent relief fund to pay half the unemployed tenants' rent until they could find other work.

In August 1932 the landlord evicted forty tenants anyway. The whole building went on a rent strike. Bess and her sisters and cousins helped on the picket line after school. The landlord responded by evicting the strikers. The tenants went to court, threatening to move in one large body to another building. Finally the landlord agreed to a rent reduction and the creation of a fund to reduce the indebtedness of the unemployed tenants.

Bess and her childhood friend Ruth Singer both have memories of evicted coop owners on the streets, with all their worldly possessions and their crying children.

"We would be coming home from P.S. 24, our first school," Bess recalled, "and as we rounded the corner of the courtyard entrance, we would see the contents of someone's apartment on the sidewalk. Our hearts would stop. We'd be breathless with fear that it might be *our* belongings out there, our furniture, our baby sister or brother in the carriage. We all knew perfectly well that we could be the next ones in the coop to go broke.

"However, no coop member ever wandered homeless, even in those hard times. If a family was evicted, someone took the children, someone else took the living-room sofa, another neighbor housed the mother and father until they could find jobs and provide for themselves again."

In addition to mutually held social ideals, Sholom Aleichem residents shared an overriding belief in education. They expected their children to attend college. They had given up their interest in religion. Ruth Singer cannot remember the presence of a rabbi in the coop. However, their cooperative in particular was inspired by a love of *Yiddishkeit,* the Yiddish language and the wit and wisdom of its literature and more generally by a dedication to *Kultur*—the arts.

From their inception, the buildings included a large auditorium where a musical ensemble or a drama group could perform and where dances and other festivities could be held. Special studios were built to encourage the membership of artists in the cooperative. Bess remembered Aaron Goodelman, a sculptor; Abraham Maniewich, a painter; a poetess named Malka Lee; and Isaac Raboy, who wrote Jewish cowboy stories. "I loved the artists," Bess said. "I would hang around their studios hoping they would invite me in to see a painting in progress, or hear a new poem. They enchanted and inspired me. They never made me feel I was intruding."

The idea that you could bring artists into a community, let them sit and work under the noses of your children and thus inspire your children to a greater appreciation of artistic achievement was not unique to Jews or socialists. Examples abound in all societies that recognize that public appreciation and an understanding neighborhood are probably as important to the working artist as money; the return on such an investment has virtually no limit.

The artists in the Sholom Aleichem complex did not bring with them an ethic of professionalism. Who would dare to claim superior status by virtue of being a professional when most artists in the 1930s were only working thanks to the dole of such agencies as the WPA or the Federal Writers Project? At the Sholom Aleichem, success was not the measure of the artist. Participation was. Anybody who wrote poetry could call himself a poet. Anybody who made paintings could display them in the public rooms.

Such an egalitarian atmosphere may not have raised up more great artists than, say, Italy under the Borgias. But it did raise up a great audience—personally involved, familiar with the artistic process, respectful of artistic effort—and that more than anything would work to make New York the cultural capital of the nation.

"It seemed to me that almost every child in the buildings took piano or violin," Bess said. "The place resounded with music. There was an unwritten rule that you could not practice after nine o'clock at night because the tenants—truckers, butchers, garment workers, blue-collar people—rose early and needed their sleep."

Mrs. Myerson was determined that her girls should become musicians, an ambition that dominated her relationship with them to the exclusion of almost everything else.

"Mom never sat still in the house and enjoyed our practicing or talked with us. She talked *at* us," Bess said. "She was always rushing out, bringing containers of vegetable soup or old clothes to someone who needed them. Hourly journeys here and there, across the rooftops. Then she would return suddenly from one of her forays and just shout random orders—one-word orders: 'Homework!' 'Practice!' Or if the three of us were eating supper and talking, she would command us from her station at the stove, *'Finish!'*

"In that crowded little apartment, Mom managed to install a secondhand grand piano, which dominated our living room. My father found remnants of carpet on different jobs he did, brought them home, and stitched them together with this enormous needle. Then he slipped the patchwork rug under the piano so that the neighbors downstairs would not be disturbed by our practicing.

"The fact that my mother and her neighbors might need to spend their money for clothes and shoes did not deter them from spending it on music lessons instead.

"The fact that their children might have no musical talent did not deter them, either.

"Music was like politics, and politics was like eating: an ordinary, integral part of daily life."

The politics of the Sholom Aleichem houses were simple. There were no Republicans or Democrats. There were the so-called Communists—known as *der Linke*, the Left; the so-called socialists, known as *der Rechte*, the Right; and that was all. The socialists were generally trade unionists and labor Zionists, members of the Workmen's Circle (the *Arbeiter Ring*). They read the *Jewish Daily Forward* and *The Day*. The Communists read *Der Freiheit* and *The Daily Worker* and often belonged to the International Workers Order.

Sophie Smith, a former neighbor who often hired Bess to baby-sit for her children, laughed about the politics in the Sholom Aleichem. "You couldn't call our communists 'Communists,' " she commented. "They were just sort of left of the socialists. We also had an anarchist group in the buildings. Their main activity during the year was to go down to the cafeteria on Yom Kippur, when all the rest of the Jewish people in the whole world were fasting, and have a nice big dinner."

Each group had a *schule*—a folk school—where many Sholom Aleichem children would study Yiddish language after regular hours at the new public school, P.S. 95. During the elementary grades, Bess was sent to both *schules* consecutively. As far as she was concerned, the principal difference between them was that the right-wing *schule* was on the right side of the courtyard and the left-wing *schule* was on the left side.

"I remember the teachers: Aaron Bromberg on the right and Itchy Goldberg on the left. Goldberg liked me because Dad had taken great pains to teach me Yiddish and I could speak it fluently. He would ask me to go to the head of the class to recite verses by Heinrich Heine or the various funny poems my father had taught me. One poem was about a serious dignified scholar who locks himself away from the world. Along comes a girl who teaches him to dance. He gets married, neglects his scholarly pursuits, and is soon pushing a baby carriage in the park like all the other henpecked husbands. Which just goes to show you that the flesh is weak and we are all vulnerable.

"I loved standing up and reciting those poems at the head of Itchy Goldberg's class.

"It wasn't until years later, when I read Irving Howe's *World of Our Fathers*, that I realized Itchy was supposed to have been teaching us Stalinist doctrine."

If Louis Myerson sent his daughter Bess to both *schules*, it was probably because he had made it his political policy to participate in everything and commit to nothing. Bess recalls sitting up half the night in the auditorium, painting placards that proclaimed "Justice for the Workers" and "Jobs for Everyone" and then going down to Union Square the next day to march with her class in the May Day Parade. On the other hand, she also recalls that Louis joined the IWO primarily because of its excellent burial society program. "His interest did not go deeper than six feet," she said with a laugh.

For those of Bess's childhood friends who came from truly politicized families, the right-left split was no laughing matter. Ruth Singer, for example, attended a left-wing summer camp called Kinderland, where the children's bunks were named for Soviet Socialist republics.

In 1929, Jewish cooperatives like the Sholom Aleichem, the Coops, and the Amalgamated were divided into warring factions by Arab attacks on Jewish settlers in Palestine.

Der Freiheit, the Yiddish-language newspaper of the far left, supported the Arabs and carried what looked to its readership very much like anti-Semitic cartoons.

The readership reacted with fury. Leading Yiddish writers

stopped writing for *Der Freiheit.* In short order the newspaper dropped the anti-Zionist aspect of the party line.[4]

Ten years later, the ever-smoldering conflict between the left and its Jewish adherents would erupt again around the Stalin-Hitler pact. Ruth Singer remembered one neighbor at the Sholom Aleichem who said she would continue to support Joe Stalin if he made a pact with the devil himself. However, the nefarious pact and the subsequent Soviet hostility to Israel caused the large majority of Jewish leftists to abandon the letter of their old political faith.

Bess's father, Louis, stayed aloof from the party divisions. He took that path that, as Irving Howe pointed out, was common among thoughtful moderates—"to be a nonparty leftist engaged in 'cultural activity.' " This "probably made it a little easier to tolerate political doctrines that a strict scrutiny might have found intolerable."[5] He enjoyed hearing the visiting playwrights like H. Leivick (*The Golem*) read from their works on a Friday evening. He enjoyed seeing Joseph Buloff performing one of his satirical theater scenes.

"Dad read incessantly," Bess recalled, "both Jewish authors and American writers like Poe and Hawthorne whose works we were studying in school. Mom read very little because her reading skills in English were poor and also because she was not relaxed enough to sit and read. Dad loved to have a cup of tea with his friends after a performance, to sit around expounding on everything from Henry Wallace to the war in Spain to the destiny of the Yankees. Mom despised this kind of schmoozing, just as she opposed any effort we made to stop and chat with the kids in the park. She felt: Why waste your time socializing when you could practice, or study?

"I empathized with Dad's need for company and entertainment. I knew how frustrated he was that Mom could not share that aspect of his life, but I had no inkling of the complex emotions that bound them to each other."

For Louis Myerson, the magnetism of the cooperative came

---

[4] Irving Howe, *World of Our Fathers* (New York: Simon & Schuster, 1976), p. 342.
[5] Ibid.; see "A Network of Culture," pp. 341–47.

not from politics but directly from Mr. Sholom Rabinovitch, Sholom Aleichem himself.

Born in 1859 in the Ukraine, Sholom Aleichem (it means "Peace Be with You" in Hebrew and Yiddish) was a government rabbi, a clerk, and a business speculator who finally gave it all up to be a writer.

He turned out hundreds of wonderful Yiddish stories and novellas and poems and little plays; he became the king of comedy, the Jewish Mark Twain. It was Sholom Aleichem's stories of Tevye the Dairyman and his many daughters that formed the basis for the phenomenally successful musical *Fiddler on the Roof.* His tales of the Wise Men of Chelm, whose monumental stupidity reminds people of bureaucracies and banking institutions in all times and locations, are frequently given to Jewish children to arm them with the precious lesson that life is often best illuminated by the bunglings of fools.

When Sholom Aleichem died in New York on May 31, 1916, more than 150,000 people came to his funeral. Like the funeral of the great Egyptian singer Oum Kalthoum in Cairo fifty years later, the enormity of this spontaneous outpouring showed that the people—so often ridiculed as ignorant and callous—were neither; they simply save the full measure of their love for those few great artists who have a real handle on the collective soul.

With characteristic wit and prescience, Sholom Aleichem left an ethical will. Among his dicta was the request that on the day of his death, his descendants dispense with the mourning and the heavy candles and just get together and tell each other funny stories.

And so in all the years since then, pockets of Jews—some of them related to Sholom Aleichem, some of them relating simply to his spirit—assemble at the end of May and make each other laugh.

The point, of course, is that when you are blue and down and you have reason to weep, your best bet is to go out and seek the healing powers of comedy. This is precisely what Louis Myerson would do. He would come home late at night, knocked out from painting and repainting walls, and in the warmth of his little kitchen he would relax and share a laugh with his favorite daughter, Bessie.

From my earliest years, as long as I can remember, my father always returned from work very late. I would lie awake, watching the passing headlights shine on the ceiling of our room, listening to Helen's asthmatic breathing, waiting for Dad. At ten or eleven o'clock, the lights from his old car would finally hit the ceiling. He would flick them on and off to let me know he was home. I'd slip out of bed, put on my bathrobe, and tiptoe into the kitchen, trying not to wake my mother in the living room, and I would meet him at the door.

He'd be spattered with paint. He'd have splinters in his fingers. He'd be hungry but smiling. He'd wash up and I would reheat his dinner.

I'd pick the paint out of his hair and off his ears; I'd sterilize a needle in the gas jet on the stove, then very carefully remove the splinters from his fingers. To this day I can picture my father's hands, strong and calloused, heavily veined. Beautiful hands. While he ate, I would review my homework with him. Then he would ask me to read to him from his newspaper, first in Yiddish, then translating into English. He would always ask me to turn to the humor page with the cartoons and the funny stories.

Like this one . . . this is an old story. . . .

"A son does very well in his business and moves up in the world. He Anglicizes his name and rents an apartment on the posh Upper East Side. Then he invites his mother to visit.

"Well, the elderly mother journeys uptown and she arrives at the building. However, she doesn't go upstairs. She remains in the lobby.

"Meanwhile, the son is getting worried. Where's Mama? He calls home; no answer. Where's Mama? He goes downstairs and sees her sitting there.

" 'Ma!' he says, 'what's the matter? Why didn't you come upstairs?'

"She says, 'To tell you the truth, I looked on the tenants list to find your apartment number but I couldn't remember your new name.' "

21

Every summer, when Bess and Sylvia and Helen were away working as camp counselors, Louis Myerson would come home with some wallpaper left over from one of his decorating jobs and he would paint or repaper the girls' bedroom. To alleviate the feeling of claustrophobia in the small apartment, he invented innumerable space-saving devices. He covered a nook in the foyer with the bindings of books, glued over bas-relief carvings of books so the effect was indistinguishable from the real thing. From out of this *trompe l'oeil* library one could pull a drop-top desk. A typewriter would slide out on a shelf. Above that, a section of the faked books was made into a trapdoor that concealed a telephone. Louis placed a one-legged brass monkey on the trapdoor.

"He was always challenging visitors, especially the boys who would come to take us out, to find the telephone," Bess said with a laugh. "And these unfortunate young men would frantically grope the walls like Gene Wilder in *Young Frankenstein,* looking for the trapdoor.

"Of course they never found it, because to get the telephone to slide out on its little shelf, you had to pull the leg of the brass monkey. . . ."

Louis had an old jalopy (named Molly) in which he transported his paints and brushes; his stiff, spattered drop cloths; and his daughters. Molly smelled of turpentine. She often broke down. Bess and her sisters never worried, because Louis could fix anything. "He would lean over the sputtering motor and say, 'Molly, Molly, how could you do this to me? What have I done to deserve this bad behavior from you?' Soon Molly would be started and we would be chugging down the road again."

In the summertimes when the girls were little, Bella would rent a room in the Catskills and take the family for a short vacation. The highlight of these trips to the mountains was a stop at the Red Apple Rest, a watering spot famous among Bronx residents who typically vacationed northward toward such towns as Liberty and Middletown.

"Mom and Dad would drive up early in the spring to scout

out a suitable room for the summer. On one occasion my father stopped to get some gas for Molly. He thought Mom was stretched out on the backseat, asleep. Dad got out to go to the bathroom. He returned, paid for his gas, and went on his way. He was halfway home before he realized Mom was missing. She had gotten out of the car at the gas station to go to the bathroom and missed his departure. For years afterward, whenever Mom gave him a hard time, he would snap back, 'I should have left you at the Red Apple Rest.' "

In the summer of 1932, in one of the rented rooms in the Catskills, Bess became very ill. The family and the other boarders thought it was polio, a disease whose very name in the 1930s had the same terrifying impact as cancer in the 1950s and AIDS in the 1980s.

In time, Bess recovered. She dragged her left foot for a while, but that soon stopped. Superstitious that talk of trouble might summon it back to reality, Bella Myerson insisted that no one speak about the "polio" incident. Bess herself began to doubt that it had ever happened. When she grew up and had a lot of trouble with her left knee, she went to a leading sports doctor. He said, "Oh, you have a congenital problem . . . or maybe once long ago, you had polio. . . ."

In later years, when the girls were grown, Mrs. Myerson would rent a boardinghouse—known in Yiddish as a *kocha-layn*—with rooms that she would let to vacationers on a weekly basis. It was known as the Old Turner Boardinghouse and Farm in Sullivan County, near South Fallsburg.

"On weekends, Dad would be called upon to bring up the boardinghouse guests in his old car. Then he would set about fixing everything in the place. There was no question that this man who worked past ten o'clock every weekday should rest on the weekend. Mom didn't rest and she wasn't going to let him rest either.

"Not that he ever complained. He believed that work was life itself, that the worst thing you could do to a man was to prevent him from working. If you did, you kept him from his self-esteem. You made a mockery of his freedom.

"Dad's clients loved him. He was proud that they appreciated his work. He would take me sometimes to see it, make me feel the walls he had painted. 'Smooth as glass,' he would say. 'Not a bump. Not a pimple.' His clients often sent him letters. 'Dear Mr. Myerson. You did such a splendid job on the dining room. It's rare that a craftsman takes such pride. . . .'

"Meanwhile, of course, Mom complained bitterly that he was bringing home letters of appreciation while others in his trade were making twice as much money."

The interminable arguments between Bella and Louis often concerned money.

"Dad would lend money to some member of the family. Mom would not cease nagging him and the borrower until it was paid back. I recall one incident in which he gave her fifty dollars out of his own pocket and told her it was the repayment of a debt, just to assuage her anger."

Sylvia and Helen did not intervene during these arguments. But Bess would stay in the thick of the battle, trying to mediate and smooth things over.

"I would say to her, 'Mom, don't scream. Listen to what he's trying to say.' To make her feel better, I would give her a kiss. The corners of her mouth would turn up, just a little. . . ."

Bella's hold over Louis extended to his special relationship with Bess. On one occasion that Bess would never forget, she even managed to goad him into an act of uncharacteristic violence.

"When I was in my last year at the High School of Music and Art in 1940, I became acquainted with a young man named Frenchie. He was some sort of labor organizer. Very bright. Very attractive. But not Jewish. That posed a problem.

"We may have had socialists and the IWO and hundreds of ostensibly radical people at the Sholom Aleichem. However, if they found out you were a dating a fellow who wasn't Jewish, their hearts would break. It was an age of sectarianism, of groups living separately in self-made ghettos. Frenchie's mother would most likely have been deeply disturbed to find her son was dating a Jewish girl. In the same way, I knew that if I started dating Frenchie, the liberal, my father, the liberal, would kill me."

Bess went off to a labor meeting, hoping to meet Frenchie

again. She told her parents that she was going to a high-school orchestra rehearsal.

She returned home very late and calculated that Louis and Bella would be sleeping. They were wide awake.

" 'Where have you been?' Dad said.

" 'At rehearsal,' I said.

" 'She's lying!' my mother yelled. 'She was with that boy from the union.'

" 'I'm not lying,' I said, lying.

" 'Hit her!' Mom yelled. 'You've got to show her who's boss!'

"My father rolled up his newspaper and hit me in the face. My gentle scholarly funny father.

"He came to me later and apologized, wiped my tears, said that she made him do it, he couldn't cross her because he had to keep *sholom bais*, peace in the house. But I was growing up. I understood now that my father would not protect me against her, that he was her husband and would always be on her side.

"Deep in my heart, I was in awe of my mother for the power she had over Dad. She drove him crazy, but he loved her, committed himself to her, and could not leave her. I believe that when I married, I looked for men who had my mother's controlling powers. . . ."

BELLA MYERSON HAD BEEN A BEAUTIFUL WOMAN. THE GIRLS have pictures that prove it. But they are old pictures, from a previous life.

"People who knew Mom when she was young told us that she was a vivacious, pretty, affectionate woman," Bess's sister Sylvia Grace explained. "They said she loved to flirt and dance, that she was always laughing and telling jokes. Unfortunately, we never saw that side of her. Never."

Born in Odessa, Russia, Bella was brought to New York by

her father when she was only ten. She received very little formal education and could read and write in English and Yiddish only with considerable difficulty. Perhaps it was a sense of loss about her own education that made her so passionate about the necessity for educating her children.

"Mom didn't just want literate daughters," Bess said. "She wanted brilliant daughters. She loved the sight of an A on a report card. She loved achievement and glory. Ultimately we gave her what she wanted, each of us in our own fashion."

Sylvia was Bella's first baby. Her second was Joseph, called affectionately in Yiddish "Yosseleh."

"Shortly after Joseph was born, Dad had an opportunity to move to Mobile, Alabama, and open a variety store with a friend," recalled Sylvia. "Mom was very reluctant to go, but we went. For two years she used every excuse to make Dad come home. She used to complain of the lack of refrigeration in Alabama—you had to keep the meat in a bucket with ice around it, that sort of thing.

"Soon after we came back to live in New York, Joseph became ill. I suspect it was diphtheria. Mom blamed Alabama. She would leave me with one of her sisters and go and visit him in the hospital. And when she returned, she would be in a terrible state, because the boy was delirious and had not recognized her. I remember her screams of grief when he died. He was three years old.

"I was so pained by my mother's anguish that at times I thought it would have been better if I had died instead."

The death of her son killed the beauty in Bella Myerson. At first she became almost catatonic, staring out the window, refusing to eat, to dress, to care for her five-year-old little girl. Louis finally threatened to call for an ambulance to take her to the mental hospital at Bellevue. Terrified of that possibility, she pushed herself back into her life again.

But her life—her vanity, her sense of security and self-worth— had been all but destroyed. Her health deteriorated along with her appearance. Over the next few years, she lost her teeth. Sylvia and Bess eventually convinced her to have dentures made, but she rarely wore them. She also lost much of her hearing and complained of a noise in her head that nagged her constantly.

Doctors advised Bella to have another baby, and she did, hoping for a boy. Instead she got Bessie, who was named for Louis's mother. Two years later, Bella tried again.

"When I wasn't a boy, she just gave up," said Helen Weiss.

Contemporary mothers may find it difficult to understand why a vivacious, ambitious woman should descend into a bitter and premature old age because of the loss of her boy-child. Listening to stories about how girl babies were drowned, or sold, in traditional societies, so valueless were their lives, we say please, come on, Bella Myerson was a progressive woman living in a socialist cooperative, and she had a supportive and loving male partner in the house.

But her daughters—modern, sophisticated, educated—insist that it's true, Bella never recovered from the loss of her only son. She had no religion to comfort her, no distractions or hobbies except the education of her children. Being irascible and argumentative, she alienated any family and friends who might have comforted her.

Her husband, trying to compensate Bella for her loss, and her daughters, trying desperately to be whatever Joseph might have been, never could find any way to comfort her. It filled them all with an abiding sense of failure and guilt so unfairly placed that it turned to anger and then just endured, for all the world like that nagging noise in Bella Myerson's head.

Sylvia tried to escape it through an early marriage.

Bess may have needed to become famous because of it.

Helen seems to have avoided it, staying safely in the background while her big sisters struggled with their mother and, in all the dust and mayhem, slipping quietly away.

Bella almost never hugged or kissed her children. She never praised them to their faces, although they heard from others that she constantly bragged about their accomplishments to her neighbors.

Her main way of showing affection was to cook and clean for her family. By all reports, she could do neither very well. Helen remembers gagging on the powdery lumps in her breakfast cereal. Sylvia recalls pot roast so overdone that it was unrecognizable. ("We called it mystery meat," Bess said with a laugh.) Barra Grant, Bess's daughter, said that Bella once sent her brownies at summer camp. They had paint chips in them. Bella's granddaughters attest that she served glasses of warm, still-liquid Jell-O with dinner because, she declared, it prevented cancer. "She was an early health-food fanatic," Bess explained. "Every time she cooked vegetables, she saved the liquid and made my father drink it." (Who knows? Maybe Bella had something. Louis Myerson lived past ninety.)

"Mom constantly washed the floor," Helen recalled, "but the floor was always dirty."

"She was always washing dishes," Bess said, "yet there were always dirty dishes in the sink."

"She would launder and iron our father's shirts," Sylvia remembered, "and then cram them into the drawers, so they became wrinkled all over again. Dad never had a properly ironed shirt unless one of us prepared it for him."

Bess sighed. "She didn't like us to help with the housework because it took time away from our studies."

"But the minute she left the house," Helen laughed, "we would rush around, straightening up. Then she would return and bring the mess back with her."

All her daughters remember Bella's tone of voice, high-pitched and strident.

"Helen! Come inside, it's late!"

"Sylvia! What are you doing? Read something!"

"Bessie! Come upstairs and practice the piano!"

Bella insisted that Bess and Sylvia practice their piano for hours every day. She was obsessed with the idea that her daughters must be music teachers. She lectured them constantly about how every woman had to be able to earn her own living.

"Mom did not believe that a woman could always count on being supported by her husband," Bess explained. "He might lose his job; he might become ill and die. . . ."

"Or he might want you to do something you didn't want to do," Sylvia laughed. "And if you had a profession, you could say the hell with him and walk out."

"Music was to be our profession," Helen said.

"Well, I had no ear for music," Sylvia continued. "I had no

relative pitch, couldn't tell if one note was higher or lower than the next. I can't sing a tune."

"But Sylvia played anyway," Bess marveled. "It was astonishing. She played, with brilliant dexterity, all these complicated Bach toccatas. . . ."

"And when we had to perform in a concert, I was in a panic," Sylvia admitted.

"Mom would always invite someone to see us perform at these concerts," Bess remembered. "The trip would always start with us crisscrossing the Bronx to pick up some woman she hardly knew, to whom she had bragged about us."

"We would be in the backseat," Helen said, "me with my violin practicing my fingering, all of us terrified of being late. We all hated the tension of those times. The pressure. The anxiety. And Dad shouting at Mom for having to go out of his way."

The greatest part of Bella Myerson's control and ambition was invested in her two oldest daughters. The youngest, Helen, was shielded by her sisters. Her social life, for example, was simply not subject to the same rigorous control applied to Bess and Sylvia.

"If I got a phone call from a boy," Sylvia chuckled, "Mom would never quite get the name right.

"I'd ask, 'Was it Marvin?'

"She'd answer, 'Yes, maybe it was Marvin. Say another name.'

"I'd say, 'Norman.'

"She would think. 'Yes, maybe it was Norman.'

"By now I'd be at my wits' end. 'Well, was it Marvin or Norman, Mom?!' I would holler.

"And she would answer, 'How am I supposed to know whether it was Marvin or David when I have so much trouble hearing and they all sound exactly alike?!' "

Even shopping, in which Bella had no interest, came under the control of her rigid, highly individualistic standards.

"When I bought a dress with the money I made baby-sitting or teaching," Bess testified, "I would cross out the price and write in a lower price so that Mom would think I had bought it on sale. Because if our mother thought we had paid full price for something, she would accuse us of wasting money and make us take it back. The only way to keep what you bought was to change the price tag."

If Bella didn't want one of her daughters to get something, her will alone could stop them. Louis Myerson was fond of saying that she could reverse the flow of Niagara Falls just by holding up her hand.

Sylvia wanted to go to a Chinese restaurant.

Bella was absolutely sure it was a white-slave den.

So much for the Chinese restaurant.

Helen wanted to go to Europe. Sylvia helped her acquire the passport and then kept it a secret. Bella was not told about Helen's trip until virtually the moment of departure.

"And then," Bess grinned, "there was the time Rose and Rockefeller were trying to convince me to run for Mayor. . . ."

My mother had a completely unique perspective of things. Nothing, but nothing, impressed her.

Back in 1974, Alex Rose, the head of the Liberal Party, and New York's longtime governor, Nelson Rockefeller, had a poll prepared to tell them who might be the most popular mayoral candidate to replace John Lindsay. The poll was done by Cambridge Survey Research. There were many prominent names on it. Respondents were asked to say whether they had a generally favorable or unfavorable opinion of the names.

George McGovern and Jacob Javits were on the list. Richard Ottinger and Howard Samuels and Allard Lowenstein were on it and so was I. When the results were tabulated, it turned out that I was the top candidate in the poll, with a 90 percent favorable rating. The next highest was Javits, with 68 percent.

Rose and Rockefeller met with me and asked me if I would be interested in running for mayor.

I said, "Thank you, gentlemen, I am flattered, but I am not running."

I had just left four years of being Commissioner of Consumer Affairs. I was tired. What I did not tell them at the time (nor did I ever tell my parents) was that I had ovarian cancer; I was facing a long, difficult siege of chemotherapy, and my priority was to get well.

In his usual blustery way, Nelson Rockefeller waved the poll at me. "What am I supposed to do with this?" he exclaimed.

"It's my mother's birthday," I answered. "I'd like you to autograph your poll and I will send it to her as a present."

On this impressive printout, Governor Rockefeller then wrote, "Dear Mom, Happy Birthday! Love, Nelson."

My mother was not impressed. Not with Rockefeller. Not with the poll. Nor with the idea that these powerful men wanted me to be the mayor.

My sisters and I and our children went to visit Mom and Dad for one of our usual Friday night dinners. Sylvia tried to coax Mom out of the kitchen by describing all the fantastical and miraculous events that might "occur" if I became mayor.

"Think, Mom," Sylvia said, "if Bess becomes mayor, I can give up my job as speech therapist and school supervisor and become Secretary of Health, Education, and Welfare!"

"Think, Mom," Helen said, "if Bess becomes mayor, I can stop teaching violin at the High School of Music and Art and take my place as conductor of the London Symphony!"

My mother was not impressed. She continued to stay in the kitchen, preparing mystery meat. However, Sylvia, the great psychological manipulator, remained undeterred. She said, "Think, Mom, if Bess becomes mayor, she will live at Gracie Mansion! When Golda Meir and Moshe Dayan visit New York, they will stay with her! You and Dad will go over and have Friday night dinner with them. Your sisters-in-law will faint from jealousy!"

This prospect was finally too much for my mother to resist. She came out of the kitchen. She said, "It's dangerous to be mayor of New York. People blame the mayor for everything."

Sylvia responded, "Bess won't be in any danger. A policeman guards the mayor's door all day and night."

"And when your granddaughters get married," Helen added, "imagine the receptions we can have on the lawn at Gracie Mansion! You can have a thousand people on that lawn! Think of all the relatives you'll be able to leave off the guest list!"

By now a gleam of ambition had been kindled in Mom's eye. We had a short silence.

We had a bite of mystery meat.

At last my mother concluded, "All right. Bessie can become mayor. I give my permission." Then she turned to me and said, "You'll try it for a year. If you don't like it, you can always come home."

CHAPTER 3

The Yearnings of a Young Musician

FOLLOWING THE PATTERN OF THE OTHER YOUNG MOTHERS AT the Sholom Aleichem project, Bella Myerson launched both Sylvia and Bess on piano lessons at the age of nine. Helen started the violin at eleven, under much less pressure, and turned out to be the only child who made a *career* out of music.

"Our mother brought with her from Russia the idea that music was a way of getting out of the ghetto," Helen commented. "The Jews in Russia were not allowed to go to universities. They had to stay in the little towns. But a musician was able to go to Moscow or Petersburg, wherever the conservatory was. The musician could get out."

For her part, Bess believed the stress on music to be more a product of expedience and her mother's "need for us to be somebody."

"She didn't go to the concert and understand. She had no musical ability, no ear, no taste, no joy in it. However, she needed to feed her pride, and by playing well, my sisters and I nourished it."

Since the Sholom Aleichem child went to public school with her neighbors and to Yiddish schule with her neighbors, like as not, the music lessons provided the first contact with the "outside world." Ruth Singer went for dance lessons at the Ruth St. Denis-Ted Shawn studio (known in the neighborhood as "Denis-Shawn"), in a yellow stucco building on Sedgwick Avenue

33

situated among the single-family houses whose Gentile inhabitants resented the intrusion of the socialist Jews from the mammoth buildings on the hill.

"We danced in our bathing suits," Ruth recalled. "Then we changed to go home. Once when I was ten, I forgot my suit and had to run back to get it. It was Halloween. The kids from the private houses had collected 'clinkers'—those jagged ash rocks left over after the coal burned in the furnace. The kids had clinkers in socks. They hit me with them and chased me and called me a dirty Jew. I ran and ran, crying. I don't know which hurt me more, the clinkers or being called 'a dirty Jew.' "

Bella found Bess and Sylvia's first piano teacher in the Sholom Aleichem itself. "Mom would march me across the rooftop to the section where my lesson was," Bess said with a smile, "wait for me to be finished, and then march me back across the rooftop to our section."

When Bess was eleven, Bella discovered the Heckscher Foundation for Children, then located at 105th Street. There she found a new piano teacher, Dorothea Anderson LaFollette. To reach Mrs. LaFollette's studio, the girls had to journey into the exciting world of Manhattan's Upper West Side. In due time, Helen began studying the violin there with Mrs. LaFollette's husband, Chester.

Although in later years Bess would write lovingly of Bella's firm insistence that the girls practice and practice for hours every single day,[1] in still later years she would admit the *deeper* truth—which was that Bella didn't insist lovingly, she insisted like the drummer on a galley ship.

"Mom stood in the kitchen and while I would practice, at regular intervals, she would shout *'Wrong!'* Even if I hadn't made a mistake. She knew nothing about the music! It was her way of keeping me at the piano.

"She never allowed us free time for game playing or fun activities, wouldn't let me hang around the candy store or roast 'mickeys'—potatoes—in the vacant lot with my friends.

" 'Those children in the park will be nothing when they grow

---

[1] Bess Myerson, "My Mother, My Piano—and Me," *Redbook* (June 1974), p. 63.

up,' she said, 'because they wasted their time just hanging around!' Of course, some of 'those children' grew up to be Abe Rosenthal from *The New York Times* and the late great writer Paddy Chayevsky. If Mom looked out the window and saw me stop to play she would yell down, 'Bessie! Come inside and practice!' I would go upstairs, humiliated because everybody had heard."

Unknowingly, Bella was now sowing the seeds of her own defeat. Although *she* thought of music as work, Bess did not. To her—and to her sister Helen—music was the high of highs, the greatest distraction, and the greatest comfort.

"Sylvia, who was tone deaf, played and played under the gun of Mom's nagging and finally escaped by marrying Bill Grace and moving out. She never touched the piano again. But I escaped long before then. Because I could *hear* the tune, I could *savor* the harmonies. With the help of my teacher, Mrs. LaFollette, I escaped *through* the music. Mrs. LaFollette unlocked the gates."

The LaFollette studio on 84th Street and Central Park West was run with decorum and grace. When a recital was held, a uniformed maid would answer the door, welcome the guests, and see to it that they were seated comfortably in a spacious living room filled with fresh flowers, graceful antiques, and *two* Steinway baby grands. Ruth Singer remembered going to hear Bess play there and being impressed with the marble foyer, the plush draperies, and the parquet floors.

"Mrs. LaFollette was tall," Bess said, "and she stood very straight. She had a beautiful, calm, Scandinavian face, a milky pink-and-white complexion. She wore her long honey-colored hair wrapped around her head and looked like a statuesque heroine in one of Ingmar Bergman's movies.

"Every month she and Mr. LaFollette held recitals at the studio," Bess said. "If you were working on a concerto, you would play your part on one piano, and she would play the 'orchestral accompaniment' on the other. Then twice a year, her students would perform at Steinway Hall or at the Carnegie Chamber Hall. Those of us who had mastered a sufficient repertoire were asked to give solo concerts, people like Harriet Josephs, Jeanne Mitchell, and Emma Ricci in the violin group, and the pianists Willie Kappel and little Byron Janis . . . and *me.*

"Can you imagine being in a school with geniuses like that? It would have been far for me to go to 84th Street, but the talent of those children took you to *another world.*"

Bess felt a tremendous insecurity as she grew older in the LaFollette studio. First of all, the parents of the other children invariably knew more about music than the Myersons did; they were richer in all ways, as were the LaFollettes themselves.

In addition, Bess had a special problem.

"I was terribly self-conscious about my height in those early pre-adolescent years. All through public school, I felt awkward because I was so tall and gawky. I towered above the other children. I was sure I would always be ugly.

"Mom enrolled me at Denis-Shawn for dancing lessons, but I felt like a freak among the smaller girls. I soon stopped dancing and ended up playing the piano as accompanist for the classes and recitals.

"On one occasion P.S. 95 held a festival of fairy tales and comic strip characters. Each one of us was assigned a role to play. We had to put together our own costumes. All the other little girls were asked to be characters like Bo Peep or Snow White. I was asked to be Olive Oyl, Popeye's girlfriend.

"Some people may not remember Olive Oyl. In the comic strip she was a long stringbean character in an ankle-length black dress and oversized black shoes. Her hair was pulled back tight and knotted in a little bun on the top of her head.

"I complained, 'I don't want to be Olive Oyl!'

"But whoever was running the show would not change my assignment. When I cried to my father, he kissed me and said, 'Don't worry, Besseleh, you're beautiful no matter what part they gave you in whatever it is. . . .' Then he went back to reading his newspaper.

"I gave up. Nobody thought I needed to be consoled because I had been cast as Olive Oyl. My schoolteachers put me in men's laced black shoes and some grown-up's black crepe dress. My black, curly hair was squashed into a bun. I already lacked confidence because of Mom's periodic raids on my storehouse of self-esteem. To be Olive Oyl made it even worse.

"I kept the picture of me and my friends in our costume parade in my wallet for years. It would be a comfort to look at the picture and know that those days were over, that I wasn't Olive Oyl anymore. At the same time, when people would say to me, 'You are so lucky to have been Miss America! How wonderful it must be to have always been beautiful,' I would look at the picture and recall that I had not always been beautiful at all. As much as anything else, that helped me keep the title in perspective.

"I recall that one of the things many of us girls had in common at the Miss America Pageant in 1945 was that at some point in our lives, we had felt ourselves to be funny-looking. We developed this idea that being beautiful would be the best thing in the world, that it would magically turn us into Snow White and Bo Peep. . . ."

As Bess entered her teenage years, her sense of physical inadequacy was exacerbated by the fact that in any given school year she had a couple of blouses and a skirt, and that was it. When the skirt grew short, Sylvia would let down the hem. When there was no more hem, the skirt was just . . . short.

Said Sophie Smith, "I remember, Bess would arrive to baby-sit for me, and I would open the door and there she would be, pulling at her skirt, embarrassed because it was almost above her knees."

Bess longed for pretty clothes. She dreamed about them.

She would say to her father, "Dad, I have nothing to wear!"

And Louis would answer, "You don't need more dresses, you would look beautiful in a potato sack!"

More than anything, Bess wanted a new dress to wear at Mrs. LaFollette's concerts. She had one dress she always wore to the recitals when she was a teenager—a wine-colored print, with a dirndl skirt and puckered smocking across the midriff.

"When we would come together to rehearse Mrs. LaFollette would always say, 'And Bess, you must wear that red dress because it does look so lovely.'

"She knew it was the only dress I had. However, she would pretend never to have noticed that, so that I would feel good about myself in it, so that I would have confidence.

" 'It's not the altitude, Bess,' she would say, 'it's the attitude.

37

You must stand tall when you are walking to the piano. Pretend that God is watching you from above the ceiling over the stage, and He is reaching down through the ceiling and straightening your back by pulling the hair on the crown of your head straight up.' "

Mrs. LaFollette's stress on dignity and self-confidence was a healing balm to the troubled young girl. She clung to the warmth of the LaFollette home. Often Mrs. LaFollette would give her a lesson at the end of the day and then call Bella and ask if Bess could stay for dinner. Bella would always agree, welcoming the teacher's influence on Bess, never once resenting it.

Bess's whole outlook on her future changed when she realized that the applause she received at a concert actually made her mother happy. It wasn't that Bella loved the music. It was that she loved the *attention.*

"When Mom would come to those concerts," Bess recalled, "I was always conscious of her turning her head, looking to see who was coming in. I saw her smiling at compliments she would receive about us. However, when we got into Dad's old car to go home, she would always be just a little critical. She would ask us, 'Why did you play so short? And so softly? Harriet had a much longer piece and played much louder. If you practiced as much as Harriet, you would have a long piece, too.' After a while we laughed about Mom's criticism. We simply could no longer take her seriously."

In 1938, the three Myerson sisters entered a family musical contest run by the Parks Department. Sylvia played the piano. Bess had branched out into woodwinds at the High School of Music and Art and now played the flute. Helen played the violin. They got an honorable mention.

"One of my aunts told me that Mom was bursting with pride about that. However, she never let us know her true feelings. To us, she complained that we had not won first prize. She reacted like the mother in Sam Levinson's old joke. A little boy came home, proud of his test score of 98 percent; 'Who got the other 2 percent?' asked his mother."

With her increasingly expert piano playing, Bess had finally found a way to please her mother. More important still, she had found a way to please herself.

"I created my own universe with the music. I buried myself in it. Music became my great friend and companion.

"Dad would find discarded records at someone's house and bring them home to me. I would play them on the Victrola, pretend that I was the conductor, and conduct the music with my baton. The music took me to a place where I could dance in my heart and Mom's unhappiness could not reach out to spoil my joy."

The key figure in this miraculous escape, never to be forgotten, was the nurturing teacher, Dorothea LaFollette. She was Bess's second surrogate mother, after Sylvia. She was Bess's mentor, her inspiration.

"Mrs. LaFollette made it so much easier for me to accept myself," Bess said, "because, you see, she was as tall as I was growing to be, and she was graceful and classy and cool. When you're a teenager, a role model like that can save your life.

"Years later, she committed suicide. People said it was because she was depressed . . . because her students this . . . because her family that . . . Can one ever know the truth about such a terrible tragedy?

"I did not attend her funeral. I simply could not bear to bury her, to have my last memory of her be the coffin lowered into the cold ground. I wanted to remember Mrs. LaFollette as she was when I was young and she was the person I wanted to grow up to be.

"She used to sit at the piano and play Bach and Schumann with those long, white fingers, and she would say, 'A woman has to give up a great deal to do serious music, Bess.'

"I thought it was just advice.

"I couldn't imagine that a woman as lovely and gifted and successful as Dorothea Anderson LaFollette could ever know despair."

THE HIGH SCHOOL OF MUSIC AND ART WAS MAYOR FIORELLO LaGuardia's pride and joy, the fulfillment of his most grandiose dreams for New York—indeed, the human race. Created in 1936 as a *public* high school, it offered a special curriculum to the artistically gifted children of the city, providing them not only the basics of a "regular" high-school education but additional courses in music, art, literature, and drama.

The school was housed in a grand gothic building up on Convent Avenue and 135th Street (known as "the Castle on the Hill"), and the artistic community of New York followed the mayor's lead, adopted it, and called it, as he did, "Baby."

A product of the Depression, like all its students in those early years, Music and Art carried forward several ideas that had gone national with such endeavors as the Federal Writers Project—that the community that was rich in artistic product could never be poor no matter how poverty-stricken its members and that it was the responsibility of government by and for the people to fund and encourage artistic expression.

More particularly to New York, the school embodied the experience of Jewish and Italian immigrants who did menial work in dark, dingy sweatshops all day long and then at night and on weekends flocked to theater and opera. These were the people who invented the American rendition of the cultured work force. Their influence was felt as far away as Detroit, in Walter Reuther's singular United Auto Workers Union and its programs to bring education and culture to the rank and file. In New York, their home, their port of entry, the High School of Music and Art was the gift they gave their children.

The school hummed with vibrant patriotism. It rejected the elitism of the "old" artistic establishment. It welcomed the young, native-born artist and extolled the American artistic product. If you had made a movie about the High School of Music and Art in 1937 (*Fame* was made in the 1970s, a different story for a different time, all about careers), you might

40

have used the music of Woody Guthrie and Aaron Copland for the sound track, you might have used Ben Shahn for your production designer, you might have given the actors lines by Clifford Odets. LaGuardia himself, "the Little Flower," whose father had been accompanist for the great opera diva Adelina Patti, who had been raised on the public concerts of the Goldman Band, used the proletarian enthusiasm of the times to build the school and came there often to conduct (arriving like gangbusters aboard a howling fire engine) and sow his proud working-class philosophies.

Bess Myerson was accepted as a music major into the second class at the High School of Music and Art. She started in 1937 and graduated in January 1941.

"Getting into Music and Art was the most wonderful thing that had happened to me up to that time," Bess said. "Many students I knew from P.S. 95 applied and didn't make it. Being selected on merit, according to an outside standard, gave me an extraordinary feeling of achievement. It was my first encounter with the thing about me that was very much like my mother— the thing that loved competing . . . and loved winning."

All music students at Music and Art were required to study more than one instrument. Since Bess was so tall, her teachers wanted her to take up the double bass. She refused.

"First of all, I had to take the subway every day. I was allowed to take my second instrument home, and I certainly did not want to haul a double bass through the subway. I wanted to study some instrument I could carry. Helen already played the violin. I felt that if I studied a woodwind, we sisters could play as a trio. That's why I chose the flute."

Helen Weiss typically offered a more complex historical explanation.

"You have to remember that a woman had no future in performing music in those days unless she could do something rare and special. No major orchestra took women (except for specialty groups like Phil Spitalni's all-girl ensemble), and there were very few minor orchestras. Minneapolis, Denver, New Orleans, all those came later. My husband was concertmaster with the Indianapolis Symphony in 1939. They would never even audition girls.

"Today the barriers are down. Look at the Philharmonic—it's full of women. But the change only took place maybe fifteen years ago, when the Philharmonic began to have auditions behind a screen, so all you were to the listeners was a musician identified by a number; they couldn't see if you were a man or a woman. Prior to that they looked at you, and if you were a woman, no way.

"Now, given that prejudice, the flute was a good thing for a girl to play in the late 1930s because there were very few American wind players at that time. Until William Kincaid began teaching at Curtis, and George Barrere made flute-playing famous, few kids *started* on a wind instrument. Kids started on the piano and stayed with it. So when Bess went to Music and Art, they *needed* flute players in the country, and I think the idea was that she should study flute because if she did and she was good, she might be able to get a job even though she was a girl."

Next to Bess in the Music and Art orchestra sat Murray Panitz, now first flute in the Philadelphia Orchestra. He corroborated Helen's feeling that there were very few good flute teachers around in the 1930s. "I went to this woodwind teacher who taught me the flute with the fingerings for the clarinet," Panitz recalled. "And when I finally started to study under Arthur Lora at the Juilliard School, he was nonplussed by my strange methods."

Bess was a quick study with the flute as she was with most new skills. She became pretty good very fast. The Music and Art faculty bumped her up into the senior orchestra when she was still an underclassman.

"My teachers' encouragement filled me with hope," Bess remembered. "Even today I can feel the gentle touch on my shoulder, I can hear those wonderful words that I never heard at home: 'You did well, Bessie. Good for you.'

"I had never been surrounded by people who had so much to give. The truth is, I had never been so happy."

At Music and Art, Bess had the opportunity to work under famous guest conductors like the revered Walter Damrosch and the twenty-nine-year-old Erich Leinsdorf, the *Wunderkind* who had just been appointed conductor of the Metropolitan Opera Orchestra. Her fellow students were people like Andrew

Toff, who is now first violinist with the Cleveland Orchestra; Bernie Garfield, now first bassoonist with the Philadelphia Orchestra; and Maurice Wilk, first bassoonist in Cleveland. Not everyone grew up and became eminent in arts and letters. But virtually all who enjoyed the Music and Art experience became members of that lifelong audience that Bess had first joined at the Sholom Aleichem and without which all artistic endeavor wanders friendless, without resonance.

"I wouldn't say we were all geniuses at Music and Art," Panitz recalled, "but we were a bunch of talented kids. We had great times. Whenever one of the newspapers came to take a picture of the orchestra, they would ask me to move aside so they could feature Bess, because she was just so beautiful."

Whether she wanted it or not, Bess's beauty began to change her life in high school. Like Buttercup, the heroine of William Goldman's classic *The Princess Bride*, she went to school one morning and found that boys were following her around and that the other girls had grown strangely hostile.

Sure she was talented, like *all* the kids there. However, everyone who remembers her during those years remembers her talent less than her beauty. Her first conducting teacher, David Ratner ("Boy, did I have a crush on him!" Bess said with a laugh), recalled that one of the high points at Music and Art was *watching* lovely Bessie lead the orchestra.

During her sophomore year, Bess received a scholarship to study flute with a teacher named Ralph Freundlich, later to be called Ray Friendly. It was a mixed blessing, this award, because although she was pleased to be studying with a fine musician, she also had the distinct feeling that she had received the award not because of the way she played but because of the way she *looked* while playing.

Freundlich fell deeply in love with Bess. Years later, when he returned home after his military service in the Second World War, he asked her to marry him. She refused—but more poignant still, she was quite astonished, for she had never even been aware of the seriousness of his feelings.

During their four years at Music and Art, Bess and her friends were bombarded with visitations from some of the finest talents in the country, and they left their impression.

43

Aaron Copland rehearsed Music and Art students for the première of his opera *The Second Hurricane*. Morton Gould wrote an opera for the senior symphony. Sam Leve, one of the first scenic and lighting designers to conquer the complexities of huge halls like Madison Square Garden, lectured about stage effects. Rudolph Serkin, William Schuman, and Virgil Thomson all came to lecture and teach.

One of the most extraordinary women in the history of music, Antonia Brico, came to Music and Art to lecture and recruit members for the Youth Symphony she was forming. A native of Colorado and a longtime companion of Albert Schweitzer, a brilliant musician and teacher, she was primarily a conductor.

"When it comes to music," Brico said to Bess and her classmates, "there is no difference in ability between men and women."

Somewhere deep in Bess Myerson's psyche, the message took hold. A girl could do. A girl could be.

"Our class was taken to observe Arturo Toscanini conduct rehearsals of the NBC Radio Symphony Orchestra. We were in the control room. Behind the glass. Pressed up against the glass. And this incredible man would be conducting *without a score*! He would stop the orchestra. He would say, 'French horns, turn back to the fourth page. You see bar three? Second horn, you hit a B flat—there.' He had it all in his head!

"We sat behind the glass with our mouths open, struck dumb with awe and admiration. And I thought, 'Someday maybe it could be me at the podium inspiring everyone to play so beautifully.' "

Murray Panitz got Bess an audition with the Columbia University Symphonic Band. She was accepted immediately. The band played classical pieces and "pops" music, all of which had been rearranged for brass, woodwind, and percussion instruments.

"We would be doing a movement from a symphony and I would be so overwhelmed by the sound of the music that I couldn't play the flute. I had a physiological reaction to it. I'd start salivating; I couldn't play. I was so moved, so thrilled by the experience. Now I knew for sure that I wanted to be a conductor."

But of course that was silly, she thought, to dream of being a conductor. Didn't the Columbia University Symphonic Band itself tell Bess and the other girls who played in it that they could rehearse with the boys and play with them at concerts in Town Hall but they could not march with the boys when it came time for the band to play at football games? At halftime on Morningside Heights, the girls sat in the stands and watched their boyfriends play, and the music of the band all but drowned out the message of lone voices like that of Antonia Brico.

Although most of the student body was Jewish in those days, there was a fair smattering of black children, too, at a time when segregated education was the rule in this country, something most of our own children cannot now imagine. The anti-elitist, democratic spirit of the school expressed itelf as well in a *personal* ethos that was fed to the students.

"Before we came to Music and Art," wrote the school paper *Overtone*, "many of us were praised for our talents. . . . We tended to feel superior to those around us and to act as though we were too good for the world. Now that we have reached Music and Art, we find that the word 'genius' is abolished from our vocabulary. . . . Our aim has changed from the purely selfish aim of becoming great artists to a sincere desire to share with others the beauty and happiness we find in music and art."

The school's political point of view ran as a slogan in the school paper: "DEMOCRACY, TOLERANCE, PEACE, AND A RICH LIFE FOR EVERYONE." When the Daughters of the American Revolution insulted the brilliant black soprano Marian Anderson by refusing to sponsor a concert in which she was to sing at the Capitol, the students of Music and Art were reminded that "Toscanini once said Marian Anderson was the greatest singer alive," and each class was urged to write a letter of protest to the DAR. Eleanor Roosevelt's decision to drop her membership in the DAR on account of this now-famous slur was considered an exemplary act of political courage and principled behavior, to be emulated.

"We became aware of the growing power of Hitler," Bess recalled, "because so many German Jewish refugees arrived in

45

the city during my freshman and sophomore years. One Music and Art student, Olive Grossman, was aboard the *Athenia* when it was torpedoed by German submarines in September 1939. She was saved on the high seas. And she returned to school with frightening tales of how terrible it was in Europe for democracy and trade unions and Jews.

"Many students in our group joined Dorothy Canfield Fisher's Children's Crusade for Children because we knew now that kids just like us were being displaced and orphaned by anti-Semitism on the other side."

In Washington and all across the country, the dispute deepened between those who felt America must defend Europe against Hitler and those who felt we must stay home, stay out, and stay safe. A city investigations commissioner dominated by the isolationists launched an investigation into the public high schools. They sought evidence that Communist teachers were convincing the younger generation to support America's entrance into the war.

Dr. Benjamin Steigman, the school's founder and longtime principal, defended Music and Art. Don't be silly, he said. We are not Communists. We are artists here, and patriots.

However, in years to come, what Steigman called patriotism would, in some people's minds, be construed as communism anyway. Many gifted people whom Bess knew in high school would find it hard to get a job in the 1950s.

It was January 1941, on the eve of war. Bess Myerson was seventeen years old. It was only a year before the Allied governments would have positive knowledge of Hitler's policy to exterminate all the Jews of Europe, some of whom would be relatives of children in the High School of Music and Art.

Fiorello LaGuardia came to the graduation exercises and made the commencement address.

"We can't be completely happy in a world which is torn with war," he declared. "We can't rest in peace when millions of children are hungry and in danger. You creators of beauty rebel against any such conditions.

"Class of 1941, I want you to shout to the whole world: 'We are confident that the destruction wrought by dictators will itself be destroyed and will stay destroyed! We insist that the ingenuity of man and the progress of science must and can be utilized for the enjoyment and welfare of humanity the world over!' Say to the dictators, 'O you brutal dictators, your end is coming, and we will continue to create beauty!' "

━━━━━━━

When Helen and I were in high school, we began to tell little tactical fibs to our watchful, overprotective mother. We covered for each other, shielded each other—because we wanted to have a life out in the wide world and there was no other way.

Pop found a bicycle and repaired it for Helen. He felt it would be good for her to ride it, strengthen her system, give her rosy cheeks. Mom said it would weaken her and make her sick again. Of course, Mom won this fight with Pop. And, of course, Helen did exactly what she wanted anyway. She rode her bike constantly.

"Where's Helen?" Mom would ask.

"Out with a friend," I would say.

"Is she riding her bike?"

"Oh, no."

One day Mom was taking the bus home. She looked out the window. Who should she see riding her bike with some of her buddies, laughing and having a ball? Helen.

Boy, did we get it that night.

Then there was the lipstick.

Mom said we were not allowed to wear lipstick at all. "If you wear lipstick at sixteen," she insisted, "what will you be doing when you're twenty-two?!"

Naturally, by the time we were in high school and all the girls were wearing lipstick, we would put on lipstick the minute we hit the second landing down from the apartment. Then we had to traverse the courtyard without Mom seeing us. Helen would stay behind and signal me for the all-clear, or I would signal her. We would dash across the courtyard with our heads down in case Mom was looking out the window. Before I came home, I'd wipe it all off.

We weren't supposed to smoke.

However, in those days everybody smoked. Bette Davis looked wonderful smoking in the movies. As a teenager, I wanted very much to be as elegant and sophisticated as Bette Davis. I tried smoking for the first time in our bathroom.

"What's that smell?" my mother said.

"What smell?" my sister Helen answered.

Mom burst into the bathroom and caught me red-handed (as well as red-faced from all the coughing and choking while smoking).

She yelled at Helen.

I pleaded: "Don't yell at Helen, Mom, she really didn't know what I was doing."

She yelled at me.

Helen pacified her: "Don't yell at Bessie, Mom, she really won't do it again."

Then we went to bed and giggled. We were co-conspirators, always supporting and defending each other. As for our mother's yelling, we had long before tuned out.

Mom didn't approve of dating. When I was at Music and Art, I pretended to have no dates when, in fact, I had quite a few (although they might not be considered "dates" by today's standards). For example, when my friend Dorothy Gelfand and I left school in the afternoon, a couple of the boys would be waiting for us. They would ride with us all the way home, forty minutes on the subway, kidding and flirting and talking. Dorothy would get off in the 170s. I would get off a few stops later, at Mosholu Parkway. Then the boys would ride all the way back downtown. That was a big date.

Helen enjoyed more freedom, by virtue of the fact that she grew up later, when Mom was exhausted from standing watch over me and Sylvia and when we ourselves had become incredibly adept at the in-house cover-up. Helen would say she was going to baby-sit for Sylvia's children. Her dates would meet her at Sylvia's apartment. Sometimes our brother-in-law Bill would pick Helen up, and her date would be right there in the car with him. I never dared to have a boy in our bedroom, but Helen's husband, Avram, recalls that when they were dating, he was there.

Helen still maintained appearances. When Mom knocked on the door, Helen pushed Avram out on the fire escape. He stayed there until Mom was gone. Unfortunately it was a very stormy night. . . .

When I look back at all the silly pretenses and fantasies we concocted in those years, I realize we were really in training then to be always aware of the impression things made. We were always trying to figure out what would please others, what would win approval.

My sister Sylvia, who had become a speech therapist after her marriage, would make me sit at the radio and try to replicate the pronunciation of the 1940s newscasters who always spoke in an important, literate, almost British way. She wanted me to be more emphatic with my consonants; never to say "pretty" as though it were written with two d's instead of two t's. Her goal was to help me eliminate my regional accent, to speak not Bronx English but excellent English. She wanted me to make the best possible impression on the world.

CHAPTER 4

The Beauty Business

IT'S AN ALL-GIRL CHORUS THAT TELLS THE STORY OF BESS MYER-son's college years. Between 1941, when she enrolled at Hunter, and 1945, when she graduated with a B.A. degree in music, virtually all the young men who might have known her well were fighting in the Second World War.

"I started half a year late at Hunter. Initially I attended night classes, leaving my days free to study piano with Mrs. LaFollette. My parents wanted me to attend a four-year liberal-arts school. 'Education is more important than food,' Dad used to say. On the other hand, Mrs. LaFollette was lobbying for me to enroll in a conservatory like Curtiss or Juilliard. I thought perhaps I would try that. First, however, I had to earn some money to cover my costs at school."

Bess baby-sat for everyone who wanted her. She worked in department stores, and as a rehearsal accompanist for Richard Fulton, an aspiring opera singer. She had already acquired about a dozen young piano students who paid fifty cents an hour for her services.

"I loved my students. Because of my own mother's extraordinary success in creating musicians by perseverance, I had a great belief in the power of practice—and the power of mothers. A woman might tell me, 'Hannah is quitting piano, Miss Myerson. The lessons are useless since she never practices.'

"I would answer with great alarm, 'Hannah doesn't practice?

Hannah is *twelve*! She has nothing to say in the matter! *You* must make her practice! One day she will thank you!' "

One of Bess's most creative pupils was a chiropodist who traded her foot care for piano lessons. He asked her to teach him the first eight measures of several impressive classical pieces. With these perfected, he would go to a party, sit down at the piano, and say, "Okay folks, what would you like to hear? Brahms?" He would play his eight measures of Brahms, then stop suddenly. "Nah, too romantic," he would say. "How about something more ferocious?" And he would tear into Beethoven, only to stop abruptly and say, "Nah, tonight's a balmy night, perfect for Debussy," and he would waft away with the opening measures of *Clair de Lune.*

By the time the chiropodist left the piano—"Don't feel like playing much tonight," he'd remark, "ask me another time" —the party guests believed he had mastered a repertoire fit for Horowitz.

Every day Bess went to 84th Street for a lesson with Mrs. LaFollette (three hours with her own students paid for one of these).

"Sometimes I went to her house just to practice, just to be near her, to talk with her and be nourished by her affection. However, I soon realized that no matter how much my dear teacher desired it, I would not be a concert pianist. I was a quick study, and maybe I'd be a fine accompanist or a teacher myself, but I simply didn't have what the Byron Janises had—genius.

"So I finally took the plunge and enrolled at Hunter full time. The Music Department had a reputation for excellence. It was one of the greatest educational bargains in history. My old college friend Lenore Miller figured out that *with* the diploma and the lab fees, we paid about fifty-seven dollars for four years!"

For the first two years, Hunter girls attended at the Bronx campus on the site of what is now Herbert Lehman College. During the war, the WAVES took over the Bronx campus; Bess and her friends spent their second two years in Manhattan.

Another old friend, Margie Wallis, recalled that she had met Bess at evening classes, when they were both freshmen. Bess said,

"I noticed Margie because she was wearing a hat. A catastrophe with a bottle of peroxide had left a big streak of platinum in her hair. She had tried to cover it with mascara, and black streams were running down her forehead from under her felt-brimmed hat."

Margie said she noticed Bess because she was so beautiful.

Lenore Miller met Bess through The 68 Club, an organization that only admitted girls sixty-eight inches tall or over. (The five-six Margie Wallis became its "mascot.") "Like Bess, I was five-ten," Lenore recalled, "and I had always felt freakish. I walked in a perpetual slouch. One day, up at Hunter, another very tall young woman, whose name was Jewel Russak, came up with a big smile and said, 'How would you like to join a club for tall girls only?' And I felt like I had been born again."

"You must understand," Bess explained, "if you were eighteen and five-foot-ten in 1941, socially you were a dead person. A blind date was an occasion for terror. You never knew whether Mickey Rooney was going to ring the doorbell."

"If we had a USO social at Hunter, I would stand up the whole time. Because if I sat down, some short soldier might come and ask me to dance. Then I would *have* to stand up . . . and up . . . and up . . . and we'd both be mortified. The members of The 68 Club discussed making a certain height requisite for young men who attended our parties. We thought perhaps we should put a six-foot marker on the door. Then we decided that would be unfair discrimination.

"The basketball players were all overseas saving England. And somehow or other, I didn't meet up with Henry Kissinger types who had the self-esteem to court a tall woman."

The widening war influenced every aspect of the girls' lives. As their brothers and cousins and young male teachers went overseas, they began to do whatever they could to obviate a sense of superfluity and helplessness.

"We were all knitting like crazy for Britain," Lenore recalled. "One of the war agencies distributed a lot of navy blue wool at the college. We'd pick it up and convert it into a hat or socks or gloves that some brave sailor could wear in the North Atlantic.

"We felt it was sort of the least we could do for the war effort, to smoke these terrible things that we got as cigarette substitutes.

They smelled like you were smoking maple syrup.

"You wore rayon hose that no manufacturer could ever make look anything other than hideous ultrared. If you got a pair of nylons, you guarded them with your life."

The Hunter curriculum was weighted down with requirements. The student body was weighted down with brains. "We had a reputation as the school with the smartest poor girls in the city," Bess laughed.

Helen entered as a freshman when Bess was a sophomore. She sought her own crowd, avoiding the bold 68 Club clique, which became rather famous on campus. But the sisters remained close.

"I was a night owl," Bess said. "I am to this day. I would always stay up late to wait for Dad and then oversleep the next day. Helen signed in for me sometimes at my early-morning classes. We had a very cooperative relationship."

On Thursday nights and Saturdays, Bess and Lenore Miller worked as salesgirls at Franklin Simon and Saks 34th Street. Impressing the store management as giant young Amazons who could restrain great crushes of bargain-hungry customers, they were invariably assigned to "the flying squad," the spur-of-the-moment crisis interveners who sold umbrellas when it rained and mittens when it froze.

"We'd meet on the subway station platform at 125th Street," Lenore recalled. "Bess would come down on the D line from the Bronx and I'd come down on the A line from Washington Heights. And we'd giggle our way to 39th Street and Sixth Avenue. And sell. I guess we were pretty good at it. The stores kept us on."

Actually, it was the best possible time to find work in the retail stores. Despite the shortage of some consumer goods, Americans were on a buying spree, spearheaded by the new prosperity of housewives. "By 1943," wrote John Morton Blum, "5 million more women were employed than in 1941, and the wages of women factory operatives were up over 50 percent for the same period. They had some $8 billion more in pocket than they had had. Retailers had doubled their sales of women's clothing and found price no barrier. . . ."[1] In 1942, Americans bought $20 million more in pharmaceuticals than they had in

1941. Jewelry sales rose between 20 and 100 percent. On December 7, 1944, the third anniversary of Pearl Harbor, Macy's had the biggest selling day in its history. Bess and her friends had all the work they could possibly want.

When girls in another era would have been dating, necking, falling in love, forming relationships, and breaking them off, gaining experience, the girls in The 68 Club were concocting their ideas of romance from all-too-brief encounters with soldiers at USO dances, and from the movies, which were rapidly changing gears. The relentlessly dewy-eyed romantic musicals of the 1930s now gave way to more literate, realistic dramas that befit the sensibilities of a nation at war.

It was hard to fall in love with a young god on the silver screen because so many major American heartthrobs—among them Henry Fonda, Robert Montgomery, Robert Cummings, Clark Gable, and Jimmy Stewart—were off fighting. Wrote *Variety,* "The war-year of 1943 will go down in motion picture history as the year in which studios scoured the country . . . in an attempt to uncover able young men who could be elevated to high prominence almost overnight."[2] The new movie heroines were strong and smart, like Katharine Hepburn in *Woman of the Year,* or strong and noble, like Greer Garson in *Mrs. Miniver.* Without men to say what *they* wanted, the wartime co-ed patterned herself on the woman who was wanted by *the times,* the independent, resilient female who could face the widening crisis alone.

The girls at Hunter grew wise and deep for their years from the horror of the war—"the horror," Bess said, "of passing Gold Star mothers on the stairs at the Sholom Aleichem, women who had once looked on me and my sisters as potential wives for their dead sons." At the same time, they stayed sexually immature and innocent as sequestered novitiates in a manless city.

[1] John Morton Blum, *V Was for Victory: Politics and American Culture During World War II* (New York: Harcourt Brace Jovanovich, 1976), p. 95.
[2] Quoted in Richard R. Lingeman, *Don't You Know There's a War On?: The American Home Front, 1941–1945* (New York: G. P. Putnam's Sons, 1970), p. 179.

On New Year's Eve in 1943, Margie Wallis's father felt so sorry for the girls because there was no one to take them out that he gave them a bottle of champagne. Bess and Margie and another friend from The 68 Club sat around the house and got drunk for the first time in their lives.

On Friday nights, club members would gather at each other's houses. The mothers would bake. The fathers would sit and read the newspaper.

"The Yiddish newspaper," Lenore specified. "Only Margie's parents and my parents were American-born. We sang, danced. Glenn Miller. Artie Shaw. Benny Goodman. 'Chattanooga Choo-Choo.' 'In the Mood.' 'String of Pearls.' We had a lot of laughs."

It is fascinating by hindsight that none of the other girls was at all jealous of Bess's extraordinary beauty. Without the forge of a male presence to sharpen it, the sword of envy apparently did not fall between the plain and the gorgeous.

And by the time she was in college, Bess Myerson was *gorgeous*.

"Bess was dazzling-looking," Lenore attested.

"She sparkled," Margie said. "Her teeth were perfect. Her smile lit up the room."

"She had a glow . . . a brightness. . . ."

"It was incredible."

Lenore shook her head and laughed.

"Our friend Bess stopped traffic in the streets, literally," she said. "In the spring of 1944, my family went to see the Giants play at the Polo Grounds and we took Bess along because she had never been to a baseball game. There was a whole section of people sitting in front of us who never saw that ball game because they just couldn't take their eyes off her."

BESS MYERSON MIGHT HAVE TURNED OUT TO BE A VERY DIF-
ferent person if her looks had not developed at a time and in a
situation where there were so few men to admire her. She did
not take too seriously the reports of her beauty, which came in
the main from her buddies. Intellectually Bess may have understood that people responded to her looks. But that didn't ever really
make her feel secure. She had too much insecurity *for starters*.

For such a lovely girl, Bess had pitifully little acquaintance
with the passions of men. She was her mother's daughter,
sheltered, prudish, uptight about sex. At one time, she had
been studying music theory at Mrs. LaFollette's studio under a
guest instructor named Vittorio Giannini. He drove her home
one night and put his hand on her knee. She was fifteen. She
never went back for another music theory class.

Her first relaxed encounters with men occurred at the all-girls
Birchwood Camp in Vermont, where she worked for four summers as a music counselor.

Bess's older sister, Sylvia, had introduced Bess to camping
back in high school. At seventeen Sylvia had gone off to a camp
to be a music counselor. As soon as she arrived in the woods
(where Bella couldn't control her choices), she gave up the
music job and joined the waterfront staff. During successive
summers she rose to become head swimming counselor at
Kearsarge, an elegant, all-girls camp in New Hampshire.

"Sylvia brought me in as a counselor-in-training when I was
fifteen and looked seventeen," Bess remembered. "As a favor to
her, the directors waived my fee. They even gave me shorts and
shirts and socks. By the time I was eighteen, I had become a
seasoned counselor myself, and I had pulled my younger sister,
Helen, into camping after me."

Camp brought the urban girl from the cramped apartment

and the crowded subway a stretch and a romp among lakes and fields and forests. She learned to play tennis, ride horses. She made lanyards and wore them as necklaces, wrote new lyrics to the tunes from hit Broadway musicals like *Bloomer Girl* and taught them to her campers. She wore her hair in long black pigtails. Her flawless skin burned deep dark tan.

"Was it work to be a counselor? Not to my mind. I loved counting the heads in the beds every night, comforting the little girls who were homesick. It didn't feel like work any more than playing the piano felt like work. And the camp food! Compared to Mom's cooking, it was so delicious! Before the bowls of food were cleared at our table, I would finish everything that was left. Camp was my vacation, my annual breath of fresh air."

For her four college summers—1942, 1943, 1944, and 1945—Bess worked as the music counselor for Sam and Tuck DuBoff, the owners of Birchwood Camp for Girls in Vermont. Most of her campers came from wealthy homes in the new Jewish suburbs such as New Rochelle, South Orange, and the Five Towns on Long Island. Many of their fathers, like so many other American businessmen, had prospered while manufacturing goods for the war effort, often in the traditionally Jewish garment industry. Bess's campers had access to clothes, not only because they were rich but also because their connections allowed them to go wholesale.

"I envied the clothes of my campers," Bess said. "They brought cashmere sweaters and fabulous slacks like the ones Katharine Hepburn wore. Many of their parents were American-born. Their mothers reminded me of the mothers of other students I had met in Mrs. LaFollette's school. Sensitive. Educated. Caring. They were friends with their children. They would come up on visitors day and swim, play tennis, go for hikes with their daughters. That comradeship between parent and child was very moving to me."

Bess's best friend at Birchwood was the drama counselor, Gloria Winter, who wanted to be an actress. Bess recalls her now as a "blond, lusty, full-voiced girl with twinkling eyes and just the right mixture of cynicism and good humor." Gloria would one day work on the radio soap operas that riveted the

attention of the country then as television soaps do today—
shows such as *Henry Aldrich* and *Transatlantic Call*. In the
summers at camp, she and Bess put on musical shows together.

"I could never get over Bess's talent as a music counselor,"
Gloria said. "In ten minutes she had those kids singing three-
part harmony. One little girl who had a glorious voice grew up
to be Judith Raskin of the Metropolitan Opera. Bess taught
them a whole repertoire of choral music. And she also knew all
kinds of funny little songs. She taught me a parody of *Minnie
the Moocher* in Yiddish that I remember to this day, and I don't
speak a word of Yiddish.

"On our day off Bess and I used to go hitchhiking together. I
can tell you, we never had any problem getting cars to stop for
us. Bess always had to sit in the middle because she was bigger
than I was and we figured it was safer that way."

Across the lake from Birchwood was a "brother camp," Green
Mountain Camp for Boys. Members of the Columbia College
football team came up to be counselors there. In addition, some
of the ex-counselors, now mobilized into the armed forces,
would come up to camp for a two- or three-day furlough in the
country. Birchwood counselors like Bess and Gloria would get
together with them sometimes for square dances, for sodas in
town. They would exchange photos. But relationships with
these men were virtually impossible. They were gone too soon.

"I met a fellow there named Sam whom I liked very much.
Then he went off to fight the Japanese.

"I remember another man, several years my senior. He said
to me, 'I can't get involved with you, Bessie, because you're a
kid and I'm going to Europe to fight but I tell you, I wish I
could put you in a cage and keep you there and save you so that
nobody else would be able to touch you before I get back.'

"I thought he was a little old. I never dreamed that this
would turn out to be a common fantasy among men, as it
apparently is.

"When I returned to New York in the winter, I would carry
pictures of these fellows in uniform in my wallet, as though
they were my boyfriends. The truth is, however, I didn't have a
boyfriend. I had a walk in the moonlight, a kiss good night after
a square dance. I believe now that many of us invented fantasies

of passionate romances with men who were stationed in Italy. And men who were stationed in Manila invented fantasies about us."

One boy named Ronnie, the brother of one of Bess's campers, turned out to be tall and handsome and very nice. She went out with him once or twice before he shipped out to the Pacific.

"He wrote a long letter to his widowed mother and his sister and me. Called me his 'sweetheart.' I loved the way that looked on the page. 'Sweetheart.' He wrote about the terrible experience of crashing in the jungle, crawling out of the plane's wreckage, getting sick from the heat and the wet and the bugs and the filth, praying to find a friendly village over the next hill. . . . He made it to safety that time. But in the end, Ronnie was killed out there.

"I still remember his mother's screams. I sat with her. Mourned with her. I hardly knew him but I felt like I had lost him, too.

"It was a very strange, surreal time to be a young woman."

Gloria and Lenore both recall even now that there was something oddly aloof about Bess's demeanor.

"There was a wall up," Gloria recalled. "With men, a little wall . . ."

"I don't know when I began to detect a pattern of behavior," Lenore mused. "But I found that if Bess opened up too much about her deepest feelings, there was a withdrawal the next time you saw her. You'd walk into a glass wall. Then that would pass, and there would be a next time and she would be her sparkling self again."

"People have always liked Bess," Margie said. "But they always think of her as sort of sanitary. Not easily touchable."

"I remember how shy she was," Gloria added. "Once at camp, we went to the shower house to get cleaned up. Bess was in the shower next to me. I discovered that I had forgotten my soap. So I stuck my head around the bend and said, 'Hey, Bessie, can I borrow your soap?' She went Gasp! Gasp! and quickly covered herself up with a towel.

"Later on, in the summer of 1945, when she left camp to enter the Miss New York City contest, I thought, 'How can this be? This shy, modest girl is going to march around in front of strangers in a bathing suit?! Impossible!' "

The dualism of Bess's personality—an electric gaiety alternating with long blue melancholies—became harder and harder for her friends to understand as she enjoyed more and more success. A reality gap yawned between the girl as her public saw her—tall, strong, striking, composed—and the girl as she saw herself.

"I basked in the praise of the parents on the weekends when they would come to visit," Bess recalled. "They were delighted to see their children singing as I conducted the choir or directed a show. They loved my flute solos. Relative to Murray Panitz, perhaps I wasn't so terrific. But there in that setting, I was the best.

"Still, I never quite felt part of things. I could never participate in that easy, chatty feeling girls have with each other. If Gloria and I were in the counselors' house at night, confessing feelings about our parents, and I opened up and said, All I want is for my dear strange mother to be happy and she will never be happy, I would instantly regret that I had revealed so much and clam up.

"I felt so empty and lost inside. I used to sit on a grassy hill in the evening and play taps on the flute, feeling sorry for myself and crying. All the praise I received couldn't substitute for the praise I had never received from my mother at home. I longed for some wonderful man to come and save me from my life— but there didn't seem to be any, at least not for me. I liked being told I was pretty. However, I was desperately afraid that people would only like me because I was pretty.

"It was very strange. To be succeeding at what I was doing. And feel like a failure."

SOMETIME DURING BESS'S THIRD YEAR AT HUNTER, SHE MET John C. Pape. He was a retired steel manufacturer from New Jersey. He said he was an amateur photographer and asked if he might take some pictures of Bess. He offered her a sitting fee of five dollars an hour. Compared to what she earned from her other jobs, that seemed like all the money in the world.

"Mr. Pape wasn't the first person to suggest modeling," Bess said. "Murray Naidich, a neighbor at the Sholom Aleichem, had taken some pictures of me when I was still in high school. They had turned out pretty well.

"So when this sweet fatherly man said he would pay me for what I had done for Murray for free, I said, 'Sure.' Mr. Pape belonged to a camera club called The Little Studio Group, which met in an office building downtown. He gave me the address and said I should come there and pose.

"Of course, I didn't tell my mother because she would never have approved of such an escapade. I was in a terrible sweat on the subway, thinking, 'What have I gotten myself into? What if they want me to take off my clothes?!' However, when I walked in, I found these five elderly gentlemen, all of them absolutely adorable and very kind.

"The pictures they took gave me a look at myself I had never imagined before. I put on oodles of makeup. I did all the sultry, sunny, languid, grinning, pensive poses that the pinup girls in the movie magazines had made so popular. I pretended to be a battleship wallflower, like Betty Grable. I pretended to be a sexpot like Rita Hayworth. I put flowers in my hair like Dorothy Lamour. I made my lips twice as full as they actually were and covered them with dark, dark lipstick so I would look like Hedy Lamarr.

"Mr. Pape thought I was terrific.

"If someone told Mom that I looked pretty, she would say, 'Poo, poo, poo' to protect me from the Evil Eye, an old Jewish superstition. In Europe, you spit three times. In America, you said, 'Poo, poo, poo.' Well, Mr. Pape wasn't Jewish. He had no fear of the Evil Eye. His praise was lavish and unguarded.

"For me, modeling was a glamorous fantasy, like my invented romances with dashing pilots and submarine captains in snow white uniforms."

As a matter of fact, Sylvia had been thinking about suggesting a modeling career to Bess for a long time, and the advent of John Pape proved a convenient catalyst to get the show on the road.

"The first time I ever really noticed that Bessie was gorgeous," Sylvia said, "was when I brought her to camp as a CIT. She was fifteen. She was standing in a canoe, tipping and laughing, the water was sloshing in, and I thought, 'My God, Bessie is going to be beautiful. She's going to be as beautiful as the girls in the magazines.' "

During Bess's junior year at Music and Art, Sylvia (who had married by then) came around to the apartment one weekend to take her to the movies.

"She was sixteen," Sylvia recalled. "I was twenty-three. When we went into the RKO, the usher said, 'Gee, she's pretty, isn't she?' And that little incident was the first inkling I had that other people agreed with me, that perfect strangers thought Bessie was an exceptionally good-looking girl.

"One of the magazines was running a Ginger Rogers look-alike contest, and I called Bess and insisted that she enter.

"She said, 'But I don't look anything like Ginger Rogers!'

"I said, 'So what? You'll go in the contest anyway. Let's find out how they work.'

"And I sent in her picture, and of course she lost, and she was very upset with me and embarrassed, she didn't like contests and she didn't like losing.

"I said, 'Why are you so upset? You know you don't look anything like Ginger Rogers!' "

The net result of the Ginger Rogers look-alike lark was that Sylvia discovered her ambition, and Bess discovered that she could survive rejection. The ice was broken. The idea of modeling, of using Bess's God-given good looks to earn maybe a few dollars or even *win* a few dollars in the beauty business had touched the imagination of the Myerson sisters.

Under ordinary circumstances, Bess and Sylvia would never have considered modeling as a career, if only because of the deep-rooted intellectual snobbery of their Jewish background. After all, what nice Jewish girl was a model? It was tacky; it was for the dumb and dishonorable; it was the next worst thing to being a prostitute.

Being an actress—which everybody *else* considered the next worst thing to being a prostitute—did not strike the same chords of repulsion. The Jewish theatrical tradition, born only a scant century earlier during the European Haskala, or Enlightenment, had the dignity of "art." Had not the great Sarah Bernhardt been a Jew? Was not Fannie Brice the most famous comedienne in the history of America? A New York girl like Bess, with a background at the Sholom Aleichem and Music and Art, could understand that acting took talent.

But modeling took nothing, or so it seemed.

For Jewish girls, the ancient ego-ideal was the concept of *eshet chayil,* the woman of valor (Proverbs, Chapter 30) whose "price was far above rubies," who supported her husband while he studied, who honored him by giving charity to the poor. "She stretcheth out her hand to the troubled," the Bible said, "she reacheth forth her hand to the needy. . . . She doth her husband good and not evil. She worketh willingly with her hands. . . . Her lamp doth not go out by night. . . . She looks to the ways of her household. . . . Her mouth opens only with wisdom. . . . She laughs at the time to come."

Of all the glorious traits the woman of valor possessed, physical beauty was nowhere mentioned. In the lives of men it might be a big plus, but in the *moral* scheme of things it just wasn't important. In fact, if there was any tradition for the uses of pretty girls that worked on the collective subconscious of the Jewish people, it was the harsh and bloody example of a series of biblical heroines—Yael; Judith; and, on the other side Delilah—who made their mark by sleeping with enemy generals and then doing them in.

But the most persuasive Jewish story of the wages of beauty was told every year at Purim, a holiday so jolly that even children from secularized families like those in the Sholom Aleichem houses could not help but feel its mighty message. The young Persian-Jewish heroine of the Purim festival, Esther (Hebraicized from the Persian goddess's name Astarte), is sent by her Uncle Mordechai to be a contestant in a kind of empirewide beauty contest, held by Persian King Ahashueres who—having slaughtered his old queen in a drunken rage—now needs a new one.

Mordechai's idea is that Esther's beauty may be a bankable asset, something to place in a savings account for possible future use. When Esther wins the contest, Mordechai instructs her not to tell the king that she is Jewish. Just hang in, he tells her; be a good queen and a good wife and hang in tight.

His advice pays off later on, when the king's ambitious prime minister, Haman, decides to do away with every single Jew in Persia. (Apparently he is jealous of their wealth, their cleverness, and their influence. Not for nothing is this cautionary tale impressed upon American children.) Esther then invites Haman over for dinner, she shames him before the king, her husband, and reveals that she, too, is a Jew and bound to die if Haman's evil plan goes through. The good-natured king cannot bear the idea of losing his Queen Esther, so he hangs Haman instead of the Jews.

All of this tradition served to place a subliminal break on any Jewish girl's desire to exploit her beauty. She might know it was powerful, but she also knew it could lead her to perdition. So when Sylvia first realized that Bess was beautiful, she reacted in the tradition of Mordechai the Wise, with limited ambition. "Let's see what we can do with this," she thought. "Let's see if we can put it in the bank where it will turn into money so that later on, when Bess wants to buy a new piano or open her own music school, she will have some cash to back her up."

The beauty thing was a matter of money for the Myerson sisters. It was never a matter of pride.

As an industry in the 1940s, modeling was divided effectively between two New York agencies. John Robert Powers had started the first in 1928; it began, in the words of the famous model Candy Jones, "as a central employment office for 'at leisure' actors and actresses who needed bread, butter, and rent money"[3] and developed over the next ten years into the single largest source of models in every medium. In 1938, Harry Conover, an ex-disk jockey who was himself one of the most popular male models in New York, started his own agency with the help of an investment from another former male model, Gerald Ford. (Yes, *that* Gerald Ford).

Powers and Conover represented power and glamour; they made some women very famous. They made fortunes in the 1940s by negotiating contracts for their models with the big Hollywood studios: Paramount, MGM, 20th Century-Fox, Warner's, and Columbia. Corporations came to them for the one symbolic female whose charms might sell their products. The WACS sent ten of their best lookers through the Conover course to try to improve the image of the branch during the recruitment campaigns of the war years. Like ambitious young women all across the country, Bess saw the *March of Time* documentary segment on fashion modeling that appeared in 1943 and the hit film of 1944 *Cover Girl,* starring Rita Hayworth and Gene Kelly. The effect was seductive.

For the model herself, the major benefit of this life of hard work and long hours was not only money but also excitement, and an entree into New York's glittery cafe society. During the war, the city seemed to explode with clubs and in-crowds whose dashing high jinks were eagerly reported by phenomenally popular columnists like Earl Wilson, Walter Winchell, and Ed Sullivan.[4]

"Life in the forties in New York was just so much fun," recalled Natalie Reid, a Conover model. "My favorite club was Armando's. . . . Also there was a club called El Bocaccio, where I had my lip prints in a room called the Kiss Room. . . . I also

---

[3] Candy Jones, *Modeling and Other Glamour Careers* (New York: Harper & Row, 1969), p. 18.

[4] Jan Morris, *Manhattan '45* (New York: Oxford University Press, 1987), p. 196 *et passim.*

[5] Carole Conover, *Cover Girls: The Story of Harry Conover* (Englewood Cliffs, N.J.: Prentice-Hall, 1978), p. 115.

[6] Noted in Brown's unpublished autobiography in the archives of the Society of Illustrators, New York.

enjoyed El Morocco and the Stork Club. . . . In the forties to be a model was to be the most glamorous person possible. . . . We walked very proudly with our hat boxes and were the envy of all the other women and girls."[5]

Powers adopted illustrator Arthur William Brown's appellation "long-stemmed American beauties" to apply to his tall, sleek, dramatic stable of women[6]—while Conover specialized in "the girl next door" types. He often changed their names to Dusty and Honey and Sunny and Windy. These seem like the names of strippers to us now, but in those days they imbued the personae of the lovely girls with all-American fresh air.

At the beginning of the war, modeling for magazines served as a stepping-stone to "Hollywood, the be-all and end-all." The magazine illustrators presided like kings over any girl's success. If Bradshaw Crandall wanted to put your face on the cover of *Cosmopolitan*, or Arthur William Brown wanted to use you in a story illustration, you were on your way. "The illustrators were the Avedons of that era," recalled Candy Jones. She summed up in one story the wonderful adventures a girl might have if she came to New York to be a model at the height of the wartime glitz.

"My name was Jessie Wilcox then," Candy recounted. "I had just been voted Miss Atlantic City of 1941. I was rooming at the Barbizon in New York with Frances Burke, who was Miss America that year, and Pat Donnelly, who was Miss America the year before.

"One night, Pat said, 'Come on, we're going to the Stork Club. I have a blind date for you. Dress formal.' So I put on my evening gown and a long red cape that I had never worn before. It was still stitched up. We couldn't open the stitches. Pat said to hurry up, so I put it over my head. I looked like a long red mummy, and I couldn't get my hands out.

"Pat was wearing my gold slippers. Frances had gone out wearing my silver slippers. So I had to wear my saddle shoes, which were hidden under the hem of the long dress and the cape.

"So off we went to the Stork Club. The doorman opened the limousine door. I couldn't move because I was stitched into this cape. He had to haul me out and stand me on my feet.

"Inside, my date said, 'Wouldn't you like to take your cape off?' I said, 'I can't because I'm stitched in.' So he picked at the stitches with this sharp knife while I held my breath, and finally he set me free.

"Sunday night was Balloon Night at the Stork Club. An enormous net held the balloons, and in each one was a number, corresponding to a prize—a hundred dollars or a magnum of champagne or maybe even a little dog. Only the ladies could catch balloons. I had an advantage because I could jump and run easily in my saddle shoes.

"I won a dinner party for twenty-four people. But I couldn't have a dinner party just yet because I didn't know anyone in New York. I figured maybe John Robert Powers would give me a job modeling for Chesterfields and then I'd meet lots of people and have lots of parties. . . .

"The next week I went for my appointment with Powers. He told me I had wrinkles in my neck and that I walked like a football player."

Harry Conover, however, had a different perception. By 1946 he had changed Jessie Wilcox's name to Candy Jones, married her, and made her his business associate and one of the most famous faces in the United States.

Candy pushed modeling. She started a cover-girl modeling school. She and other models told stories of their exciting nights in New York to women's magazines such as *Glamour, Charm,* and *Vogue*. Few pretty girls were not inspired by tales like that of Dorian Leigh, who had left her job as a tool designer in a war plant to become one of the leading cover girls in the country, earning upward of eighteen thousand dollars a year! Few did not know that Barbara Stanwyck, Paulette Goddard, Lauren Bacall, Lisbeth Scott, and Jinx Falkenberg had come through the modeling business to that greatest of all rewards—the movies.

Most important for Bess and her growing awareness of the modeling option, the business had gained tremendous respectability. Photographic reproduction by new printing processes had vastly improved. The photographers could now challenge the illustrators' monopoly on power and emotion; the well-drawn picture was being replaced by the well-lit one. Inspired by dramatic achievements in documentary photography made by war correspondents like Robert Capa, fashion photography tried for a new excitement, employed a new artistry. The "new" models had to be smart girls able to deal with expanding technology. In addition, television—a prize invented for the war, like antibiotics and nuclear power—was on its way in and required a whole new type of *animated* beauty.

What David Sarnoff, RCA's president, said of political candidates would soon prove true for pretty girls: "Their dress, their smiles and gestures . . . may determine to an appreciable extent their popularity."[7] The thin, vivacious girl with sparkling eyes and a dazzling grin who could put over a parody or improvise a tune—like Bess—had more of a future than ever before. By the end of the war in 1945, with millions of women being laid off at the war plants and sent home by the corporations that had used them as male substitutes during the fighting, secretarial, domestic, elementary-school teaching, waitressing, and pink-collar beauty shop jobs were what women could do for a living once again. By contrast, modeling now became the most inviting profession open to young single girls.

Encouraged by the new respectability of a modeling career, tempted by the money Bess might make, cheered by high-spirited magazine reports of what fun it was to be a cover girl, fascinated not so much by the distant gleam of Hollywood as by the prospect of television (centered in New York), Sylvia gathered the photos that Mr. Pape had made of Bess and sent them off to John Robert Powers and Harry Conover.

Powers didn't like Bess any better than he had liked Candy Jones.

Conover told Bess that he wanted "the all-American type," which, in his opinion, she wasn't.

That was it for Bess.

She gave up the idea of modeling at the first sign of rejection.

She figured it was a career for someone else's daughter. For herself, she determined to find another half-dozen piano students. She figured one of the five million Americans who would soon be home from the war would fall in love with her and they'd get married.

[7] Joseph C. Goulden, *The Best Years, 1945–1950* (New York: Atheneum, 1976), p. 170.

In June 1945, while Bess was preparing for her graduation from Hunter, photographer John C. Pape heard about the competition for Miss New York City that was being conducted by Radio Station WJZ, the Blue Network. He consulted Sylvia. They decided not to tell Bess but to enter her in the contest.

Bess had gone off to Camp Birchwood after graduation, to be the head music counselor. Her sister Helen was a member of the staff at the same camp. In late July, Bess was busily directing *H.M.S. Pinafore* with the girls when word came from Sylvia back in the Bronx that John Pape had called, all excited because WJZ had chosen Bess from among 1,200 applicants to be one of 350 contestants. Of these, a further selection narrowed the field to sixty.

Bess would not go. Her rocky ego had barely survived the close encounters with Powers and Conover, and she didn't want to compete any more in this beauty business, which was, she felt, embarrassing.

Refusing to take "no" for an answer, Sylvia called the camp owners, Sam and Tuck DuBoff, and secured their agreement to give Bess time off. Then she called Bess, instructed her to get hold of a flattering bathing suit, return to New York immediately, and appear in the pageant.

Sylvia's strength of purpose did the trick. Bess turned over *Pinafore* to her sister Helen, borrowed a bathing suit (a two-piece white) from a camper named Paula Hirsh, and off Bess went, to compete for the title of Miss New York City.

"Don Rich, a square, squat little fellow, was the public-relations director of radio station WJZ," Bess remembered. "He led us onto the stage of a large, empty theater, the Ritz. I quaked, thinking of appearing before an audience that size. However, as soon as I saw the piano, I felt more secure. I had been playing before audiences since I was ten years old. I had nothing if not self-assurance in a concert setting.

"I remember walking onto the stage, looking around at the other girls, feeling like I was out of another mold. They were very blond and cover-girlish. Very Candy Jones. I was tall and dark. I had no hips. I remember feeling . . . not desperate . . . but giving up beforehand, as though I were the wrong person in the wrong place. Since all the other girls were so much like each other and so different from me, I thought surely one of them would be chosen."

The girls were told the routine. Then they went backstage, changed into their bathing suits, rehearsed walking across the stage, then changed into their performing clothes. Bess rehearsed a three-minute arrangement of Grieg on the piano and Gershwin on the flute. The audience arrived. The girls did the entire routine over again.

Don Rich announced that Bess was one of the fifteen girls to make the finals. Then Sylvia took her to the train and she went back to camp.

Sam DuBoff, proud and beaming, announced at lunch that Bess had made the finals. Her friends and campers were thrilled with her success in what was to them the exotic world of the beauty business. All week long they greeted her with "Hi, Miss New York City!" as though she had already won. Bess still didn't think she would win and was pleased that the finals would occur at the end of camp, sparing her a postscript confrontation with the disappointment of her fans. She concentrated on the production of *Pinafore* that Helen had handled ably in her absence.

However, the enthusiasm at Birchwood began to get to Bess. Even the news of the world seemed to suit her exhilarated state of mind. Her own girlish notes from a personal diary she kept at the time reflect that better than anything.

> *Midnight train to New York, Friday August 14. In New York 8:00 a.m. To Sylvia's. Slept until 6:30 p.m. War over. Building ablaze with parties. Finals tomorrow.*

Bill Grace, Sylvia's husband, thought the whole thing was stupid. "What are you knocking yourself out for?" he said to Sylvia. "She'll never win. This is all just an exercise in futility."

But he stayed home with their daughters, Michelle, then two and a half, and Francine, then only six months, while Sylvia accompanied Bess to the Ritz for the finals.

Sometime after midnight, Sylvia called and said to her husband with relish, "Guess who is the new Miss New York City?"

Bess wrote in her diary,

> *August 15. Won honors. Miss New York City. Ray Knight was MC. Murray Korman presented me with watch.*
>
> *Paul Whiteman, Danton Walker judges. Photographers took pictures. Dad very excited. Mom unfortunately away.*
>
> *Met Bob Steen who manages Ritz Theatre. Tall, blonde, extremely good looking. Then to the Monte Carlo with Dick Flanagan and Bob (he's wonderful!), Sylvia, and John Pape.*
>
> *Mrs. Slaughter, head of the Miss America Pageant, there with us. Called camp from the Monte Carlo. Everyone there celebrating. More pictures. Dick Flanagan resented Bob Steen being there with me. He says he's trying to set up a deal with Howard Hughes(!) who is peculiar and likes the girls to be unattached. Left for El Moroco with Flanagan. Had champagne! Met Spanish playboys. Chauffeur drove us home at 6 a.m.!*

Meanwhile, Flanagan, the manager of the Monte Carlo, said privately to Sylvia, "Listen Sylvia, your sister is going to go to Atlantic City to the Miss America Pageant now. She's going to need someone to get her clothes. I'll introduce you to all the right people. . . . I'll take care of your sister."

Said Sylvia to Flanagan, "Look, Flanagan, *I'm* managing my sister, and *I'm* going down to Atlantic City with her, thanks very much, bye-bye."

Said Earl Wilson in his column "It Happened One Night": "Bess Myerson's sister is keeping the wolves from the door!"

When she woke up on August 16, 1945, Bess was a little bit of a celebrity. Her picture had appeared in a couple of the papers. Her name was springing up in the columns. For the next couple of days she was whisked off on a madcap spree of wining and dining and dancing and meeting new men and being flattered and hearing promises of fame and fortune unlike anything she had ever imagined before!

Don Rich was running after her. Dick Flanagan was running after her. She wanted Bob Steen, the handsome blond theater manager, to run after her, but he didn't. She invited John Pape along to everything. All her other erstwhile "managers" wished he would get lost.

"Dick Flanagan invited the new twenty-one-year-old Miss New York City Bess Myerson to the Monte Carlo," wrote Earl Wilson, "but her chaperon, an elderly photographer, told her, 'You can only stay half an hour.' They went and three hours later, the old guy was having such a good time, he had to be dragged out of the joint. . . ."

WJZ took Bess over as though she were a new hit song and played her everywhere. Her diary, scribbled on trains, in taxis, showed how impressed she was.

> *August 17: 9:00 a.m. train to Schenectady to appear on Dumont TV with Bobbie Henry from WJZ. Stayed at Van Curless Hotel. Delicious lunch with Ann Armstrong and Lee Pepper. Rehearsed at 4:00 p.m. Performed at 9:00 p.m. Television is terrific stuff!! Pictures taken. Cocktail party. McLane from General Electric says I could be great on television, he's sold on me. To bed at 2:00 a.m.*
>
> *August 18: Morning train to New York with Johnny Olsen, the announcer. Olsen wants me on his radio show! Must get outfitted.*

She had won the New York City contest on August 15, a scant month after her twenty-first birthday, and now only three days later, the fun was fading and a sense of urgency had begun to mount. She was, after all, going to Atlantic City, where they were, after all, offering a five-thousand-dollar scholarship! Lenora Slaughter, executive director of the Miss America Pageant, had made it clear to Bess at the WJZ New York City contest that she intended "to make the Pageant the first major national event of the peacetime era." Now that Bess was in this thing, she owed it to herself and the moment to do everything in her power *not to lose.*

From the Jersey shore, Lenora now sent complicated contracts (which both Louis and Bess had to sign) as well as a long form letter to all contestants. It struck terror into the heart of the Myerson household.

"We are eagerly anticipating your arrival in this resort on Monday, September 3," Lenora's letter said, "and we promise you the happiest experience of your life. We know you are going to enjoy every event we have planned for you and we also know it is going to be a grand experience for you to meet the charming and representative girls from every section of this great Nation of ours, as well as Cuba and British Columbia. We know you are going to enter into the festivities with all the sportsmanship you have already shown in your own home towns and states. Only one girl can win the title of Miss America but 40 girls will have had the experience of competing in the National Finals which is an honor each of you can remember in the years to come. I am confident that your mothers will be just as happy with your participation in the Pageant as you will be and *I am personally anticipating meeting not only you beautiful and charming girls but your mothers, for to them goes a great deal of the credit for the success you have obtained. . . .*"

Bess panicked. Her mother would never agree to go! And what would happen if she *did*?!

She would stay locked up in her hotel room.

She wouldn't want to eat what was prepared, so she'd probably try to *cook* in the hotel room.

She'd be embarrassed about her English; awkward with the other mothers. She wouldn't mingle.

Bess would have to take care of her.

And then who would take care of Bess?

But there was yet more to fear in the chatty hyperbole of Lenora Slaughter's form letter.

"Be sure to bring a minimum of three and a maximum of four evening gowns," she wrote. "You will wear evening gowns at all formal appearances where you are judged. Street clothes should be simple and youthful. At no time are you judged in street clothes. You appear in the Boardwalk Parade in an evening gown. Therefore, concentrate on your evening clothes, which do not have to be expensive but should be most flattering."

At the time she received this epistle, Bess had the one long white dress she had worn during the WJZ contest, and she had not the faintest idea where she was to get two or three more. Unlike pageants in other cities, where the Chamber of Commerce or a local department store might be sponsoring the contestant, the Miss New York City contest brought no immediate investment in the wardrobe of the participating girl. In her naïveté and fright, Bess imagined thirty-nine other contestants outfitted from head to toe in designer clothes bought by rich men from Birmingham to Boston.

Her heart sank. When John Pape stepped in with an offer to have a seamstress make her daytime clothes, she was enormously relieved and grateful. But her brother-in-law Bill was suspicious of Pape. He wondered aloud why "the old guy" was spending so much money on Bessie. His suspicion was catching, and it spoiled the fun.

To mix the blessing even more, the tabloid displays and articles about her in the newspapers had attracted some unwanted attention. Her diary entries were shifting focus.

> *August 19: Received letter from crank. Filthy notes made on picture. Letter contained derogatory statements. Must not think about this.*
>
> *August 20: Down town to meet Pape for fittings on dresses. Up to see Rich. He's being divorced by his wife. Declined his invite for dinner at Toots Shor's. Never rains but what it pours. Call from crank. Asked me to guess what he had in his hand. I hung up on him. Dad found a condom around the doorknob in the morning; it wasn't empty.*
>
> *Dad wants to call the police. Don Rich said not to call the police because that might draw attention to the situation and invite yet more dirty letters. He said he'd take care of it. Mom came home.*

With characteristic bad luck, Bella Myerson—having missed all the fun of the first days after Bess's victory—returned just in time to find it sullied by the proliferation of disgusting letters and phone calls coming in from nuts around the city.

Bella accepted a big hug and a kiss from Bess and congratulations on being the mother of Miss New York City. "I'm not going with you to Atlantic City, Bessie," she announced. "You'll go with your sister Sylvia. Sylvia, you'll send your children to me so they'll have a decent meal."

John Pape met with Bess and Sylvia to discuss the all-important matter of a picture for the Pageant booklet. "Most contestants submitted poses of themselves in traditional swimsuit cheesecake," Bess remembered. "Pape wanted me to have some picture that would distinguish me from among all the others. We decided that we should submit pictures of me in the academic cap and gown I had worn for my graduation."

It was a brilliant idea and the first stroke of victory, but nobody knew that yet. Bess herself was too busy nurturing a brand-new crush, and her uptight family was too busy guarding her against the perverts who seemed to be lurking around every corner.

> *August 22: Spent restless night. Downtown with Sylvia and Bill. Met Mr. Pape for pictures in robes. Spoke to Bob Steen . . . he's really very nice. To dinner at McGinnis's. Appeared as guest artist. Mom there this time. I think she enjoyed herself! She said fellows have been annoying the super at the Sholom Aleichem to find out where I am. Told Don Rich. Brother-in-law Bill contacted FBI. Said they'd take care of it. Out with Bob Steen for drinks.*
>
> *Sylvia doesn't want me to come home alone with any of these new guys, so she sent Bill to pick me up at 1:20 a.m.*

Not all the people who read about Bess in the paper were having X-rated thoughts about her. Samuel Kass, a Seventh Avenue fashion manufacturer, turned out to be a savior. Moved by patriotic feelings for his city, stirred by the photos of Bess that had appeared in the papers, aware that she must be a poor girl without much to wear (Giles Place in the Bronx was not known as the ritziest of addresses), he called and offered her whatever she wanted from his line of evening dresses. Bess was overjoyed. A perfect stranger had taken it upon himself to rescue her.

"So down we flew in the worst heat of August to the Kass

showroom on Seventh Avenue," Bess recalled. "I was introduced to this distinguished, dark-haired man who smelled of
fresh lime aftershave. He was impeccably dressed, with cuff
links and manicured fingernails, surrounded by many models
and seamstresses who were so wonderful and welcoming to us.
My heart was pounding; I thought I was meeting royalty. And
when Mr. Kass opened his mouth to speak, he spoke with one
of those sort of 'I'm trying to sound like Sir Laurence Olivier,
but I'm really a tailor from Minsk' accents that Myron Cohen
always used in his comedy routines. God bless that wonderful
Mr. Kass. He was the first person I ever met who really understood that even a pretty girl can't make do with a potato sack."

On the twenty-fourth of August, she again boarded a train for
Schenectady, where WJZ was promoting its newly selected Miss
New York State, June Jenkins. For the first time, someone let
Bess climb up *behind* a television camera, an early, burly
version of today's sleek models. The two Miss New Yorks, Bess
and June, horsed around with it, pretending to be shooting
scenes of each other, feeling themselves on the cutting edge of
the infant industry. On the radio, Bess played the Chopin
"Fantasie Impromptu," and this time she was given a chance to
talk. For months her sister Sylvia, the speech therapist, had been
training her to pronounce her consonants, to deregionalize her
accent. It had worked to a degree. She sounded good on the
radio.

However, a panic had begun to seize her as the Atlantic City
Pageant approached. With Bella's suspicions of all things joyful
to discourage her—it was too good to be true; there must be
something wrong; the promoters promising wealth and fame
must be lying; there must be an Evil Eye lurking, poo, poo,
poo—Bess pulled back from her own joy. She began to derogate
her own appearance, afraid to believe that she was as beautiful
as all the sharp guys said she was. She thought constantly about
finding a man and getting married. She wrote in her diary,

> *August 26: Babs Sobel says Phyllis Brand from camp is
> getting married September 6th. Lucky girl. I'm losing my
> tan and getting thinner.*

August 27: On roof sunning with Helen, trying to stay tan. Don Rich sent me down to Hollywood Model school for a lesson in walking in high heels. Mr. Pape took me down to the Allan Young show. Young says he wants to make me another Hildegarde. Fat chance.

August 30: Felt kind of low. Postponed appointment with P.M. Magazine photographer. Bad night. Even hoped I wouldn't win.

In a scant two weeks, Bess had ingested her mother's mood, hunted down her own confidence, and shot it out of the sky like a bird in midflight. Other girls were getting married. Why was she spending her time with con men and fools?

Even the jolly little mayor of New York, Fiorello LaGuardia, asked what a girl like Bess Myerson from Music and Art and Hunter was doing en route to a low-life event like the Miss America Pageant.

August 31: Met Mayor LaGuardia. He asked me if the Miss America Pageant was merely another fanny-shaking contest where I'd have to compete with a lot of empty headed females who show their legs. Made me promise I'd stick to my music and write and tell him what school I was going to attend. Pics by Press. Standing behind a desk next to Mayor LaGuardia. One of the photographers asked the Mayor please to stand up. "I am standing up, dammit!" yelled LaGuardia. Don Rich working on a deal to put me and June Jenkins on Aquacade Saturday and Sunday evening for $75.00. But of course it won't go through.

The first casualty of this downward mood was John Pape. He had given Bess her big break; she was bound to him by affection and loyalty. But her new "managers" didn't like him. He was too old, too much of an amateur, and although she didn't understand why, they thought he was in their way. She wrote,

Don Rich really let Mr. Pape have it over the phone. Full of anger at why Pape is hanging around, wants Pape to

clear out. Pape is obviously annoyed by my overcrowded schedule. I can't just drop him. . . . He's been too good to me.

It was September 1. In forty-eight hours she would have to pack up all her new clothes and her new fears and head out for Atlantic City. Don Rich and John Pape would be with her, but they were distracted by their battle for control of her career. Sylvia would be with her, but Sylvia was almost as scared as she was.

Her father tried his usual brand of philosophical comfort. "So you'll lose," he said, "at least you'll have a vacation at the beach. When you *win, THEN* we'll worry."

Bess's friends from Hunter, Lenore Miller and Margie Wallis, came over for the afternoon. "It was a slow easy day," she wrote in the last entry of her diary. "But my nerves are drawn taut as piano wires."

In this state of aggravated tension, Bess Myerson went with her sister Sylvia Grace to the Miss America Pageant in Atlantic City.

CHAPTER 5

The
Occupation
of Atlantic City

Sylvia and I were both tremendously excited about going to Atlantic City. We had never seen the Boardwalk or stayed in a hotel. We couldn't even imagine room service. Sylvia bought some new clothes. She had her dark hair done in a very sophisticated upsweep. The minute our train pulled out of New York on Monday morning—it was September 3, 1945, a beautiful day—she began to bounce with contagious good humor.

"We're going to have a wonderful time, Bess," she said. "At the very least, we will have a terrific time."

We knew of Atlantic City as a famous resort town, a summer playground for the Astors and the Vanderbilts, for Hollywood stars like Frank Sinatra and Judy Garland. We associated it with Easter Parades, big bands on the Steel Pier, saltwater taffy, hot-dog-eating marathons, chimpanzees in chess tournaments, Monopoly, all sorts of zaniness and fun.

Many Broadway shows previewed in Atlantic City before coming to New York. My wealthy campers went on vacations there, especially around the Jewish New Year, when the weather was still warm and the ocean still swimmable. We had both seen the movie Atlantic City, *which had appeared in 1944. It was about the Miss America Pageant, glorious gowns and gala dinners, wine and roses and true love. That movie had left me limp with desire for romance.*

The first blast of sea air that hit us when we arrived was like artificial respiration. The freshness of it. The salt and tang of it. The weather was perfect. Cloudless and sunny but not hot. Sylvia and I went out to the Boardwalk, leaned on the railing, turned our faces toward the sea, and just breathed. It was the most intoxicating breath I had ever taken in my life.

We reported to the Seaside Hotel for registration. All around us, beautiful girls chatted and laughed with their spiffy mothers. I found them extremely "put together" with their hats and their manicures. All the states were not represented in those days. A total of forty girls had entered the competition, some representing states, some representing cities, depending on the availability of local sponsors. So, for example, there was no Miss Wyoming. There was a Miss California, named Polly Ellis, as well as a Miss San Diego, named Phyllis Mathis, but no Miss Los Angeles, no Miss San Francisco.

The first girl I met was Miss Birmingham, Frances Dorn, a vivacious, chestnut-haired tap dancer. She came with two chaperones: Lily May Caldwell, a distinguished lady who reminded me of one of the Gish sisters; and Jimmy Hatcher, a charming, sophisticated young man with a generous smile. These three seemed to me to be quite comfortable everywhere they went. They showed none of the tension that the rest of us were feeling.

Miss Florida, Jeni Freeland, was blond and cool. Her mother looked so young that at first I thought she must not be a mother but an older sister, like Sylvia. I was pleased to see June Jenkins, Miss New York State, whom I already knew from our television trip to Schenectady; and Gloria Bair, Miss Philadelphia, who would turn out to be my next-door neighbor all through the Pageant. A pretty, petite brunette from Minnesota, Arlene Anderson, told us she played the marimbaphone and that she had been studying music for many years. I remember thinking that the talent part of the Pageant was not going to be so easy to win as in the New York City contest.

A woman introduced herself as my chaperone from the official Hostess Committee. Although she was perfectly polite, Sylvia and I both felt that she was rather cold compared to the other girls' chaperones.

Lenora Slaughter, the Pageant director, seemed to be everywhere, giving orders in her high-pitched southern voice, sending us here and there, patting everybody. I am sure she was trying to allay our obvious nervousness. However, Lenora had a way of smiling perpetually, even while she talked, and that conveyed a feeling of insincerity that made me even more nervous than I had been in the first place.

Lenora told us to wear our identifying badges at all times, to make it clear to everyone around that this flood of pretty girls had been brought in courtesy of the Miss America Pageant. The vacationers with their children did not resent the invasion. On the contrary, they loved it. They spoke to us in a friendly, welcoming way, as though we were a good omen.

And we were. We were the first harbingers of peace.

Everybody in Atlantic City felt a little bit like me and Sylvia at that moment in September 1945. Released, like in the end of Beethoven's *Fidelio*. Out of jail. Breathing free. Because the terrible war was finally over.

We Americans had won at last, at a cost we had not yet been obligated to face. In our minds, we carried the image of heroic soldiers raising our flag on Mount Suribachi at Iwo Jima. We did not realize that Joe Rosenthal's picture was taken after seven thousand Marines had died and twenty-one thousand had been wounded, after twenty thousand Japanese soldiers had been killed, all on that one island.

On V-E Day the previous May, we had celebrated and cheered. General Eisenhower had promised us "no more doleful lists of death and loss" from the European Theater. It would take us years to understand that forty million people had died in Europe and to have any real sense of connection with them.

We had no comprehension that the surrender of Japan only three weeks earlier, on August 14, had been purchased by unleashing weapons that could destroy all humanity. We thought the atomic bomb was just a bigger bomb than the ones the Germans had dropped on London. We were brokenhearted that President Roosevelt, whose death in April had sent me and my Hunter friends staggering into Central Park to weep with thousands of other New Yorkers, had not lived to see the glorious day of victory. When I think now of our innocence then, I am overwhelmed with sorrow that we should have been so joyful.

But we were. That is the truth; we were all joyful. The soldiers on the Boardwalk who whistled at us and waved to us knew they weren't going to have to go back to fight again. They are in my scrapbook and forever in my memory, with their uniforms and their medals, grinning with relief and, just like us, full of hope.

━━━━━━━
───────

ON THE EVE OF THE MISS AMERICA PAGEANT OF 1945, ATLANtic City, New Jersey, was in the grip of a transformation. It had been occupied by the U.S. Army.

From the onset of the war, the Armed Forces command had fastened on Atlantic City with its dozens of hotels and thousands of beds as one logical place to house and train America's new soldiers quickly. Between 1941 and 1946, 350,000 military personnel passed through the town.

During that time, the whole look and feel of Atlantic City changed. Instead of strolling vacationers, the Boardwalk was phalanx-deep in khaki-clad men running in double time under the watchful eyes of barking sergeants. The security forces insisted that at night all the Boardwalk shop windows be covered with blue cellophane, which made the coastline stores as iridescent as the night sky and all but invisible to German vessels lurking (*now* they tell us) only a short distance out to sea.

The normal influx of vacationers shrank to a trickle when the war began. Most people were too busy in these tense, troubled days—working overtime, gearing up, cutting back—to enjoy the luxury of a week at the shore.

The Boardwalk shops that traditionally offered furs, fancy clothes, jewels, and objects of art started going broke. The food wholesalers, the mechanics, plumbers, and cement and building materials vendors started making fortunes on government orders. The hotels were in big trouble, and in many cases, the

Army—far from being an invasive billeting force—appeared as *deus ex machina* to save the day. All in all, the U.S. Army took over forty-seven resort hotels and paid them on the basis of a dollar a day per bed. This may seem a patriotically low price, but it was real money. "Whether they'll admit it or not," one owner told *The Saturday Evening Post* at the time, "some of the big hotels were operating in the red. But if the Army stays here three years, they'll be in the black."[1]

The first soldiers to arrive in Atlantic City were raw recruits. Cavernous Convention Hall became their basic training center. If you went through the door marked "Ladies' Bathhouse," you found not ladies bathing but the desk of the post intelligence officer.

With the advent of the troops, the prostitute population of the city skyrocketed. The Army immediately banded together with the City Fathers (and the many local mobsters) to halt the influx—fearful that the young warriors would contract the dread venereal diseases of that day, gonorrhea and syphilis, and be debilitated long before they had had a chance to die for their country. The City Council issued an edict that girls under eighteen could not be on the streets unchaperoned after nine (this sounds like a law written more to protect the young ladies of Atlantic City against the soldiers rather than vice versa), and the police drove all but the most circumspect whores into the hinterland.

Significantly, it was in 1941 that "Nucky" Johnson, the head of the Atlantic City mob, the man responsible for political patronage, illegal gambling, bootlegging during Prohibition, entertaining Al Capone when he came to visit the shore, and the administration of the red-light district, finally retired.[2]

The entire city participated in the process of welcoming and nurturing the servicemen. The Catholic Daughters of America opened its Stella Maris clubhouse to all soldiers who wanted to drop by. Since the Jewish Community Center had been taken

---

[1] Martha S. Woolley and Pete Martin, "Camp Boardwalk," *The Saturday Evening Post* (February 27, 1943), p. 35.
[2] Vicki Gold Levi and Lee Eisenberg, *Atlantic City: 125 Years of Ocean Madness* (New York: Clarkson N. Potter, 1979), p. 191.

over by the Coast Guard, a new JCC opened on South States Avenue and became a drop-in center for military personnel seeking latkes on Channukah, matzoh on Pesach, and an invitation for dinner on Shabbos.

Colonel Robert T. Glassburn, the Basic Training Center commander, had to issue public pleas warning goodhearted citizens in local bars not to buy drinks for the men in uniform. Since the men had to be back in their hotel barracks by nine o'clock, saloonkeepers were asked to push them out the door around eight-thirty.

A group called The Sewing Moms from Absecon Island put in thousands of hours altering soldiers' uniforms. This turned out to be a vital task, because by 1943 the spiffy dress uniforms of the young recruits often no longer fit very well. Said Jean Bartel, Miss America of 1943, "It was the year we were losing the war. The year my friends were getting killed." It was the year the Army turned Atlantic City from a Basic Training Center into a giant convalescent facility for returning veterans, some of whom had been grievously wounded.

On August 15, 1943, the Chalfont Haddon Hall and Traymore hotels were rechristened into Thomas M. England General Hospital—known to all as England General—the largest amputee hospital in the world. The hospital was named for a former Surgeon General of the Army who had done heroic service in the fight against yellow fever in Cuba during the Spanish-American War.

Into the lavish corridors of famous hotels came some of the best young physicians in the country, men like Howard Rusk of New York and Rufus Aldredge of Alabama, who would use their wartime experience to coach great advances in prosthetics and rehabilitative therapy. Rusk went on to found the Institute for the Rehabilitation of the Disabled in Manhattan and became a medical editor of *The New York Times.* Aldredge became a professor of orthopedic surgery at Tulane and received the Legion of Merit for his work at England General.

"At the time my husband took over command of amputee surgery at England General," Mrs. Lib Aldredge recalled, "he was thirty-five years old. Now I have a son thirty-three and a son forty-one and I can't imagine either of them doing what he was doing at that time. The hospital was filling up fast—with all these eighteen- and nineteen-year-old boys, they were just babies, with both legs gone, one arm gone, two arms . . . oh, it was a terrible thing."

One of the surgeons who worked under Aldredge in the twelve-hundred-bed amputee unit at England General was Dr. Calvin Terwilliger of Pennsylvania.

"Part of our problem was encouraging those boys who had lost both arms," he said. "To help us, we had civilian volunteers, like Charlie McGonegal.[3] He was a veteran of World War I who had lost both arms and had learned to use prostheses. When World War II came along, McGonegal would show the boys how he could use his artificial limbs—shave himself, dress himself, make change, get on a streetcar, drive a car. It wasn't just talk, it was something the boys could *see*. It did great things for morale."

Two WAC nursing companies supplemented the overworked nursing staff of England General. The 31st WAC Hospital Company was comprised of black women who had been trained as medical and surgical nurses. The 32nd WAC Hospital Company was all-white, predominantly physical therapists. Although they had trained together and they mopped up the blood and carried the bedpans and administered medication to Americans of all colors in an integrated hospital, these women were housed in separate hotels.

May Satchell was a postsurgical nurse who worked "on the floor," one-on-one with the recovering men.

"The town of Atlantic City just opened its doors to the veterans," she remembered. "They were invited to everything. We took them everywhere. I remember that we always carried a screwdriver in our pocketbooks, because sometimes their artificial arms or legs would warp and the screws would come loose. And we'd go into the opening of a store that was closed for the night and give the screwdriver to the patient so he could tighten up his knee or his ankle.

[3] In his autobiography, Harold Russell related how inspired he was by an Army-issue film called *Meet McGonegal,* which was shown to amputees (see page 126).

"Sure we got depressed. My roommate Millie and I used to cry in our room and say we couldn't take it one more day. But we did take it, we went back and back. Because the patients didn't cry. They helped each other.

"The minute the war ended, it was different. People didn't treat the veterans right. I remember one incident very well. During the war, they always closed the railroad stations until all the patients and medical personnel were on the trains . . . because it took time to board those boys who were on crutches and in wheelchairs . . . and now that the war was over, they opened the stations, no preference for veterans. Well, I was getting on the train with one of my patients. And a woman came by with a suitcase; she was in a big hurry. She knocked the crutch right out from under him.

"I could have killed that woman.

"But during the war, at England General . . . the spirit . . . the being together . . . it was wonderful. To see a man get well and go on with his life, that meant everything to us. I tell you there was something about that hospital . . . in a million years, you could never find it again."

The idea behind England General—firing the imagination of every single member of its staff, from the top surgeon to the lowliest gray lady—was the idea of rehabilitation. Men who in previous wars would have been given up to vegetable lives were now to be offered every chance to participate in the society they had fought to defend.[4]

The England General complex provided occupational therapy and physical and recreational therapy as well as courses in business English, history, French, German, motion picture projection and repair, music, radio repair, shorthand, and typing. At the Traymore there were special gym classes for "upper-extremity cases and lower-extremity cases." At the New Brighton, there were "pretechnical shops" to instruct men without legs and sometimes without hands in auto mechanics, carpentry, sheet metal work, and cabinetmaking.

[4] Gen. Ref. RG 112 Office of the Surgeon General/Army, WWII Administrative Records, 1940–1949, 319.1 Unit Annual Reports, Box 66 and "Final Historical Report of Thomas M. England General Hospital."

Special Services put on shows almost every day; boxing matches were staged at the Traymore rec hall; patients took music lessons; cheery figures such as Donald O'Connor, Vera Zorina, and Ann Baxter entertained the wards. The men strapped themselves to stationary bikes and pedaled on the sun roof; they played pool and Ping-Pong with prosthetic hooks; they got massages, whirlpool treatments, sunbaths, and dancing lessons from their physical therapists, and roller skating lessons from their gym teachers. They rested their leg stumps on cushions and beat at punching bags.

"From the moment we arrived at the train station, we were aware of the disabled soldiers," Bess said. "White boys and black boys, they were everywhere. Nurses pushed them in their wheelchairs down the Boardwalk. They leaned on their crutches and limped from store to store. Of course, the work at hand took our attention right away. We immediately started worrying about our hair, our clothes, our talent, all the things beauty contestants worry about. However, not for one minute could I forget the presence of the soldiers, sad background for all the gaiety and silliness of our pageant."

In September 1945, when Bess Myerson and her sister contestants arrived in Atlantic City, Thomas M. England General Hospital had 4,924 patients, 1,250 enlisted men in the medical detachment, 445 officers and nurses, and 900 civilian employees. By the time it was deactivated in 1946, the hospital had served nearly 61,000 patients.

Never before in the history of military medicine in America had a single institution tried to do more to atone to its wounded for the horrors of war.

THE THIRTY-NINE OTHER CONTESTANTS WHO REPORTED WITH Bess to the Seaside Hotel for registration on Monday, September 3, all received, as she did, background information forms to fill out and a little booklet with a blow-by-blow, day-by-day schedule and an opening message from the president of the Pageant Board, Arthur Chenoweth.

"We have carefully selected our judges for their experience in appraising beauty and talent," Chenoweth wrote, "which assures every girl an equal opportunity for the coveted title of 'Miss America.' In all contests, there must be winners and losers, and true Americanism prompts us to win or lose graciously. The hearts of the people of Atlantic City are open equally to the winners or to the losers."

Lest any of the girls imagine that this emphasis on "true Americanism" was mere rhetoric, the Pageant's registration forms wanted information on such things as each girl's war work record (Dorothy Louise Johnson, Miss South Carolina, said she sold ten thousand dollars in war bonds in the seventh war loan drive), information on her favorite food (for slender beauty queens, they sure did tend to mulligan stew and hot fudge sundaes an awful lot), and the genealogical particulars of her family's background in America. Four decades later, it is clear that many of the girls may have felt compelled to embellish.

Miss Arkansas, Leslie Hampton, traced her ancestry back to 1783. Polly Ellis, Miss California, said her forebears had come over on the *Mayflower*. Betty Ann Lackyear, Miss Indiana, said she was a descendant of John Quincy Adams. Surrounded by all these self-proclaimed blue bloods, Bess figured she'd go for broke and say she could trace her ancestry back four generations.

"I figured it this way," Bess laughed. "Sylvia is the first generation, I'm the second, Helen is the third, and Sylvia's little girls are the fourth."

Mary Louise Weaver, Miss Atlantic City, said her favorite dish was mashed potatoes and gravy. Miss Northern British

Columbia, Georgina Elizabeth Patterson, said she grooved on breaded veal cutlets and chocolate cake. Bess deduced it was not the time to admit that she was mad for kasha knishes and schmaltz herring. She put down that her favorite food was southern fried chicken (which was naturally the dietary mainstay of the menu at the Sholom Aleichem houses).

All the girls said they wanted a career. It was the first year of the Pageant scholarship. Many of them had been drawn to Atlantic City with the scholarship in mind, just like Bess. They wrote, "I want to be a singer" or "I want to be a fashion designer." The bold traditionalist Miss Utah (Dorothy Holohan) put down that "a career is not necessary" and that she "prefers happy marriage." As truthfully as anyone, Bess wrote, "Would like to continue with music (flute and piano); work for my M.A. degree and perhaps go on for additional training. Would include dramatics courses while working for Masters."

Fearful of appearing grandiose, she did not say that she wanted to study orchestral conducting.

Lest anyone think these girls in 1945 were unique in their tendency to embroider the facts, Karen Aarons, the current executive director of the Miss America Pageant, commented with a laugh, "Listen, it's a lot worse today. The girls give us false grade-point averages, they say they're members of honor societies, and then it turns out not to be so. Our local pageants spend enormous amounts of time just checking facts, to find out if what these girls have put down is truthful."

As soon as the contestant was finished registering, her chaperone escorted her and her mother to the assigned hotel.

"Our assigned hostess saw to it that we were settled at the Brighton," Bess remembered. "I was relieved to find that the Brighton wasn't one of those Boardwalk palaces I had seen in the movies but a nice clapboard hotel, with a congenial owner-manager named Alan Graf. June Jenkins, Miss New York State, was housed there. So were Miss Maryland, Miss Philadelphia, Miss Pennsylvania, and Miss Washington, D.C. Mr. Graf sent fruit up to our rooms. He did everything to make us feel comfortable.

"I shall never forget the whiteness of the starched sheets on the bed, the crunch of the white wicker furniture, the way the floral chintz curtains billowed in from the windows.

"The members of the Hostess Committee wore hats and gloves. They spoke in an upper-crust Philadelphia accent. The whole atmosphere at registration that first day was so silk-stocking, so silver-spoonish, that I felt I had fallen into the Atlantic City chapter of the DAR. I worried about it. If they wouldn't have Marian Anderson, what were they going to do with *me*?!"

Lenora Slaughter had started developing the hostess concept in 1937, as a response to the Federated Women's Clubs of New Jersey, which were then attacking the Pageant as an obscene and disgusting degradation of American girlhood. Her plan was to out-women's club the women's clubs.

"My training had always been working with civic leaders and proper people," Lenora said, "and I realized that the best way to protect the Pageant was to protect the girls from scandal, and the best way to do that was to get the best people in town on my side."[5]

Adrian Phillips, one of the earliest members of the Pageant Board, recalled that the origins of the Hostess Committee were quite pragmatic. "In the 1920s and 1930s the contestants were selected by the newspapers and the radio stations as a circulation promotion gimmick. We had girls who represented amusement parks and so on. You got a weird variety of females. Some were professionals and others were not yet dry behind the ears. Then you began to have this influx of so-called agents, some of them legitimate but most of them questionable. These agents would make prostitutes of the girls, lead them into entertaining in cheap bars. It was pretty bad. It became obvious that we had to take some responsibility here for the protection of the girls. From that need to be protective, we got the hostess situation."

Lenora laid siege to the society ladies of the town, many of whom were members of the Quaker elite that had founded the resort and owned some of its finest hotels. She enlisted the wife of the mayor, Mrs. Charles D. White, to be the head of her new Hostess Committee. "She was the Quakerest of the Quak-

---

[5] Frank Deford, *There She Is: The Life and Times of Miss America* (New York: Viking, 1971), p. 270.

ers," Lenora remembered. "Why one time I went to see her, I was so scared I took off all my nail polish and lipstick."

Mary Corey, former secretary of the Atlantic City Press Bureau, recalled that the hostesses in 1945 were handpicked by Lenora Slaughter and Arthur Chenoweth.

"To be a hostess, you had to be a member of the elite," she said. "You had to have a good reputation, which meant you had to be wealthy and do work with charities. Those women would be with the girls almost the entire day, until they went to bed. They met them when they registered, took them to their hotel, led them to the Boardwalk for the panorama shot, they would go with them to the dining rooms and everywhere."

Adrian Phillips pooh-poohed the idea of a bona fide society club. "In Atlantic City, it's the height of the ridiculous to speak about any '400.' There were numerous little circles and each considered itself the top one. It became a status symbol for young matrons to be on the Hostess Committee, it was an honor, a sacrifice . . . they gave their time, their cars, devoted themselves wholly to the contestant in those days. The real phenomenon is that we found so many volunteers to offer their time and money to this program."

Gilbert Katz, an insurance man who has lived in and around Atlantic City all his life, recalled that "to be a hostess was a big feather in a woman's cap, and only the social upper crust of the city got on the committee. You never heard of a Jewish woman chaperoning for the contest, except for the one or two Jewish ladies who were so rich they were acceptable as tokens."

Bess quickly assembled a pretty accurate picture of intergroup relations in Atlantic City. She knew she was the only girl in the entire Pageant from a minority ethnic group. Except for the black soldiers who had just come home from fighting a war to defend democracy, the only blacks on the Boardwalk were pushing sedan chairs and/or working as waiters and charwomen. Not until after the Pageant would she run into the two Jewish members of the Pageant Executive Committee, Max Malamut, who owned the Breakers, and Joseph Wagenheim, who was in the meat business and who was serving as treasurer of the Pageant in 1945.

"At that time there was still a definite feeling in the minds of some Atlantic City people," Lenora said, "some of the Quakers, the leaders in town . . . they didn't say things about Jews but they just didn't encourage. . . . A lot of them didn't have Jews in their hotels, they didn't this, that, and the other."

Gilbert Katz, the insurance man, recalled that Atlantic City possessed a large, vibrant Jewish community in 1945, whose relations with the Gentile majority were "friendly but separate." Neighborhoods were carefully guarded against encroachment by Jewish people. The country club was closed to Jewish members. But the Jews didn't fret over that, they didn't sue or go to the newspapers; that wasn't what you did in 1945. They started their own country club. They built their own houses in their own neighborhoods. If they had a bar mitzvah or a wedding, they went to one of the Jewish hotels, the Breakers, the St. Charles, or the Strand. "You went there because you were accepted there," Katz recalled. "What did you want to cross a line and break a barrier for?"

As she hit her pillow in the Brighton on the night of September 3, Bess Myerson found herself wondering the same thing.

———

I couldn't sleep. I was concerned. I thought it was just my paranoia, my lack of ease in the big WASP world . . . but it wasn't just that . . . it was that something had happened back in New York that preyed on my mind and made me uneasy from the outset.

Back in New York, Lenora Slaughter had asked me to change my name.

I had met Lenora for the first time on the night of the finals at the Miss New York City contest. She had come down to watch us rehearse, I think because Don Rich of WJZ called her and asked her to. So she was there in the afternoon watching the rehearsal, and when it was over, she asked me to join her in the third row in the empty theater for a talk.

You must understand what an impressive woman Lenora was to me at that time. I had literally never met a Southerner in my whole life. If I had some decorous, swooning, Gone with the Wind stereotype in my mind, she exploded it right then and there. She didn't speak or move slowly. Her clothes were flashy. Her teeth were big. She didn't dissemble or approach by indirection. She was who she was, a bright woman who knew exactly what she wanted. She scared most of us because she was so self-assured and flamboyant.

In the Ritz Theatre she told me all about the history of the Pageant. She declared it would be the first major event of the peacetime era and reminded me that the winner would receive a five-thousand-dollar scholarship. "There is a very strong chance that you might become Miss New York City tonight," she continued, "and then you'll have a good chance at being Miss America and winning that scholarship. If that happens, what would you like to do?"

I answered that I would continue studying piano. Go to graduate school. Buy a new piano.

Lenora smiled and said, "You might also decide to go into show business or the movies, many girls do, and Bess Myerson is just not a very attractive name for a career in show business."

Now, I had thought—if I ever had a career modeling—I might change my name, it was an ordinary thing to do in those days. People with ethnic names changed them from Betty Persky to Lauren Bacall, from Archie Leach to Cary Grant, from Issur Danielevitch to Kirk Douglas.

"What would you suggest?" I asked Lenora.

She thought for a moment and said, "Betty" or whatever, "Merrick" or something.

I thought that sounded fine. However, something happened to me in that moment. Some heat of reality peeled off Lenora Slaughter. I knew suddenly that I was not dealing with just a name change, that I was dealing with Lenora's fear. I wasn't sure what she was afraid of, but I knew she was afraid.

So I said no.

I tried to explain to Lenora.

"If I win this contest tonight," I said, "the only people who will really care are my girlfriends from Hunter, my friends from camp, my family, the families I've grown up with. And if I win and I'm Betty Merrick, they won't know it's me, and I will want them to know it's me. So I think I have to keep my name. Bess Myerson."

Lenora wasn't happy about it. She persisted in her argument, but I was adamant. Don't ask me why. An instinct. Some five-thousand-year-old defense mechanism. I knew that there was more at stake here in my relationship with this woman than immediately met the eye, that how I presented myself to her and to the world she came from would be vital from the word go.

You're walking through the corridor of life, and you know that there are doors, that if you open up the wrong one, you're going to fall down a black hole. It takes so much energy to preserve self and maintain focus without being distracted. Already I was losing my sense of who I was; already I was in a masquerade, marching across stages in bathing suits. Whatever was left of myself in this game, I had to keep, I sensed that. I knew I had to keep my name.

It turned out to be one of the most important decisions I ever made.

———

WHEN BESS MYERSON MADE HER FIRST LITTLE STAND AGAINST the wishes of Lenora Slaughter, she did not realize that she was taking on one of the more formidable American women of this century. Their relationship would span almost three decades, during which Lenora served as the executive director of the Miss America Pageant and Bess would become its television mistress of ceremonies and its most illustrious symbol.

To judge from the memories of those who knew her when,

Lenora Slaughter was a great prude, a prattler of niceties and one of the fiercest business managers of her time, an exploiter of women and their most devoted defender, an elitist snob and a down-home buddy. However free people may gag on the antics of the Miss America Pageant during Lenora's thirty-year reign there, from 1937 to 1967, her tireless advocacy of the huge scholarship program it now embodies—five million dollars each year to winners and contestants in state, local, and national contests—has made her in retrospect one of our country's more effective crusaders for the advancement of women.

"When you look at Lenora in that light," Bess said, "it really doesn't make too much difference if she embroiders history or forgets it entirely. In her day, she did a job."

Lenora Slaughter was born in Live Oak, Florida. By the Depression years, she had made her home in St. Petersburg. Although nice southern girls weren't supposed to go to work in those days, necessity bred revolution: Lenora took a job with the Chamber of Commerce in St. Petersburg, and she was very good at it.

"It was one of our civic projects to make our winter visitors have a pleasant season," she said. "They registered with the Chamber of Commerce and joined the tourist society for their state. Pennsylvanians belonged to the Pennsylvania Society and so forth. I ran those organizations. Well, in 1935, there was an Associated Press story in the newspapers about my running a parade pertaining to our Festival of States."

They read that article in Atlantic City. Eddie Corcoran, a PR man and newspaper reporter, had been charged with reviving the Miss America Pageant, which had sunk into poverty during the Depression. As far as he could see, Lenora Slaughter might be able to help, all the more so because she was a woman and it was women's groups especially who were attacking the Pageant in the 1930s.

Corcoran immediately wrote to Al Lang, the baseball commissioner for Florida, a Philadelphian wintering in St. Petersburg. He asked Lang if Lenora could be borrowed for a while.

"Mr. Lang was a member of the St. Petersburg Chamber of Commerce and fond of me because I did his work for him,"

Lenora said. "He gave me a thousand dollars to go north for six weeks."

When Lenora arrived, the Pageant had been renamed "The Showman's Variety Jubilee" and was operating under the aegis of the Variety Club of Philadelphia. Corcoran liked her work and asked her to stay on full time. She says she took a salary cut to do so. Shortly after she returned to Atlantic City in 1936, Corcoran died. George Tyson, a "theater official" from Pittsburgh, was brought in to supervise. ("He was a promoter and a con man," current Pageant chief Al Marks now says with a long sigh. "Ah, this Pageant was very different then, I can tell you. . . .")

Lenora immediately impressed the board with her getup and her frank espousal of any number of measures to improve the image of the Pageant.

"Lenora was a master salesman and very persistent," said the dignified Adrian Phillips. "She was a hundred percent sold on her program. She was extremely articulate and persuasive, and very determined. She went after the so-called big wheels, the hotel operators, the utility officers, the people who had influence. She had an innate sense of diplomacy. But there was another side to Lenora. She could be really rough and tough if the situation called for it."

The board soon named Lenora associate director. Within a year or two she had begun to bring nationwide publicity to the Pageant and put it on the solid business footing that had eluded the Board of Directors since its inception in 1921.

"The director [Tyson] . . . was running these pageants all over the country in amusement parks, fairs, things like that," she recalled. "In the state contests they had the girls parading around in swimsuits in front of the theater before the pageant. It was awful. I wanted to throw out all the cheap promotions. I said I believe I can get civic organizations to run the pageants and we can get the class of girl that we should have."

Lenora befriended the chic Hollywood director of fashion news features, Vyvyan Donner, and cooked up a piece on the Pageant that made it into *Movietone News*. In 1938, millions of Americans who went to the movies saw Marilyn Meseke being crowned. After that, enough people showed up for the Pageant

lla Myerson before her wedding.

Louis Myerson as a young man.

The Sholom Aleichem Cooperative Apartments, unchanged today.

My sister Helen, Dad, and me...with "Molly" in the background. Circa 1936.

The Myerson girls—Helen, Bess, and Sylvia —around 1940.

The traumatic Olive Oyl masquerade. I wa[s] twelve years old.

With fellow counselors-in-training at Camp Kearsarge.

As a flutist in the orchestra at the High School of Music and Art.

Pals from the 68 Club at Hunter College, 1942. From left: Margie Wallis, Lenore Miller Baker, and me.

Pictures taken by John C. Pape. I was paid $5 an hour for modeling.

*Playing piano for the talent
presentation at the Miss New
York City contest in 1945.*

*The winner with
Mayor Fiorello LaGuardia.*

In the Boardwalk Parade,
September 1945.

Sylvia Grace, my chaperone-
sister, in Atlantic City.

The contestants advertising Catalina swimsuits from the hip.

Frank Havens' unforgettable photograph of the U.S. Army training in Convention Hall.

THESE GREAT LEADERS SPONSOR MISS AMERICA SCHOLARSHIPS FUND

The F. W. Fitch Company is proud to be a contributor to the Miss America Scholarship Fund. By doing so, we feel we are helping Miss America to develop her special talents to their highest degree. For, no matter what talent an individual possesses, it must be trained and used in order to make it of greatest value to the individual and to others. Our congratulations and sincerest best wishes for your future success, Miss America of 1945.

F. W. FITCH
Founder, The F. W. Fitch Company

My sincere congratulations go to the deserving winner of the 1945 Miss America scholarship.

The future which faces American womanhood is filled with opportunities on the one hand and fraught with dangers on the other. Certainly the training and incentive which this scholarship provides will go far in enabling the recipient to meet the challenge of that future successfully and constructively!

H. H. WHEELER, President
Sandy Valley Grocery Co.

Catalina takes special pride in contributing to the Scholarship Fund. There can be no question but that this great annual classic has vastly increased swimming as the peer of all sports in developing healthy and coordinated bodies.

In my opinion the Scholarship Fund is the finest approach to further the idea of the wisdom and necessity of developing sound minds in sound bodies. "The Flying Fish" of Catalina is proud to adorn the swimsuit worn by the first MISS AMERICA SCHOLARSHIP FUND winner.

E. W. STEWART, President
Catalina, Inc.

"It is a pleasure for us to be among those sponsoring the "Miss America Scholarship Fund." We are sure the judges' choice for "Miss America 1945" will necessarily have ambition, talent, beauty and charm and we believe the scholarship will help her to win many more triumphs, both in her career and in this, our 'American Way of Life.' "

W. RALPH MACINTYRE, Executive Vice-President
Joseph Bancroft & Sons Co.
Originators of "Everglaze" Process for Fabrics

Our association with the Miss America Pageant dates back several years. It is, therefore, with considerable pleasure that Harvel is again participating in this event, and it is with great enthusiasm that we contribute to the sponsorship of the Scholarship Fund. We are confident of the success of this great project and consider the program a vital contribution and inspiration to every fine American girl.

HENRY H. HARTEVELDT,
President, Harvel Watch Company

The sponsors of the first Miss America scholarship.

THEY ARE ALL POTENTIAL WINNERS

"MISS NEW YORK CITY"
Bess Myerson

"MISS BIRMINGHAM"
Frances Dorn

"MISS TEXAS"
Polly Below

"MISS NORTH CAROLINA"
Dorothy Louise Johnson

*John Pape's cap-and-gown picture of me set me apart
in the Pageant program.*

On display for a sea of photographers.

Breakfast with judges Bradshaw Crandall and Vyvyan Donner.

The judges in 1945.

Gathered in our evening gowns after the Parade of States.

The finalists. I am fourth from left.

Sharing the moment of victory with Jimmy Wilson and Ernie Sardo.

Venus Ramey, Miss America 1944, "crowns" me for the press. Top row, left to right: Arlene Anderson, Phyllis Mathis, Venus, me, Francis Dorn, and Jeni Freeland. Gloria Bair, my hotel neighbor, is in the center bottom row.

itself so that the budget was balanced and the financial doldrums finally overcome.

In 1939, for the first time, a majority of the girls represented not just beach resorts and amusement parks but states of the Union. In 1940 the Showman's Variety Jubilee moved into Convention Hall and was officially redubbed the Miss America Pageant.

No sooner had this been accomplished than the war broke out and the U.S. Army took over Convention Hall. Hearing that the bathing beauties were looking for a home, Madison Square Garden made Lenora an offer. She and the board resisted; a move to New York would have undone all the intentions of Atlantic City's Fathers to use the Pageant as a way to extend the summer season past Labor Day. It seemed wiser to discontinue the event until the war's end rather than move to another town.

Lenora saved the day by using her connections to force her way into the Warner Theatre.

"The local manager didn't want to rent to us. My board couldn't get anywhere with him. But I went to the top. Rose Coyle, Miss America of 1936, had married Henry Schlesinger, who was one of the important men in the Warner chain. I went to New York to see him. I told him that the manager in Atlantic City wouldn't rent to us since we needed it for two weeks and he felt he would lose money if he stopped showing movies for that length of time. Schlesinger got hold of the big boys in Hollywood and called me and said, 'You've got it, dear.' It was a great break for Atlantic City and a great break for me."

Lenora's coup with the Warner Theatre literally prevented the Pageant from closing down, and the board was duly impressed with her. Clearly a woman who had a *relationship* with the contestants could use her ongoing contacts with them to benefit the Pageant. "The story was put out that George Tyson had resigned. In fact, he was fired right after the Pageant of 1941," Lenora said, "and I got his job."

Luckily the usurpatious military understood that there might be an advantage in keeping the Miss America Pageant alive in Atlantic City during the war years. "The War Finance Department knew we could do a good job of selling bonds," Lenora recalled. "They agreed to pay if I would chaperone Miss America on a trip around America selling war bonds in 1943. The girl was Jean Bartel. Jean and I sold bonds in about a hundred cities. We raised millions of dollars in Series E bonds.

"Now, this girl Jean Bartel happened to be a Kappa Kappa Gamma from UCLA. So when we were selling war bonds in a big department store in Minneapolis, she was invited to the University of Minnesota by her sorority sisters, who had a tea for her. While she was at the tea, I was invited to talk to the Student Council. They let me know in a hurry that no college girl would enter a contest that afforded as few opportunities as the Atlantic City Pageant.

"And that's when I got the idea for the scholarship.

"I never went to college. I wanted to go to college more than anything in the world, but I didn't have the money. Now I wanted my girls to have a scholarship, something *constructive*. I knew the shine of a girl's hair wasn't going to make her a success in life, and I knew good and well that the prizes Miss America had been getting were a joke . . . a fur coat that couldn't have been worth more than two hundred dollars, the Hollywood contract that they got for fifty dollars a week—why, they couldn't even live on that in California.

"To get through to a better class of contestants, I had to raise money enough for education and training, for the opera, to be a judge, a doctor. I was rabid on the subject of the necessity for education.

"I left Minnesota with the determination to give a scholarship to Miss America."

Jean Bartel has a slightly different version of the Minnesota story. "We were just all sitting around at this tea with Kappa Kappa Gammas," she said four decades later in a sunny Los Angeles restaurant, "and I was the one who suggested it might be a good idea if Miss America got a scholarship."

Jean Bartel had won as Miss California in 1943 by being cool, blond, beautiful, gracious, and singing "Night and Day" very well.

"There was a very low expectation of the girls in the contest

in those years," Jean said. "We weren't automatically respected—
that took a long time. The year I won, Lenora set up an
interview and this newsman came into the hotel room to talk to
me and he led off with 'Okay, chippie, what's your story?'

"I went to forty key cities in 1943–44. I was billed as 'The
Girl Back Home.' I worked twenty-four hours a day, seven days
a week, christening ships, leading bands, doing theater perfor-
mances for the war effort.

"Lenora had a beaver coat, and she had a silver fox cape, and
she was very generous, she would let me wear her furs anytime I
needed them. Lever Brothers paid me a hundred dollars a week
to do their promotions. Butterick let me have some of their
things to wear. I made three thousand dollars that year."

The classy, educated Bartel fit perfectly into Lenora's grand
scheme to wrest the local Miss America Pageants from the (in
Lenora's opinion) tacky hands of radio stations and newspapers
and amusement parks and place them under the more stately
aegis of the Junior Chambers of Commerce around the country.
"What better than to have the ideal men of America run a
pageant for the ideal woman?" she remarked.[6] Everywhere she
and Jean went, Lenora contacted the Jaycees. Her pitch was:
Come take a look at the ideal woman, fellas; she's 'The Girl
Back Home'; she's supporting the war effort; she's a devout
Christian Scientist; she's the living symbol of Lever Brothers;
she's a class act; and she's gorgeous! Wouldn't you young fellas
like to be part of all this excitement?

By 1945, eleven state Jaycees had agreed to sponsor the local
pageants. Lenora's plan to escalate the Pageant from a local
promotion in a Jersey seaside resort to a national institution
born and bred in the American heartland was on its way.

Now she had to deal with the scholarship.

"In 1943, when I got my board to approve . . . a scholarship to
give Miss America, I had the Second World War to contend
with. So it took me until 1944 to raise the money. I was fighting
a battle to get a thousand dollars from (each of) five companies.

"The first person I wrote to was Mr. E. W. Stewart of
Catalina Swimsuits. He gave his thousand dollars immediately.

[6] Ibid., p. 154.

He was a perfectly wonderful person. He furnished the swimsuits for all the state winners when they arrived in Atlantic City,
and they all had a Catalina swimsuit in exactly the same style.
They were different colors, but the same cut.

"Then I wrote to 230 companies, to anyone who had a
product that looked like the girls could advertise. Colgate-
Palmolive-Peet wrote me back and said, 'Your idea is excellent,
and good luck, but the Colgate-Palmolive-Peet Company cannot afford to be associated with a beauty contest.'

"Of course, they tried to get in later," Lenora continued with
glee. "But by that time we had tied up the cosmetics business.

"And I wrote to Mr. [W. Ralph] MacIntyre of the Joseph
Bancroft & Sons Company out of Wilmington, Delaware. In
1944 he was ashamed of the way Miss Delaware was going to
look, so he told his top woman to get hold of that girl and see
that she's properly groomed, and he paid for it. Mr. McIntyre
came down to the Pageant. I thanked him and told him what I
was trying to do, and he said, 'Count me in.' So he was my
second sponsor.

"I went to Des Moines, Iowa, and met with Mr. Fitch (F.
W. Fitch of the Fitch Shampoo Company). He asked if I was
related to [major-league baseball player] Enos Slaughter. I said
he was my second cousin. He said his grandson adored Enos
Slaughter. I spent the afternoon telling Mr. Fitch about the
scholarship, and he liked it very much, and said, 'I'll go in with
it, but I want you to have dinner with my son and his wife and
the little boy who loves Enos Slaughter.'

"The fourth sponsor was Henry Harteveldt of Harvel Watches.
His company, which imported diamonds and watch facings
from abroad, had supported the Pageant since the 1920s.

"Now I had four. I couldn't get the other thousand dollars. I
was absolutely desperate. It was getting very close to Pageant
time. I put the other thousand dollars in the bank out of my
own money to make the five-thousand-dollar scholarship we
had publicized. One week before the Miss America Pageant, I
got a call from Mr. Wheeler (Henry Harrison Wheeler), the
president of the Sandy Valley Grocery Company, out of Kentucky. He had employed Bette Cooper, the winner in 1937, the

one who walked out,[7] and Marilyn Meseke, the 1938 winner, in his public-relations program. He said, 'I'd like to get into your scholarship fund, and I understand that it costs a thousand dollars.' So there I had the fifth scholarship certificate just before Pageant week, and I could put my money safely back in the bank.

"I knew I could not build without the background and recognition of colleges and universities. Guy Snavely was executive director of the Association of American Colleges and Universities. I hied myself up to New York to see him. He agreed to head up the scholarship program. He opened the door to any-place I wanted to go to talk to a college, so that universities would understand we weren't a leg show, and they would encourage their girls to participate in the Pageant."

Jimmy Hatcher has a slightly different version of the Guy Snavely story. Chief of Protocol for Alabama under Governor Wallace and a major entrepreneur in the arts who would often produce the Miss America Pageant in the 1960s, Hatcher says the original contact with Snavely came from Lily May Caldwell.

"Lily May Caldwell was the arts and amusement editor of *The Birmingham News,* Alabama's largest newspaper," he said. "She was influential in all phases of life in the state and knew all the great educators, of which Dr. Snavely was probably the most prominent. He had been president of Birmingham Southern, and out of her friendship with him she persuaded him to become involved with the scholarship program."

The scholarship was a tremendous departure for the Pageant, and many of the people on the board did not support it.

"They were geared too much to Hollywood," Lenora complained, "and not enough to what I wanted. They liked the publicity and they wanted to make a movie star. And in fact there have been quite a number. But I wanted to see girls who

---

[7] Bette Cooper came to Atlantic City as Miss Bertrand Island in 1937. In a crowd of contestants that included a stripper and a member of a traveling dance troupe, she was sweet and innocent and she won. But she was *so* sweet and innocent that she freaked out from the various pressures of victory and convinced her driver to help her escape. This story is told in detail in Deford, pp. 140–46.

turned out to be doctors, lawyers. To give every girl in America who had ambition the chance to study and have the education to be what she wanted to be."

———

IN THE FOUNDATION OF LENORA'S NOBLE DREAM THERE WAS a glitch, an inbuilt self-destruct mechanism that would work ultimately to frustrate her ambitions. For this was a beauty contest. Above all, beyond all, no matter what amounts of money it produced for the education of women, it was a *beauty* contest. Edward Stewart of Catalina, for one, could never be convinced by Lenora to forget that, nor could the tourism-conscious hotel operators on the Boardwalk.

The Pageant required beautiful women who, by the time they arrived in Atlantic City, had been altered and conditioned by the pressures that beautiful women must endure in a society that was then (and apparently still is) infantile on the subject of women's bodies. Most of these girls did not generally want to be doctors and lawyers; at best, they wanted to *marry* doctors and lawyers. If they were brilliant, they had already gone through much of their lives trying to *prove* that they were brilliant despite their beauty. And appearing in a beauty contest was the last thing they would tend to do, for it would further compromise them in their struggle to be taken seriously.

Lenora's dream for the girls was a projection of her own greatest frustrations. The great Art Nouveau fashion designer Erte once commented to Diana Vreeland that he designed clothes for the woman he would have wanted to be if only he had been a woman. Perhaps Lenora Slaughter tried to design the Pageant to produce the Miss America she would have wanted to be if only she had been beautiful. Thus, over the years, her girls became more and more religious, Christians from the South and the West, who professed conservative politics.

In the 1950s, Lenora's tastes dictated that Miss America should grow increasingly *less* sexy. By the 1960's, in the era of miniskirts, the clothing required by the Pageant was so dowdy and dated that the girls couldn't find it in the stores. By the time Lenora retired in 1967, the rise of feminism was beginning to discredit the Pageant so among educated women that no self-respecting, bona fide intellectual would go near it. She bequeathed to her successors Ruth McCandliss and Al Marks a vision fundamentally undone by the sexism of the country at large, and they had to rebuild it as carefully as cosmetic surgeons lifting an old face.

Never in the whole history of the Pageant had Miss America turned out to be a doctor or a lawyer, and in the era of television it was time to drop the rhetoric. In 1970, returning to the Pageant for a special tribute in her honor, the now-married Lenora Slaughter Frapert told her girls: "Remember, all of you, that the most important thing in your lives will be your marriage, and the main test, as a woman, will be how much of a success you make of yourself with your husband and your family."[8]

But in 1945, with the inception of the scholarship, Lenora's dream was fresh and new, supported by a tremendous swell of confidence and ambition among American women. With Rosie the Riveter as their symbol, they had spent the war years working in a vast variety of jobs never before available to them. They had their own money now. In the absence of their men, they had grown as citizens. Jean Bartel raised 2.5 million dollars in war bonds on her trip around the country in 1943–44, and *80 percent* of those had been purchased by women.

It was a peculiar indentation in psychological time, set exactly between the ascendance of Rosie the Riveter and the advent of the Happy Homemaker, a perfect time for Lenora's dream of a well-educated, professional Miss America to flower, the perfect moment, perhaps the *only* moment when a girl like Bess Myerson—the closest thing to a bona fide intellectual ever to cross a stage in a bathing suit—would be moved to show up in Atlantic City.

---

[8] Deford, p. 260.

CHAPTER 6

Apparently Cool, Inwardly Quaking

The official judging did not begin until Wednesday night, September 5. Before then, we were issued our swimsuits by Catalina and scheduled to rehearse our talent and the appearances we would make at the Warner Theatre. We had our pictures taken again and again, participated in events for the benefit of the military, and tried to remain calm despite the mounting tension.

I was filled with foreboding. Once again, most of the other contestants were shorter than I, with rounded hips. I felt strange, different, a departure from the national standard of beauty. I worried about my looks, their clothes, the Pageant rules, Lenora Slaughter's moods. Nervousness closed my throat; I couldn't swallow, picked at my meals, or passed on them altogether.

Sylvia was so nervous she ate her food and mine, too.

We rescued ourselves from anxiety by going to the beach at every opportunity. We were determined to have a good time, no matter how the Pageant turned out.

On Tuesday morning, September 4, we were told to report to the City Press Bureau at Convention Hall to hear one of Lenora's lectures on the Pageant rules and then to pose in our bathing suits for the panorama picture.

They don't take those pictures anymore. At that time, though, they were the single most recognized symbol of the Miss America Pageant. They were wide horizontal photos of the girls arranged on makeshift bleachers set up against the background of the ocean.

The photographers took forever to prepare the photo because they had to keep lugging their equipment along the line of girls. We had to keep smiling and not move. Our long hair blew in the breeze and became unruly. We were constantly brushing and combing. It was before setting lotion, before gel and mousse. If you had long, black, curly hair, as I did, you used beer to keep it under control. Whenever I was scheduled to go outdoors, Sylvia would order a beer from room service and set my hair with it. As often as not, the effects of the beer dissipated the minute my head hit the humid ocean air, and there I would be, just as in that panorama picture, curling and frizzing.

Thousands and thousands of those panoramas were produced. Some of them were six feet wide, hung like murals in barbershops, poolhalls, and saloons. A fellow I knew from camp wrote to me that he saw one in Okinawa. Another fellow saw one in Berlin. We couldn't have realized it, standing on the bleachers, sucking in our bellies, fixing our smiles, but we were at that moment becoming the cheesecake that followed the flag.

It was no wonder, then, that so many of us in the Pageant would receive letters, ranging from the tender to the lewd, from soldiers who had seen our pictures in some lonely outpost.

FRANK HAVENS, THEN SECOND IN COMMAND TO ATLANTIC CITY'S official photographer, Al Gold, remembered that the panorama shots irritated Lenora Slaughter no end. "She didn't want the pans made," he recalled. "She said these girls of hers were not horseflesh and were not going to be exhibited as such.

"Well, this caused a big revolution with the two major photographers in town, Fred Hess and Central Studio. Because if Lenora was going to lay down the law that those panoramic pictures could no longer be produced, those photographers were going to be out thousands and thousands of dollars. So they fought her . . . they fought like hell. . . . But I don't know of anybody who ever succeeded in challenging Lenora for long. If you did, somebody clipped your wings."

Allied with the photographers was E. W. Stewart of Catalina, who much valued the publicity the panoramas brought his company: forty beautiful girls hip to hip, each hip carrying the Catalina emblem. In all of Lenora's efforts to sanitize the Pageant, Stewart would prove her most formidable opponent. Her successor, Ruth McCandliss, remembered a letter he sent to Lenora in which he roared, "If you have your way, soon they'll all be marching down the runway in caps and gowns!"

Lenora finally got rid of the panoramas in the late 1940s. Meanwhile, she tried to placate the fiery Stewart as best she could.

"She told us very sternly never to refer to our Catalina bathing suits as 'bathing suits,' " Bess laughed. "Instead she said we should call them 'swimsuits' because Mr. Stewart preferred that term. He insisted that you bathe in your skin and you swim in a Catalina."

Lenora's lectures to the girls became legend at the Pageant. Gloria Bair, Miss Philadelphia, remembered that "everybody was scared of her." Arlene Anderson, Miss Minnesota, said she was "tough and not too sincere." Jeni Freeland, Miss Florida, dubbed her "The Mother Superior." Al Marks called her "a dictator." Frank Havens said, "She was the law. That was it. You didn't ask why."

Bess attempted an imitation of Lenora, as do many of the women who remember her.

"She had a Holy Roller way of reeling out the encourage-ment, like Jimmy Swaggart or Oral Roberts, exhorting us in this high-pitched southern voice.

"Now you are all perfectly beautiful girls, she would say, you are all extremely intelligent and I daresay you will learn more from the experience of being in the glorious Miss America Pageant than from any other single thing you do in your whole entire lives! You are the living symbols of American woman-hood! No matter how the voting goes, you must never, never be discouraged, for you must remember the Pageant is not over until the very last vote is counted on the very last minute of the very last day! So chin up! Forward! Onward!

"Of course, in an attempt to appear egalitarian, Lenora would always refer to us by our titles. Move into the back row, Miss New York City, you're blocking Connecticut. Do not speak to your neighbor while I am talking, Miss San Diego, it makes me very very cross! Out of my way, New Hampshire, I'm coming through!

"She told us there would be absolutely no drinking, absolutely no fraternization with men, absolutely no falsies or other artificial padding. She said anybody who was under eighteen and had lied about her age would be disqualified. Anybody who had ever been married would be disqualified. The most frightening thing she said was that you could be disqualified for some sinful act and no one would tell you! They would just let you go on through the whole week, performing your talent, parading in your swimsuit, trying to impress the judges. Meanwhile, however, you would be out of the running, and you wouldn't even know!

"We were all terrified of making a mistake by *mistake!*"

Was anyone ever disqualified?

"Oh, sure," Jeni Freeland Berry remembered with a laugh. "One very sweet kid, they found out she was sixteen and sent her home. Another girl was caught having a drink and they threw her out, too. One of them they sent home because she saw a guy that she knew.

"Well, I saw plenty of guys that I knew. My mother would call down to the desk at the hotel and say, 'My nephew is arriving this afternoon. Will you show him to our room, please?' So I got to see all my boyfriends who had enough money to come to Atlantic City and nobody ever realized what was going on."

The daughters of Bella Myerson felt no such ease or freedom.

"If some nice young soldier tried to talk to me on the Boardwalk," Bess declared, "I would nod politely and rush past him. We were afraid that Lenora or one of her friends on the Hostess Committee would see me and disqualify me for flirting."

"We were warned not to talk to our *fathers!*" exclaimed

Arlene Anderson Low. "Because that would have looked suspicious."

When Bess saw the other contestants' many suitcases stacked up in the lobby of the Brighton, when she saw how many pretty frocks and skirts and blouses and hats some of the other girls had come with, she began to worry about being inadequately dressed. All she had to wear during the daytime hours for seven days were the two two-piece outfits Mr. Pape's seamstress in Newark had made for her: one a royal blue, the other a chartreuse.

"Every morning I would roll out of bed and groan, 'What in the world am I going to wear today?!'

"Sylvia would start running back and forth to the closet, pulling out the separates, throwing them on the bed, imitating Lenora. 'Oh, but you have so many many choices, my dear Miss New York City!' she would ooze. 'You can wear the royal blue skirt with the chartreuse top or the chartreuse skirt with the royal blue top or the royal blue scarf around your chartreuse hair. . . .'

"Sylvia was incredible. My house jester. I was so frightened, I felt as though I was drowning, and she kept me afloat with laughter."

Early Tuesday afternoon, after the panorama shot, Bess headed back to the Brighton for lunch. In the lobby, an elderly couple timidly approached her.

" 'Du bist a yid?' the lady said to me in Yiddish. She was asking me if I was Jewish.

"I answered, 'Yes.' She laughed as though she had won the jackpot. She and her husband hugged me, they patted me on the back, they hugged each other. They told me that they lived in a nearby suburb, where they had heard a rumor that a Jewish girl had entered the Pageant for the first time. They had come to the Brighton to see me and check out the rumor.

" 'Well, it's true,' I said.

" 'So you've got to win,' they insisted.

" 'But it's just a beauty contest,' I protested.

" 'And you're *our* beauty, darling,' they answered. 'You've got to win, for all of us.'

"I was delighted by this encounter and very touched by it, but also bewildered. Five minutes before, I had been worrying about how my hair was going to stay neat throughout Victory Parade on the Boardwalk, which was scheduled for that afternoon. Suddenly these strangers had arrived to remind me that I was not merely a girl seeking a scholarship but also a symbol of Jewish yearnings for good news. For a victory. Any small victory.

"You see, we were just discovering the full scope of what had happened to our people in Europe. Ovens. Gas chambers. Mass graves. It was inconceivable. The numbers: a million, two million, four million, later we learned it was six million, and a million of those were little children. What could winning or losing a beauty contest mean in the scope of that nightmare?!

"Sylvia rescued me. She thanked the old couple for their good wishes and led me to lunch. She said, 'Eat something, Bess. You don't want to lose any more weight than you already have.'

" 'How will they feel if I lose, Sylvia?' I asked.

" 'Don't worry about it,' she answered. 'These people are our friends, your supporters; they love you.'

"We went upstairs and she set my hair again.

"Wherever we went after that, we always met up with groups of Jewish people who wanted to hug me and shake my hand, who wished me well and said, 'You're *our* beauty queen, Bessie, you've got to win.'

"They made me feel vindicated in my strong stand against changing my name. I knew full well that Lenora would have preferred me to disguise my origins. But to have given up my name would have been like masquerading in someone else's skin, would have cut me off from my own people and the outpouring of affection and support that now greeted me everywhere.

"As I think back on it, I know I would not have missed the smiles of those strangers in Atlantic City for anything in the world."

Later that day, all the contestants reported in their gowns to the Breakers Hotel for the Victory Parade down the Boardwalk. The 1945 version of this well-loved annual event was dedicated to the victorious armed forces. Each girl had her place on one of a long chain of elaborate rolling chair floats, and thousands of locals and visitors lined up on the Boardwalk to watch and cheer their hometown favorite.

Bess was experiencing a new sense of elation because of her lunchtime encounter with the old couple. All her tension dissipated suddenly. She waved to the crowds. Her black hair rippled in the wind. Wheelchairbound veterans who had parade-side seats out in front of England General still remember her dazzling smile. An ex-POW named Murray Sklaroff felt overwhelmed with pride when he heard that the black-haired beauty in the pale green gown was actually a Jewish girl.

That evening, September 4, all the girls attended the Military Ball being given in their honor at Convention Hall by the creative officers who ran Army Air Force Redistribution Station 1—AAFRS 1. More than two thousand servicemen—many of them ex-POWs—and their guests were present. To suit the proprieties of those times, a Jewish date was found for Bess— Sergeant David Gerber of Brooklyn. "From a prison camp to this," he said. "Don't wake me up."

Morley Cassidy reported in the *Philadelphia Bulletin*[1] that, with the war over, enlisted men had the edge over officers at the dance: "A rough count found 312 commissioned officers standing at the side lines with their hands in their pockets while approximately 42 corporals, technicians fourth grade and privates first class had a perfectly wonderful time."

Corporal Leslie Spitznagle of Portland, Oregon, was dancing with Frances Dorn, Miss Birmingham, when a major tapped him on the shoulder with the intent to cut in.

"Do you mind, soldier?" asked the major.

"You're damned right I do, sir," answered Spitznagle, and he kept on dancing.

The master of ceremonies, Donald O'Connor, spent most of the night dancing with Miss New York State, June Jenkins.

Gilbert Katz, at that time assistant to the Jewish chaplain at AAFRS 1, was at the ball. "I remember as I'm sitting here Bess Myerson dancing by in a long white dress, with silver shoes," he said. "She seemed to me and my wife head and shoulders above all the other girls."

---

[1]*Philadelphia Bulletin* (September 6, 1945).

The Military Ball was a typical shindig of AAFRS 1, which was mandated to be a kind of temporary "Club Med" by the Atlantic, a hotbed of rest and recuperation for men from the northeastern and mid-Atlantic regions who had been "separated from their units" and who needed to recover and reorganize their lives before being reassigned. Sometimes the Army's rotation system brought men in for furlough before reassignment. AAFRS 1 saw to it that they and their wives were treated to a *cheap* seaside vacation.

Headed by Colonel A. W. Snyder, AAFRS 1 employed psychiatrists, USO comedians, great cooks, and some of the more sensitive paper pushers in the Army. (It is no minor thing to send a man who has survived the first round back into battle. Frank Havens vividly remembered at least three suicides among men despondent at the notion of having to fight again.) AAFRS 1 would entertain its soldier guests with concerts, comedy shows, athletic events, movies, and such fantastic glories as the Military Ball before the Miss America Pageant of 1945.

On this occasion, each girl was taken to the executive offices of Colonel Snyder and introduced to her escort. Then she took a turn across the Convention Hall stage and received a key to the city from Mayor Joseph Altman. At the end of the evening, the soldiers at the dance took a straw poll on their favorites to win the Miss America Pageant. They decided that Phyllis Mathis of San Diego, who had been sponsored by Larry Finley's Mission Beach Amusement Center, took third place. Miss Wisconsin, Ellen Christy, took second. And Bess Myerson, feeling a little safer tonight in the arms of a guy from Brooklyn, was the soldiers' choice for the girl most likely to win the Miss America Pageant.

So Bess had scored with the soldiers, and she came home to the Brighton elated from their admiration. Her sister Sylvia, *éminence drôle,* reminded her that the soldiers were not the judges.

WITH HER HANDPICKED HOSTESS COMMITTEE, LENORA HAD gone far toward controlling the Atlantic City elite and the overall direction of the Pageant's development. With her indomitable personality, she easily controlled the nervous girls. The corporate sponsors gave her no trouble unless aroused, and she took great care not to do that.

"Lenora had lots of power," Press Bureau secretary Mary Corey recalled. "Lots. But there were limits. For example, she couldn't always control the judges."

The judges in 1945 comprised an odd assortment of men and women who straddled the past and the future of the Pageant, bringing Lenora both wonderful connections and big headaches. The job of judging entailed no fees but it was a week's paid vacation, and for some of the judges a valuable opportunity for personal publicity. The majority came because it was their *business* to discover good-looking, gifted young women.

In the early years, they were invariably people whose decisions on *beauty* would be accepted by the public—among these, artists and illustrators formed the largest group. In 1945, Arthur William Brown, Bradshaw Crandall, and Dean Cornwell were the illustrator judges; another artist, Vincent Trotta, art director for National Screen Service, had moved from the world of print art to Hollywood.

For the illustrator judges, 1945 posed a new challenge. Almost five years of fighting had denuded the country of its entire young male population and subjected the definition of "beauty" to a dramatic, even traumatic, change. The illustrator, accustomed to judging beauty by and for male tastes, had now to adjust to feminine priorities.

No one could roll with these timely punches better than Arthur William Brown, president of the Society of Illustrators in 1945 and a judge who had been associated with the Miss America Pageant since its earliest days. Known as "Brownie" among the New York glitterati whose parties he enlivened for forty years, Brown was a jaunty little man with a moustache who wore snappy jackets and ascots. Some of his models achieved extraordinary success, among them Fredric March and Joan Blondell.

Brown's illustrations for three of Booth Tarkington's novels— *Seventeen, The Magnificent Ambersons,* and *Alice Adams*— made him nationally famous. For twenty-five years he illustrated *Saturday Evening Post* stories by such luminaries as F. Scott Fitzgerald, Arthur Train, O. Henry, and Sinclair Lewis.

By the time Brown reached the Miss America Pageant of 1945, he had mellowed until, in the words of one journalist, he was "mild as chicken broth," acknowledging with a sigh that the poorly paid, poorly educated models of years past were now being replaced by savvy college girls who would insist on their own style no matter what men said. The war had changed the American woman for all time, as far as Brown could see, and he was philosophical about the revolution. Let it come; he was ready.

Another of the artist judges was Bradshaw Crandall. Not yet fifty in 1945, he had been selling drawings of beautiful girls for more than thirty years. To be rendered by Crandall was to achieve a kind of immortality, if only because few artists' styles were more copied.

Although it is hard to judge the sincerity of anyone's comments in the babble and claptrap of beauty columns in any era, Crandall seemed to long for individuality, some verve and distinction among his homogeneously regular models.

"Our American girl potentially has more charm than any other type of feminine beauty in the world," he said. "She just doesn't develop it. And I'll tell you why. . . . She isn't sure of herself. . . . Just because a pair of shoes happens to be the mode of the moment, she will buy them even if she ruins . . . the beauty of her legs. Originality is construed as oddness, and the most characteristic American trait is to shun oddness of any kind. . . . When our girls know how to play and work and live their own lives, only restrained by what is good taste, they will be remarkable creatures."[2]

---

[2] *New York World-Telegram,* (February 16, 1933).

The third illustrator judge, Dean Cornwell, had become rich and famous in the 1920s for his illustrations of, as Norman Rockwell called them, "swashbuckling romantic costume stories." Frustrated by the short-lived nature of magazine illustration, Cornwell quit at the peak of his fame, studied mural painting and concentrated on historical docudramatic art until his death in 1960.

Cornwell's portraits of the Founding Fathers now hang in the Capitol rotunda. His incredibly dramatic series for Wyeth Pharmaceuticals called "Pioneers of American Medicine" decorated pharmacies and doctors' waiting rooms for a decade, inspiring aspiring physicians and intimidating their future patients. Whatever may have been his tastes in the 1920s, by 1945 Dean Cornwell had made the decision for substance. Like the jaundiced Brown and the bored Crandall, Cornwell wanted something more from the new Miss America than he might have wanted in the past.

Lenora Slaughter was not impressed with the illustrator judges. As far as she was concerned, the illustrators were the collective enemy. "I always had trouble with those artists," she told Frank Deford.[3] "All they saw was legs, and I was a Baptist and my board was Quakers."

Lenora's battle with the illustrators, seemingly cultural, was actually an ideological struggle that cut to the heart of the American way of looking at women.

In 1923, when all seventeen of the Pageant judges were artists (they included Norman Rockwell, James Montgomery Flagg, and Howard Chandler Christy), the standard employed was literally a hundred-point body breakdown to measure the "beauty" of each contestant. The judges gave fifteen points for construction of the head; ten points for the eyes; five points for the hair; ten points for facial expression, and on and on. Whether the woman had talent, what she might say, certainly what she might think concerned the illustrators not at all. In this regard, a hero of American folk art like Rockwell proved no different

[3] Frank Deford, *There She Is: The Life and Times of Miss America* (New York: Viking, 1971), p. 63.

than a sometime villain of American feminism like Brian DePalma, who was once heard to say, "When you look through the camera, a woman is a series of circles."

Only in the fullness of time does the illness discover its precedents.

Lenora couldn't have known it, because she hadn't studied the obsessions of François Truffaut and Alfred Hitchcock, but the fact is she was doing battle not just with a bunch of legmen but also with something much more subtle and strong—the abstract technological mode of seeing women, the impulse to look at them through the cold lense of professionalism, as a series of circles . . . a construction of face bones . . . a set of measurements.

Even by the lights of her own era, Lenora had an excellent case for the lasciviousness of the illustrators. Their high times and randy life-style were best exemplified by the activities of the Dutch Treat Club.

Founded in 1905, the DTC was a high-class literary-man-about-town stag association specializing in that kind of ribald *macho* camaraderie that mutated in the 1970s into the *Playboy* bunny culture and is now usually reserved for college humor magazines. By the standards of the 1980s, its illustrated annuals during the war years are astounding, if only because of the importance of the contributors. A certain wartime issue called "Total Offense," and clearly dedicated to that proposition, listed on its membership roster George M. Cohan, Howard Taubman, Lowell Thomas, Nathaniel Benchley, Cass Canfield, Russell Crouse, Max Eastman, Clifton Fadiman, Rube Goldberg, Jasha Heifetz, Condé Nast, Ogden Nash, Grantland Rice, Teddy Roosevelt, Jr., and Mr. Simon and Mr. Schuster. In these pages you could find a picture by Arthur William Brown depicting frolicking cuties who wore nothing more than Japanese hats and high-heeled red shoes, titled "Hors de Combat." Bradshaw Crandall's illustrated lady straddled the centerfold, one leg outstretched on each side.

Among the speakers at a DTC meeting was the political analyst Louis Fischer. Colonel "Wild" Bill Donovan gave a report on the war. And in the program booklet, an accompanying illustration by John Falter titled "War Map" pictured a prone, somnolent nude with troop movement arrows driving toward her genitals and anchor pins in her breasts.

This was the leisuretime activity of the most influential group of judges who came to Atlantic City. No wonder Lenora Slaughter, who called herself "a little girl from out of the Southland," was in a tizzy.

FROM THE MOMENT SHE ARRIVED IN ATLANTIC CITY, LENORA began to chip away at the priorities of the illustrator judges by supporting every possible expansion of the basis on which girls were evaluated. And the instructions to the judges, written in the spirit of Lenora's stateliest rhetoric, bristled with a certain aura of warning.

"The modern American conception of Beautiful Womanhood minimizes the ancient classic standards of height and other physical measurements in favor of a generally well-proportioned figure plus these other important characteristics:

1. Beauty of face
2. Voice, manner of speaking
3. Wholesomeness, disposition, general culture
4. Special talents
5. Health, care of the body, dress

"The Miss America Pageant, aside from serving as a worthwhile civic event for Atlantic City, offers the young women of America real opportunity to attain recognition of their natural beauty and their acquired talents. Most of the girls who compete in the Miss America contest are seriously interested in a career on the stage, screen, radio, or in some other profession in which they can adapt their beauty and personality. In their behalf, we ask your sincere interest and unbiased judgment."[4]

Talent had been introduced into the Pageant in 1938 mostly as a way of making the stage show more fun to watch. Lenora tried to get the local pageants to take it seriously.

She also did her best to dilute the illustrator majority with judges whose tastes would reflect different standards.

Vincent Trotta was an illustrator whose long association with the Pageant was more paternalistic than opportunistic. From 1912 to 1946, Trotta served as advertising art director for Famous Players, Paramount Pictures, and National Screen Service. He is remembered now for the more than two thousand portraits of military personnel, from generals to privates, that he made and gave as gifts to his subjects during World War II and the Korean "conflict."

Jolly and kindhearted, Trotta treated the contestants like daughters. He would take them out in New York and pay a visit with them to one of his favorite hangouts—the Stage Door Canteen. He was definitely not from the lascivious wing of the Society of Illustrators.

In 1945 the most important new group of judges challenging the "legmen" were women.

"The women judges proved the biggest mystery," Bess said. "We simply had no idea what they would like in a winner, and we had the nagging suspicion that Lenora controlled them completely.

"Lois Wilson was a former contestant, very pretty, a starlet in Hollywood. We figured she was there to inspire the girls with the idea that being in the Pageant could lead them to the gold in the hills of California. Then there was Prunella Wood, who wrote fashion news for King Features. She wore peasant blouses and seemed tight with Harry Conover, the model agency executive who was also a judge. In my self-absorption I feared that Conover would recognize me from my modeling audition photographs and tell Prunella Wood that he had already rejected me."

---

[4] "Method of Judging for the Selection of Miss America," published by the Miss America Pageant Committee, Atlantic City, New Jersey, 1945.

The third woman judge was Vyvyan Donner of *Movietone News.*

Tall, sweet-faced, with an upswept pile of tight curls on the very top of her head, she was one of the few women ever to make it in Hollywood as any kind of director. By 1945 she had already produced over six hundred short features. Her newsreel capsules on world fashion influenced farm girls in Iowa and secretaries in Detroit to notice what they were showing in Paris, what they were wearing in New York. She did as much as any single person to internationalize the fashion market.

Donner brought Lenora a valuable connection to Ethel Traphagan, who had a fashion design school in New York (and whose students ultimately created a line of fancy dresses for Miss America of 1945 to wear during her year as the symbol of "beautiful womanhood"). Most important, Vyvyan Donner could give a girl a job in Hollywood. In fact, she employed Venus Ramey, the controversial Miss America of 1944, in a 1945 *Movietone News* capsule on the postwar swimsuit.

"The judges made valuable business connections at the Pageant," Bess commented. "Harry Conover wasn't there for his health; John Robert Powers wasn't coming as an honorary judge on Saturday night just because he wanted to chase sea gulls. They were there looking for girls for their modeling agencies; they hoped that Vincent Trotta or Vyvyan Donner or one of the Hollywood scouts who came, like Zelma Brookhov of Warner Brothers, would see a contestant who was already under contract to their agencies and want to buy out her modeling contract for thousands of dollars and make her a movie star."

Bess assumed that contestants who had worked before as models had a tremendous advantage because a whole group of judges in the Pageant might actually benefit from their success. "I figured that with no record as a fashion model, I'd better try to impress the judges who were interested in *talent.*"

Foremost among these were Conrad Thibault, a handsome radio tenor who enjoyed great popularity and who had often judged the Pageant, and a newcomer to Atlantic City, Sidney Piermont. Piermont worked for Loew's Theatres as head booker for all the vaudeville from 1920 to 1942. At the time of the 1945 Pageant, he was working for Mike Todd Productions.

"Dad was a real show-business personality," his son Denis said with warmth. "He actually *lived* in the Hotel Astor. He hung out at Toots Shor's. A friend sent him a telegram addressed only 'Sidney Piermont, Times Square, New York,' *and it got to him.*

"I remember he was very unimpressed with the Miss America thing. He never served as a judge before or again. The only justification he could have had for going that year was that he was always looking for talent."

Recalled Bess with a laugh: "When I realized that Mr. Piermont the talent expert represented *the musical hall circuit,* I figured I was washed up with the judges. After all, I was a *classical* pianist! Perhaps I could pound out a little boogie-woogie in a pinch, but believe me, it wasn't my *forte.*

"On Tuesday afternoon and Wednesday afternoon when we went to Convention Hall to rehearse our talent presentations and I saw Frances Dorn, Miss Birmingham, whirling by in her tap shoes or Miss Detroit singing the blues, I thought, "That's it. Sidney Piermont and Conrad Thibault are looking for *them.* I ought to go home.""

Bess could not have been more off base in her judgment of the judges. They were operating under pressures of which neither she nor her sister Sylvia could have been aware.

The experience of recent Miss Americas informed Lenora Slaughter's tastes in a winner, and she duly informed the judges. They could take it or leave it, but she told them what she thought.

She didn't want another borderline starlet.

She had grown seriously suspicious of the commercial Hollywood connection because of the experiences of Rosemary LaPlanche, Miss America of 1941, and of Jo-Caroll Dennison, Miss America of 1942. Both had won film studio contracts, and Lenora was disappointed with the results. Said LaPlanche in later years, "I showed I had a certain value to the studio that did not help me. They would send me out on the road to publicize RKO pictures and somebody else would get the good roles back in Hollywood." She said she had made about $150,000 in 1941–42, and because of the bites of agents and managers, had not seen one third of it.

If Lois Wilson, the starlet, was serving as a judge, it was probably because the Pageant board wanted her as a role model, *not* Lenora Slaughter. Lenora's role-model choice was Miss America of 1943, Jean Bartel, soon to appear on Broadway in *The Desert Song* by Sigmund Romberg. "Look how far a girl with real musical talent can go," Lenora suggested . . . at every opportunity.

The scariest tale circulating among the judges in September 1945 concerned Venus Ramsey, Miss America of 1944. In her wide-eyed desire to make it in show business, Venus had believed the lavish promises of several "agents." She had been locked in hotels by them, placed in degrading and low-paid gigs by them, and then dropped by them. Bitter and broke, she harbored great rancor against the Pageant, calling it "an entree into oblivion." When Lenora asked Sidney Piermont to introduce her to Harry Kalcheim of the William Morris Agency, it was because she wanted once and for all to settle the agent mess, to make sure that whatever the proclivities of future winners, they would be signed, booked, paid, and protected.

The judges to whom Lenora brought all this accumulated wisdom were already inclined to feel friendly toward change. Arthur William Brown, Bradshaw Crandall, and Dean Cornwell had long since passed the pretty-girl stage and possessed a more sophisticated vision of what the great American beauty might look like. Harry Conover had his eye on television. He figured any Miss America from here on in would need the vivacity and wit to make the transition from the page to the home screen. Piermont thought more like Conover than Bess might have imagined. He, too, was heading for television and would soon become the talent booker for all CBS variety shows except Ed Sullivan's. Vyvyan Donner was less interested in Hollywood than in the postwar Paris collections and the demanding world of high fashion. More than any other judge, Vincent Trotta had been upset by the unpleasant experiences of the previous year's winner, Venus Ramey. He felt it reflected badly on the judges and his honor. He supported Lenora's efforts to elevate the Pageant's reputation.

No judge could ignore the presence of Guy Snavely. Although not a judge himself, the dignified educator from Alabama reminded everybody that in this first scholarship year, the winner must be a young woman whose "poise and personality" suited her for an advanced education.

The net effect was a board of judges predisposed to look for a winner who, besides being beautiful, could be trusted to make a good impression during public appearances, who actually had some real talent and some verifiable intelligence.

To the great good fortune of Bess Myerson, they were inclined to listen to Lenora Slaughter when she grinned and said, "Honey, just pick me a lady."

UNAWARE OF ANY ADVANTAGE SHE MIGHT BE ENJOYING, BESS *worked* at becoming Miss America. Her sister Sylvia took copious notes on all Lenora's speeches, and when Sylvia and Bess were alone in their hotel room, they would study the notes as though they were cramming for a math final.

The other contestants appeared to Bess to be beautiful beyond beating. Compared to them, she felt like the Chrysler Building.

"Sometimes when we had to line up onstage for a rehearsal of an entrance or an exit, the laws of alphabetical order would put me next to Miss Minnesota, Arlene Anderson, who was five-three," Bess recalled. "I longed to collapse on my knees, to crouch, to slump over. Then I'd look out into the empty theater to the seat where I knew Sylvia was sitting. She would pull her hair up from the crown of her head to remind me of Mrs. LaFollette's old dictum, and I would stand up straight, look straight ahead. . . . Like an acrophobiac who is trying to avoid vertigo, I tried desperately not to look down at Arlene."

As helpful as Sylvia was to Bess, both young women regretted that their mother couldn't be there. They knew that they would never have arrived in Atlantic City were it not for Bella's ambition.

"I wanted my mother to enjoy the Pageant the way the other mothers did," Bess said. "They had brought their daughters this far. Hadn't my mother brought me here, too? With her 'Practice! Practice! Wrong! Wrong!,' with her sheer will, hadn't she made me into a disciplined person with enough nervous energy to maybe make dreams come true? I wished for Mom to be there . . . and at the same time, I was so glad she wasn't."

Bess was quite correct in her assessment of the typical mother's role in the beauty pageant. Many of the girls had come to Atlantic City almost entirely on the strength of their mothers' dreams.

"I never wanted to do anything," Jeni Freeland said, "but my mother made me. When I was three years old, I was Little Miss Georgia. We traveled all the time. My father was a sales promoter. When I was seven I was Little Miss Knoxville. I looked up at the Big Miss Knoxville contestants and wondered if I'd ever be that big and if I could be a Miss Something.

"When I was older and we were living in Miami, my mother prompted me to go into business on my own. So I was designing clothes, painting murals on nightclub walls as well as working at Hartley's Department Store. My mother had big dreams for me."

Arlene Anderson had been playing the marimbaphone since she was a young girl and hankered after a career in music. However, it was her mother who got the idea that Atlantic City might advance Arlene professionally.

"My mother called up the veterans organization at the University of Minnesota where I was a student and said, 'How about sponsoring my daughter to the Miss Minnesota contest?' They said 'Okay,' and I said 'Okay,' and I won. Then my mother called the Chamber of Commerce. 'This child needs money for some gowns,' she said. 'She is going to be exposing Minnesota to a big audience and she deserves to have some backing.' And they said 'Okay.'

"She got Miss Slaughter to send an airplane ticket, and then my father cashed it in and the whole family, my mother and me, my sister and my father, all of us went by train.

". . . It wasn't that she was a stage mother or anything. She just wasn't your stay-at-home housewife type."

To Bess, these seemed the luckiest of girls. How could she know that Arlene had come, just like she had, with a donated wardrobe? How could she know that Jeni had been ready to stay home in Miami when she discovered that the Miami Chamber of Commerce would give her only two dresses?

"My boss, Mr. Hartley, came to my rescue," Jeni said. "He let me go through the store and take anything I wanted. I took an ermine-trimmed coat, hats, I took an inexpensive evening dress that had flowers all over it, and my mother sewed sequins on it the whole way up on the train to New Jersey."

As mistaken about these contestants as Bess might have been, they were even more mistaken about her.

This is what Arlene thought:

"Everybody needed a mother at the Pageant, except for Bess. Bess was the most mature individual, for her age, of any of us. Her gowns were custom-made. They were way above everybody else's. They were gorgeous. Sequined, with stones set in them. She carried them well because of her height.

"She was far and away above us. We were corny little creatures. Jeni Freeland was a little more sophisticated than me, I mean I was a bumpkin from Minnesota. But Bess was just . . . just in control."

This is what Jeni thought:

"Bess was a lot taller than we were, and she looked very groomed. She looked like she had been told how to walk and maybe how not to talk too much. She looked polished. Compared to her, we were all just a bunch of provincial little shrimps."

And meanwhile, "cool, calm Bess" was having stomach trouble, throwing up the food she managed to swallow, and losing a pound a day.

I did not want to be paranoid.

On the eve of the official competition, many girls were. They had conspiracy theories. They believed that Lenora had stacked the odds against this one or in favor of that one. They believed that the judges had succumbed to one influence or another.

Some of the girls had come from state or city pageants where talent was not judged. Of course, they would prepare a poem or a dramatic reading, perhaps something Lenora might suggest. However, they felt disadvantaged by their lack of experience. When they discovered further that they would be performing before an audience of more than three thousand, competing against well-trained, experienced performers like me or Arlene Anderson or Frances Dorn, they often felt betrayed.

My potential paranoia concerned my minority ethnic status. Where I came from, everyone was Jewish. Now I felt alien and strange, closely watched by fans and detractors. It was nerve-racking.

A crowd of newsmen and photographers followed us everywhere. We became very friendly with them. They were light-hearted and unpretentious men, never putting on airs like Lenora and her Hostess Committee. They made jokes and carried gossip.

One day one of the newsmen said to me, "Watch yourself, Bess. There are people involved here who don't want a Jewish winner. Something may happen to ruin your chances. Watch yourself."

Thereafter I was even more nervous that I might break some rule inadvertently.

My assigned chaperone had not grown friendlier as the official judging approached. She remained cool and distant. I wondered why.

To allay any prospective disappointment, I convinced myself that I would lose, despite all the kind wishes of my friendly Jewish fans and my enthusiastic soldier friends. I protected myself against the catastrophe of overconfidence by expecting the worst. It was a very valuable psychological device for me.

On Wednesday afternoon, those of us whose first competitive event would be in talent held a rehearsal. During a break, a local photographer named Frank Havens took me backstage to a roomful of scenery and props, where Miss America's throne was stored.

"Come on, Bess," he said, "sit in that chair. If you sit in that chair and I take your picture, I bet you will be Miss America."

I didn't want to. I felt almost frightened of Frank's enthusiasm. I finally agreed to pose for the picture. However, before I sat down on the throne I said, very quietly, "Poo, poo, poo." Just as my mother had always done. To ward off the Evil Eye.

CHAPTER 7

The
High Costs
of Victory

This was the way they scored the Pageant when I was competing in it in 1945.

First, we were divided into three groups, each with a different competition schedule.

On Wednesday night, Group A would compete in swimsuit, Group B in evening gown, and Group C in talent. On Thursday night, the groups would rotate. On Friday night, they would rotate once again. By Saturday—the final day, the day of judgment—every contestant would have competed in each category.

The judges voted their choice of the top five girls in each category on each night. Five points for first place, four points for second, three points for third, and so on. On Saturday morning the individual scores would be tabulated. On Saturday evening after the "Parade of States" when all the girls were gathered onstage, the fifteen highest scores would be announced, and those girls would step forward as the finalists.

There were ten judges my year. Two honorary judges— sportscaster Ted Husing and model agency head John Robert Powers—arrived for the finals on Saturday night, September 8. These twelve judges were instructed to disregard all their previous feelings and ratings and look at the fifteen finalists with a fresh eye. The fifteen girls then competed against each other in swimsuit, evening gown, and talent. The judges voted for the five they liked best. Then they voted for the order in which the five should be rated. The top-rated girl of the final five was the winner.

Vague, indecipherable elements influenced the judging.

The judges were not supposed to discuss their votes with each other. However, I am sure that most contestants believed they did. We saw them on the beach together. They went to night-clubs together. They were entertained constantly. Were we sup-posed to imagine that throughout all that drinking and eating and dancing they wouldn't talk about us?

During the week we would be given opportunities to converse and mingle with the judges, enabling them to rate us on poise and personality. We attended a formal breakfast session with them. We knew that in the final scoring they would give consideration to whatever impression we had made on them during the week.

The mystery of the evening gown competition added another variable. At the end of each night of judging, the winners in the swimsuit and talent divisions would be announced. However, the evening gown winners were never announced. Only the judges knew those results. Generally, however, the secrecy of the evening gown results proved to be a morale booster. Even if a girl had not won in her swimsuit or talent divisions, she knew she might still have a chance if she won in evening gown.

Rehearsals, on the other hand, could deal a serious blow to a girl's good spirits. Even those of us who had trained seriously were amateurs; we were all insecure about our talent. We had no idea what would entertain the judges. The limited rehearsal time left many girls feeling unprepared. They pleaded with Lenora to allow them a second run-through.

It was tremendously important for a girl to sustain her mo-rale, to weather various setbacks. We had to possess inner resources to withstand the general tendency to paranoia. All other things being equal, the strong-willed girls among us with attentive cheerful companions like Sylvia and Mrs. Freeland, Mrs. Anderson and Franny Dorn's companions, Lily May Cald-well and Jimmy Hatcher, probably enjoyed a significant advantage.

Only the Atlantic City and Philadelphia papers covered the Pageant thoroughly in those days. New York City, with its sophisticated entertainment pages, allotted little or no space for this "nonsense on the Jersey shore." Out-of-town papers depended for their coverage on photographers like Al Gold and Frank Havens and, very importantly, Mall Dodson, who ran the Atlantic City Press Bureau. Mall was a tall, lean man who chewed tobacco and treated everyone with courtesy. His staff supplied the nation with photos and stories on the Miss America Pageant.

The local press kept the audience involved with the Pageant. "Who will win tonight?" the stories would ask. "Will it be sultry Miss Philadelphia, our hometown favorite, or adorable Miss Tennessee, with the big blue eyes and the girl-next-door innocence?" The reporters would spotlight the front runners and predict the finalists, exactly like sports reporters forecasting the outcome of a boxing match.

The difference, of course, is that if a sportscaster declares Marvin Hagler will win and Sugar Ray Leonard wins instead, the sportscaster never hears the end of it.

If Morley Cassidy of the Philadelphia Bulletin was wrong about the Miss America Pageant, who cared? No one took the Pageant seriously . . . no one except us.

The most benevolent variable at the Pageant was the audience. Large, warm. Endlessly sympathetic. If you walked out onstage at the Warner Theatre and the three thousand people in the audience cheered, you felt wonderful. The judges might be sitting down in their corner near the orchestra pit giving you a "1" for your talent or a less than "0" in your evening gown; however, the public response, the applause, the whistles from the soldiers, and the cheering from your friends and supporters gave you confidence. It kept you in the race.

That first night when I played the piano and the flute in my talent competition, the burst of applause at the end of my performance hit me like a vitamin shot.

They like me, I thought.

Maybe I have a chance.

ON THAT FIRST NIGHT OF JUDGING, WEDNESDAY EVENING, September 5, Bess's group was assigned to compete in talent. Joe Frasetto, the Pageant bandleader, who often appeared at Atlantic City's swinging 500 Club, rehearsed all day with the girls. His band included two violins, three saxophones, a trumpet, a piano, a bass, and a drum. Albert Skean, the Pageant's general manager, had written Lenora in August, cautioning her to inform the girls about the exact components of the band and to make sure they brought with them the orchestrations for any music they intended to use during the show.

Better-trained musicians like Bess and Arlene Anderson brought appropriate arrangements. But some other girls just *told* the band what they wanted and then had to hope for the best.

"I told Joe Frasetto I would kill him when I got back to Philadelphia," Gloria Bair laughed. "You see, my dance was to 'Temptation,' and if I had been able to use the Perry Como record that was out then, I would have been fine. But Frasetto just gave me a piano accompaniment; he wouldn't even give me the full band. I don't know whether he was told to do it or whether he did it on his own."

The other thing that irritated Gloria was that Lenora insisted she could *only* dance, when she was fully prepared to dance and sing as well. "Bess was allowed to play the piano and the flute when I wasn't allowed to do my two talents," Gloria said. "We couldn't figure it out. But we had the feeling that there were these little conspiracies going on . . . that Lenora Slaughter had her likes and her dislikes. In 1945, she liked Bess Myerson. At least that's what we thought. . . ."

Bess was not the only one with two talents. Arlene Anderson played the marimbaphone and sang, too. Jeni Freeland had been prepared to perform as a singer, but Lenora told her there were too many singers and that she would stand out much more if she staged a fashion show as her talent. Too independent-minded to accept Lenora's word as law, Jeni went ahead with the fashion show but arranged with Frasetto to sing a song along with it.

In the group Bess and Gloria appeared with on Wednesday night, the singers came out in force. Miss Indiana sang "Indian Love Call"; Miss Connecticut sang "I'm in the Mood for Love"; Miss British Columbia sang "The Sheik of Araby." Miss Georgia sang a song called "Candy." Miss Arkansas did a torch song interpretation of "My Man."

Miss Iowa did a tap dance; Miss Utah did a ballet dance. Miss Washington, D.C., attempted the courtroom scene from George Bernard Shaw's *St. Joan*. Miss Mississippi attempted stand-up comedy. Phyllis Mathis, Miss San Diego, performed a hula dance. Years later, Lenora reported that she objected to the fact that Phyllis's belly button showed above the waistline of her ersatz grass skirt. Frances Dorn astonished the audience, which had already grown inured to appalling mediocrity, by turning out to be a tap dancer who really knew how to tap dance.

Bess played three minutes of Edvard Grieg's Piano Concerto in A Minor. Then she played Gershwin's "Summertime" on the flute and brought down the house. She and Frances Dorn tied for first place in talent.

"I had no idea there could be a tie," Bess recalled. "They announced the winners consecutively in alphabetical order of states, so Alabama was announced first. In the split second before my name was added to Franny's, I mentally took myself out of the running, concluding that as I had anticipated, no serious musician could win. In the next split second, my whole outlook changed."

Elsewhere on the stage of the Warner Theatre, Miss Tennessee, Lee Harriet Henson, took top honors in the bathing suit division. The press conjectured that the judges may have given highest ratings in the evening gown competition to Lee Wieland, Miss Chicago; Arlene Anderson, Miss Minnesota; or Jeni Freeland, Miss Florida.

The pictures of the winners that night bear out the impression that Arlene and Jeni had of Bess. Frances Dorn wore a two-piece frilly glitter costume and white high-heeled tap shoes, with a gardenia in her hair. Lee Henson looked Sandra Dee-ish in her pert Catalina swimsuit. Bess towered over both of them, statuesque in a long white dress with long sleeves and a high neckline. She was very tan. She looked like she had it together. She looked elegant and sexy. No way did she look scared.

By the end of Wednesday night, the morale crises that one bout of judging entailed had worked on the ego systems of many of the contestants, making them vulnerable to conspiracy theories. Rumors that Bess Myerson "had it in the bag" began to circulate.

Arlene Anderson says that the first time she walked across the stage for the opening Parade of States, she saw a judge point to Bess and say to one of his colleagues, "Well, there she is, that's Miss America."

"I thought, 'Gee, what a deal,' " Arlene said. "I mean, it was like it was over before it began."

One impression that has endured with Gloria Baïr until this day is that Bess was bound to win because Lenora Slaughter was on her side. "If Lenora liked you, she liked you," said Gloria. "If she didn't, she didn't. And that year, she liked Bess."

Gloria insisted, for example, that Lenora steered Bess through the interviews with the judges.

"A lot of the girls believed Bess would win because 'it was just New York's year to win,' " Gloria said. "And a lot of the girls felt Bess would get it because the majority of the people in Atlantic City at that time were Jewish and it was thought that the Pageant would just have to surrender to popular demand and give them a Jewish winner."

Frank Havens, the photographer, had a very different impression.

"Most of the young ladies that came to Atlantic City—even today—they were already Miss Prim," he said. " 'I won the state contest so I'm better than you are,' that was their attitude. But Bess was a real down-to-earth person. She wasn't in any way affected by the fact that she had been chosen for the Pageant. So naturally she became a favorite with the photographers.

"After the second day of the Pageant, Lenora saw this happening. She saw that the press was leaning toward Bess. And she came to us and said she didn't like the idea of us picking one girl and making more of her than the others, because they were all equal and every one of them should be treated absolutely alike. She spent the week trying in subtle ways to get the press off Bess. She would push the other girls. Have us concentrate on other girls. . . . In my opinion, she didn't want Bess in 1945."

Bess Myerson was completely unaware of anything that might be going on in the minds of her sister contestants or in the offices of the Atlantic City Press Bureau. In fact, the only area in which she and Gloria have similar memories concerns the Jewish presence in Atlantic City.

Gloria is mistaken about the demographics: The Jews were not a majority in Atlantic City in 1945. However, her impression of an overwhelming Jewish presence may have been created by the fact that Jewish people were buying tickets for the Pageant as never before. They wanted to see Bess. They wanted to root for *their* beauty queen.

"In the eyes of the local Jewish citizenry, Bess was a goddess," Gilbert Katz recalled. "She was our champion. Maybe we looked at it that way because of recent history in Europe; if we did, then I guess that was an awful weight to put on a young girl. But I tell you, we were all pulling for her. We were hoping and praying that she would be the one to win."

On Thursday morning, when Bess left her hotel, her fans were in the lobby, wanting to give her a kiss for good luck, pressing her hand. Coupled with her elation at having tied as the talent winner, these good wishes left her cheerful, feeling strong.

Then she got the barf green bathing suit.

———

The girls who were going to appear in the bathing suit competition on Friday night had a run-through on Thursday morning at the Warner Theatre. Lenora wanted to see how we looked walking down the runway and to give us one of her encouraging spiels.

Upon our arrival, we had all received exactly the same style swimsuit—different colors, same model. I had requested a white suit, which I thought would look flattering with my camp tan. I was working hard to keep it. Every time I would go outside, I would lift my face to the sun. We loved to burn in those days. A glorious tan was the height of chic.

Compared to the latex spandex boned body-molding suits of today, our swimsuits were shapeless tanks. They did nothing for you. In case you tried to do more for them than God intended, a volunteer from the Hostess Committee would check you out beforehand to make sure you didn't have anything extra stuffed in the bodice.

["Those bathing suits were the most unflattering things ever made!" exclaimed Jeni Freeland. "They gave you no shape, no support. They had this wrap-around panel in the front that actually called attention to your crotch and accentuated your belly. If a girl looked good in one of those, she really had a wonderful figure. There was nothing engineered or artificial. What you saw was what you got."]

At the rehearsal, just as I took my turn and began to walk down the runway, Lenora suddenly stopped me and beckoned me over to her. She leaned in close to me so that our conversation would remain private.

"That swimsuit is too small for you," she said quietly.

I looked down at myself, puzzled. "It's a twelve," I answered. "I am a size twelve."

"Well, the suit is riding up very immodestly in the back. I'll have Catalina send a size fourteen replacement over to your hotel later. Meanwhile, let's go on with the rehearsal."

Of course, it never occurred to me to argue. I certainly didn't want to make any trouble. However, the incident left both Sylvia and me on edge.

Later that day, when Sylvia was setting my hair in the hotel room, the Catalina man delivered the size fourteen suit. Sylvia had the impression that he looked suspiciously at the glass of beer she had been using to set my hair. Fearing that I would be disqualified for drinking, she grabbed the beer and downed it in one long gulp.

"I love a nice cool beer in the afternoon," she said sweetly, "although, of course, my sister Bess, Miss New York City, never touches a drop."

The Catalina man probably could not have cared less if Miss New York City was soused to the gills in her hotel room. When he was gone, I cried, "Sylvia! How could you drink that disgusting glass of beer?! Why didn't you just drop the comb in it so he would know you were using it as setting lotion?!"

She burped and said simply, "I panicked."

When we saw the size fourteen swimsuit, we both panicked.

It wasn't a pretty pale lime green like one of my Kass evening gowns. It was a repulsive green, the color of overcooked peas.

I tried it on. It was huge. Those bathing suits wrinkled on the roundest of figures. On my long, lanky frame, this one looked like a sack. Furthermore, the color gave me a certain froglike complexion.

"We're being paranoid," Sylvia reasoned. "Maybe it really doesn't look so bad. Let's get another opinion."

We showed it to the other contestants in our hotel. They all confirmed our dislike of the green bathing suit.

["Oh, it was quite horrible," Gloria Bair remembered. "A car came to take Bess and Sylvia to a dressmaker to have the waist taken in: I was sure Lenora sent the car."]

Frankly, I don't remember being sent to a dressmaker to have that bathing suit fitted, and neither does Sylvia. If I did go, it certainly did not help. The very next morning we had to appear in a swimsuit parade at Thomas M. England General Hospital before the wounded GIs. The very next evening I was scheduled to compete in my swimsuit division. I was sure that the green fourteen would signal the end of my chances to be Miss America.

Trying not to worry, I went on in my evening gown competition on Thursday night. The Warner Theatre crowd had almost doubled in size. I felt great in my Grecian-draped Kass gown.

["Judging from the tumultuous ovation given her by the audience," wrote the Daily World, *"stunning Bess Myerson, Miss New York City, would undoubtedly have won the evening gown event by popular vote."]*

The girl who won the bathing suit competition that night was Lee Wieland from Chicago, reportedly one of the front runners in the evening gown division the night before. However, the most hotly contested honors were in the talent division.

There was the usual crop of blues singers: Miss Rhode Island sang "How Deep Is the Ocean?"; Miss Maine sang "I Should Care."

Then Miss Tennessee, Lee Henson, went on. She had won the night before in the bathing suit division. She was a charming girl. The soldiers in the audience loved her. For her talent presentation she was supposed to make a speech.

She went onstage, took one look at the audience, and if my memory serves me, she said something like, "Sorry, folks, I forgot it. Can't remember one word. If you don't mind, I'll sing a song instead." She launched blithely into her song. The band followed right along. Lee was a smash.

["It was 'I Didn't Know the Gun Was Loaded,'" Gloria Bair said with a chuckle. "That was the song."]

I was sure that Lee Henson would win in talent that night, if only because she had overcome a major fluff with such aplomb. To my surprise, Miss California won instead. She appeared in a sombrero with a short fringed skirt and sang a cowboy number. I concluded that audience reaction had no influence on the judges. That concerned me. Because like Lee Henson, I was an audience favorite.

For me, the most instructive thing about that Thursday evening was the appearance of Miss Maryland. She sang "Ain't Misbehavin'" in the talent division. At the opening of her number, she was dressed in a long gown. In the middle, she stripped to a black sequined dancing brief and pranced around the stage with a top hat and cane. It wasn't the sort of costume of which Lenora generally approved. I wondered whether Miss Maryland had checked it out during rehearsal or whether she had been bold enough to spring it as a surprise in performance.

I never learned the truth about Miss Maryland's number, but I drew my own conclusions anyway. A girl did not always have to follow to the letter all the instructions of Lenora Slaughter. A girl with courage might—within limits—do more or less what she wanted.

In the privacy of our room, I shared my new insight with Sylvia. I took off my evening gown. I hung it in the closet. Sylvia was standing in the middle of the room, holding the atrocious green swimsuit in one hand and the pretty white swimsuit in the other. She looked like Justice balancing her scales. Suddenly she exclaimed, "I've got it!"

She threw the green one in a corner, peeled off her clothes, and began to pull the size twelve white swimsuit onto her own ample, size sixteen body. She tugged. She twisted. She grunted and hopped. I kept yelling, "You'll bust it, Sylvia! The seams will split!" She would not be deterred. Finally she wriggled into the suit.

Mincing across the floor, wagging her hips and strutting in a parody of the Pageant parades, she broke me up with a routine that went something like this: Miss New York City has been disqualified for speaking to a six-year-old boy, but never fear, she has been replaced by the beautiful, talented, voluptuous Miss Bronx River Parkway. Let's have a hand for our new contestant, folks! Miss Bronx River Parkway's measurements are 48, 36, 62. She's such a bombshell that the U.S. Army Air Force considered dropping her on Berlin. Her favorite food is chicken soup with matzoh balls, and she can trace her American ancestry back to the witches of Salem!

Sylvia threw her nightgown on over the swimsuit and collapsed on the bed.

All night long I lay awake in that room, listening to my dear sister Sylvia's labored breathing. I wondered if perhaps the emotional cost of competing in the Miss America Pageant was beginning to run a trifle high.

The next morning, Sylvia took off the swimsuit. I put it on. It was a little bit bigger.

I wore the white suit at the show in Thomas M. England General Hospital. Luckily, Lenora was not there. I was careful never to turn my back to the audience, and walked sideways, leg over leg, as though I were dancing in a very slow hora. Sylvia sat out in the audience, watching me carefully. She concluded that the suit was still too small and would never get past Lenora that evening.

So she put it on again and wore it for the rest of the day, right *until the time we dressed to go to the Warner Theatre. When I put on the bathing suit, Sylvia said, "It still needs three-quarters of an inch more in length."*

She removed the buttons from the suit, sewed up the button-holes in the straps, and sewed the strap ends directly to the suit. At last the suit fit. Not a trace of cheek showed in the back.

There was only one problem.

I was now sewn into the bathing suit. I couldn't take it off.

Very carefully, I put on the evening gown I had to wear for the Parade of States. Very slowly, I walked down the runway at the Warner Theatre. Just before the swimsuit competition, I slipped into the bathroom backstage and took off the evening gown. Trying to appear relaxed and casual, I then slipped out of the bathroom with my evening gown over my arm. I didn't sit down. I was afraid that the stitches holding the straps to the bathing suit would pull out. I tried not to breathe very hard.

In the talent division, Jeni Freeland presented a fashion show of clothes she had designed and decorated. While other girls modeled her creations, Jeni sang "Rum and Coca-Cola."

One of the contestants from the Deep South portrayed all the characters at a black religious revival meeting. It was a sort of one-woman minstrel show. Do a number like that today and you would probably end up in court with the Urban League for the rest of your life.

Then Arlene Anderson played the marimbaphone. She started with "Flight of the Bumblebee"; segued into "Tea for Two;" and ended with "Ah, Sweet Mystery of Life," which she also sang in a lyric soprano.

She won hands down in that Friday night talent competition.

At the appointed time, trying to look calm, I went onstage to compete in my stretched, stitched white Catalina.

My fans in the audience cheered. I didn't pay too much attention because I had already convinced myself that audience reaction counted for nothing.

When Bob Russell, the MC, announced that I had won in the swimsuit division, I was beside myself with excitement, because now I was the only contestant who had tied to win in the talent division and won outright in the swimsuit division. The press had reported that I had done well in the evening gown competition. I realized that on points alone, I must be one of the fifteen finalists.

My heart was very full at that moment.

I looked out into the audience for my wonderful sister Sylvia. I couldn't find her.

"Oh, I was on the phone," Sylvia said. "I was calling Helen in New York. I told her she had better get herself down to Atlantic City, because our Bessie had made the finals."

———

ON FRIDAY MORNING, THE GIRLS HAD BEEN ASKED TO APPEAR in a swimsuit parade for the wounded veterans at Thomas M. England General Hospital. Forty years later, Francis Ford Coppola would suggest in *Apocalypse Now* that this is not the most tasteful way to entertain men who are wondering if they will ever have a date with a woman again. However, to be honest, no one who was there—not the nurses or the soldiers— remembers being offended.

Bess recalled, "From our vantage point onstage in the lighted hall, we could clearly see the men. On stretchers. In wheelchairs. With nurses standing among them like white candles. We were in the biggest amputee hospital in the world. When we were asked to stay the afternoon and visit the boys from our home states, some girls demurred. They said they needed to rehearse. Or rest. Any excuse not to remain in that sad place.

"It was not a simple thing to sit down on the beds to talk to those veterans. To see where the sheet dropped, where the leg ended. To reach out to shake a hand and find a hook. I saw one nurse carry a maimed boy down the hall on her back."

It was before mainstreaming. It was long before blue signs with white wheelchair insignia reserved the parking spaces right out in front of every supermarket for the handicapped. It was before anyone had even thought of building ramps alongside steps so that disabled people might have access to public facilities. In the years after the war, veterans would band together and lobby in Congress to pass laws making the nation more responsive to the special needs of handicapped citizens. But in 1945, the handicapped were hidden.

Added Bess, "Most of us felt completely unprepared to meet them with an easy gaze."

"They told me there was a young man in the hospital who was a quadruple amputee," Jeni Freeland recounted. "He was from Florida and they wanted to take my picture with him. It would really thrill him, they said. So I said 'Okay.' And when I saw him, I was just devastated. He was such a darling blond curly-headed boy. And I was just . . . just overcome . . . it was all I could do to hold back the tears. Whoever was with me, this officer or someone, kept poking me and saying, 'Straighten up.' And when we got into the open convertible to leave this young fellow and drive down the Boardwalk, the officer said, 'Turn around and smile at him and don't you dare cry.' So I did. But as soon as we were out of sight, I broke down and sobbed. It was the first time I'd ever seen anything like that."

When Bess saw this same young man, Jimmy Wilson, she was with her old friend Miss New York State, June Jenkins. They had been assigned to visit Jimmy's roommate, Ernie Sardo, a triple amputee from Elmira.

"I had spent the entire night brooding about *my swimsuit!* Suddenly I was confronting two cheerful, optimistic fellows my age who had been torn to pieces by the war against the Nazis. It certainly put things in perspective."

Jimmy Wilson started out the Second World War as an eighteen-year-old recruit learning to be a radio operator and a top turret gunner in the Army Air Force. On October 16, 1944, the B-24 in which he was training crashed at night on Camel's Hump Mountain near Burlington, Vermont. Nine men were killed. Jimmy was thrown clear, the only survivor. Badly hurt, he languished for two days and nights on the snowy mountains. It took another day for rescue workers to bring him down by litter.

By that time he had suffered severe frostbite of his hands and feet, requiring amputation.

"It looked rather bleak for me when I was sent to England General," Jimmy said. "I had been told by an Army colonel at the base hospital in Westover, Massachusetts, that I shouldn't expect more from life than to be able to feed myself and dress myself.

"Years later, I decided that colonel must have known what he was doing, because he made me so mad that I worked harder at proving him wrong than I might have otherwise. I think that was his intention. It took me five or six years to recognize what he had done for me. His name was Benjamin Custer."

More than anything, what resurrected Jimmy Wilson from the harsh prognosis of Colonel Custer was the positive ambience at England General.

"Dr. Rufus Aldredge was responsible for the atmosphere," Jimmy recalled. "He exuded competence and yet he was very easygoing. Unlike most Army doctors. Unlike most doctors.

"He made England General one of the most unmilitary establishments in the whole Army. It was an informal arrangement, never spoken out loud, but we got out of the hospital every chance we could. The only time we really had to be there was if we had some current medical treatment.

"We spent a lot of time on the Boardwalk. The weather was beautiful. The place was full of pretty girls. And they were all very patriotic.

"I had been there a couple of months at least before Ernie Sardo arrived. A triple amputee. He couldn't have weighed more than eighty-five pounds, and he's six feet tall. I thought, 'Ah, the poor bastard, the only guy in this hospital worse off than me.' Ernie and I were good for each other because he looked at me with the same thoughts.

"Sometimes the Army did things right. Not often. But sometimes."

Ernie and Jimmy were medicine for each other, the best medicine that England General could provide.

"I was a machine gunner," Ernie said. "I went overseas in 1943 as a replacement, turned nineteen on the boat. We fought all through the fall and the winter in France, and in January 1944 I got wounded in the German counterattack in Alsace-Lorraine, in the Battle of the Bulge.

"I was in a foxhole with another guy. Somebody threw a grenade, right in the hole. Our troops retreated and left the two of us up there. I don't know what ever happened to the other fellow who was in the hole with me.

"The blast blew off my left leg. Not completely. It was just hanging from the knee. I laid out there all night. Then I got hit a couple of times by American artillery. I think I laid out there about twenty-four hours before the Germans took me back to a first-aid station.

"I didn't know that I had been picked up by Storm Troopers, that I was in an SS hospital. I mean, we didn't understand about the SS, we weren't aware of what was happening with the Jewish people until after the war, when names like Buchenwald and Dachau started coming out. I finally wound up in Heppenheim, Germany. There were many Americans in the hospital. And Serbians. About a hundred Russians in the basement. It was an old insane asylum before the war. If I'd known anything about the SS, I would have realized that they had wasted the people who were mentally ill and emptied the hospital that way.

"We lacked medical attention. We didn't get the necessary drugs. Our diet was under six hundred calories a day. The Americans liberated us on March 27, 1945. It was . . . it was a very heavy . . . heavy emotional . . . We were all crying.

"To this day I don't know why I was spared.

"At England General, they put me in a room with Jimmy Wilson; Bernie Wagner from New Oxford, Pennsylvania; and Tony Levandowski from Hartford, Connecticut. My folks came down to see me. They walked in the room and didn't even recognize me. They thought they were in the wrong room. They turned around and started to walk out. I had to call to them and tell them who I was.

"I remember when the Miss America girls came to visit. June Jenkins and Bess Myerson, sure, I remember them. They were in their bathing suits. It was a shock to see them. We were in bed, we sat up, a photographer named Sam Belasco took pictures of us. The girls were beautiful. I still have the pictures.

"It was one of those things that happened in Atlantic City that seemed like dying and going to heaven."

I took it all very personally. In the same way that one is supposed to take Passover personally and say at the seder "God brought me out of slavery in the land of Egypt. . . ." I felt that the soldiers in England General had saved me and my family from the Nazis, that Hitler had been stopped by their arms and legs.

Ernie and Jimmy were so brave and cheerful. They had no fear of death anymore. What they may have feared most was life, living, going outside of this haven in Atlantic City where every single soul was dedicated to their rehabilitation. As I went to more and more veterans hospitals in the year that followed, I tried to tell the boys that it would be all right on the outside, they'd be fine.

To be honest, I never really believed that. I couldn't imagine what was going to become of these terribly wounded men. How could I know they would one day conduct businesses? Conceive children? Drive cars? As far as I was concerned, there was just no way you could make it up to them for what they had lost.

So I did what I could. I sat at their bedsides and signed their casts. And I tried to imagine how I could help to overcome the hatred and racism that had caused such inhuman slaughter so that we would deserve Ernie Sardo and Jimmy Wilson and their sacrifice wouldn't be meaningless.

ON SATURDAY MORNING, THE GIRLS HAD BREAKFAST WITH THE judges. It was a fairly terrifying experience.

"We were all gathered on the sundeck of one of the hotels," Bess said. "Two judges would sit down at a table with five or six of us and ask us questions. Then a bell would ring and the two judges would move on to the next table and another two judges would sit down in their places. We called it 'musical judges.'

"I was mortified because at the age of twenty-one, I was still a milk drinker. It would have been a disaster to converse with a judge with a milk moustache over my upper lip. Therefore, I took little tiny sips. I took little tiny bites.

"We all tried not to bore *each other* to death by telling the same stories over and over to the successive duets of judges. The dishes and the silverware became like an obstacle course. Our hands shook. Our cups rattled."

Wrote Morley Cassidy of the *Philadelphia Bulletin:* "Forty potential Miss Americas were called on this morning to prove that they can juggle buttered toast and a dish of tea, look beguiling, carry on a sprightly conversation without saying 'ain't,' and drink a glass of orange juice without getting lipstick all over the glass—all at one and the same time. Who passed and who didn't is a secret now locked in the breasts of the ten solemn judges charged with the responsibility of naming Miss America 1945. . . .

"The results, though secret, will have a lot to do with naming of the fifteen finalists who will appear tonight, to compete for the crown that will be awarded at midnight.

"And since these scores are known only to the judges, experts who were making book today on the outcome could venture only one definite statement: The new Miss America will either be Miss New York City, Bess Myerson, of the Bronx, or somebody else."[3]

The "somebody elses" (according to press reports) included Miss Tennessee, Lee Harriet Henson, the first swimsuit winner, who had recovered so charmingly in the talent segment; the tap dancer Frances Dorn, Miss Birmingham; Miss California, Polly Ellis, the cowbgirl singer; Miss Chicago, Lee Wieland, the second swimsuit winner; Gloria Bair, Miss Philadelphia, the sultry "Temptation" dancer; Jeni Freeland, Miss Florida, the blond singer/designer; and Miss Minnesota, Arlene Anderson, the brunette marimbaphone player.

---

[3] *Philadelphia Bulletin* (September 8, 1945).

Some of the women who participated in the Pageant recall it now as a lighthearted romp, an adventure whose major component was fun.

"I just did it for a lark," Arlene said. "I never expected to get anywhere, that's just pie in the sky. The other girls were all very nice. Everybody was friends."

"We had the most wonderful time," recalled Gloria Bair. "Me and June Jenkins, we had so much fun kidding around with Bess and her sister. I remember Bess sang us this parody of 'Stormy Weather,' it was very risqué, it was just a scream."

Bess laughed and sighed. "I guess it was fun," she said. "We did have some good times. But quite honestly, I believe some may have forgotten the intensity of feeling we experienced at the time. I know that I and the other girls in my hotel became increasingly serious about winning as the Pageant proceeded. We were young, insecure, ambitious. A five-thousand-dollar scholarship could unlock the world for us. We all wanted it."

"Once two ladies came up to the me in the lobby of the hotel where Mother and I were staying," Arlene recounted. "And one said to me, 'Oh, my dear, you are so pretty!' And her friend said to her, 'But she's *young*, Agnes. When you're *young*, you look like that.' "

"We talked among ourselves," Jeni said thoughtfully, "about being frightened of what we might be exposed to. I had never read any of those books about the girls who became movie stars on the casting couch, but I just had a gut feeling that these guys with all these offers were not going to do all this for me without something in return."

"I really believe that the way each of us remembers the Pageant is conditioned by how it turned out," Bess commented, "and what our lives were like after it was over."

Gloria Bair Kienle briefly worked at modeling and in nightclubs before settling down to raise a family. Arlene Anderson Low pursued her musical vocation, completed a degree in psychology, traveled, and then married and started a family.

Jeni Freeland Berry became one of the top models in the country. She worked with Conover. She was everything from Miss *Police Gazette* to the symbol of Blue Bonnet margarine.

Her face appeared on the covers of myriad magazines and became a familiar fixture on Florida television. Like Bess, she was a little more serious than some of the other girls, a little more ambitious, and by hindsight her experience in the Pageant counted for a great deal in later life. Like Bess, she would experience the difficulties of juggling marriage and career in times before "having everything" was an acceptable option for women.

"There is another reason I don't remember as much of the fun we had at the Pageant," Bess admitted. "And that is because I was so tense and frightened; I had the feeling that something was going on behind the scenes that concerned me but that I did not fully understand."

"I FELL IN LOVE WITH BESS MYERSON WHEN I ATTENDED THE pageant at WJZ where she became Miss New York City," Lenora said. "She had a white scarf tied around that glorious black hair of hers, she had gorgeous eyes, she was one of the most beautiful girls I had ever seen. She played the piano beautifully. I had sense enough to know immediately that this girl had a wonderful chance to be Miss America. She was a good candidate. A college graduate. Lived up to everything I wanted.

"I also knew she was Jewish. But that didn't worry me."

This Lenora said forty-two years after the fact.

Other eyewitnesses have a very different impression and suggest that as the Pageant moved to its conclusion, Bess's enthnicity may have caused great worry indeed.

Photographer Frank Havens remembers that one day a Pageant official came into the press office and declared that the swell of support for Bess had to be stopped. "This official insisted that there had never been a Jewish winner or a Negro winner and there never would be." Frank chuckled. "Of course, that proved wrong on both counts."

Zelma Brookhov, then a young movie scout who had been sent to Atlantic City by Warner Brothers, remembers being seated at a table where two ladies connected with the Pageant were discussing its progress.

"Maybe they didn't know I was Jewish," she said. "Why should they know? But I ended up at dinner with these two miserable bitches and I was absolutely sick because they're talking and they're moaning and groaning, 'What are we going to do if this Jewish girl becomes Miss America?! It'll be the end of the Pageant! We can't allow it to happen!' Well, I almost dropped dead from hearing that.

"Let me tell you, honey, that whole contest scene that year was the most anti-Semitic thing you could imagine. But they couldn't screw it up for Bess. What could they do? They had a good judging system, a point system, and a lot of judges. All the judges were in the pit there, in the theater, rating every girl on bathing suit, talent, evening dress, the interview at breakfast, poise and personality, the score was a matter of points. The judges had to hand in their papers with their names on them; could they possibly give Bess only one point for talent when she's the most brilliant pianist there and played the flute, too? You can give her four points, maybe, but you can't give her just one. So she won. They couldn't prevent it."

It appears that at the eleventh hour "they" were still trying.

Candy Jones, an old friend of the Pageant, had come to Atlantic City at Lenora's invitation after ten months of island-hopping and entertaining soldiers in the Southwest Pacific. As one of the leading models in the country, she was a close friend and colleague to many of the judges, socialized with them and their wives, and went out to "Jimmy's" with them after the night's performance. "You weren't supposed to, but naturally everybody talked about what was going on at the Pageant. People weren't supposed to discuss their votes, but they did . . . in a very unveiled fashion." From Harry Conover—who was later to become her husband—she heard about the mysterious phone call that came just as the judges were leaving their hotels for the finals.

"Harry said he got a phone call from an anonymous man who was calm but threatening," Candy recounted. "This man made it clear that any judge who voted for Bess Myerson would never be invited back to the Pageant again." Ruth Patterson, Russell Patterson's widow, attested that she had also heard this story, which was passed on to her husband by colleagues in the Society of Illustrators.

It is not clear which or how many of the judges received the phone call. Sidney Piermont's son was sure that his father, for example, had not received one because despite the patrician name, Piermont was a Jew.

"Supposedly the voting was to be so that no one was to see the ballot," Candy continued. "But the guys felt all along that someone was looking at the way they voted. Prunella Wood did not have the phone call. Vyvyan Donner did not have the phone call. It was just those who had been voting for Bess. Harry Conover. Brad Crandall. Dean Cornwell. Arthur William Brown. Vincent Trotta was particularly upset about it. (Piermont had been voting for Miss Tennessee.) And the number who had voted for Bess put Bess ahead."

If the Pageant did not want a Jewish winner, it was reacting no differently than much of America in 1945. It was an anti-Semitic time. A vast range of American institutions, from the medical schools to the statehouses, did not want Jews. For pragmatists who were building an empire based on elitism and money and the marketing of women, the overriding goal was to deliver a Miss America who could be *sold.* And some powerful folks associated with the Pageant may not have thought they could sell a girl named Myerson.

It may have been on this basis—the crucible of hard dollars—that all efforts to rob Bess of the title finally foundered. Henry Harteveldt, president of Harvel Watches, was the only Jewish sponsor. He had been a great supporter of the Pageant for many years. Sitting in her lovely old Park Avenue apartment, his elderly widow probed the outreaches of her memory and summoned what *she* recalled of the Miss America Pageant of 1945.

"Lenora Slaughter was very nice, very nice," said Mrs. Harteveldt. "She and Henry became very good friends. She and I became very good friends. . . . Henry was particularly interested in Bess because there was a problem. He had a big upset and I remember he told Lenora Slaughter . . . you see Bess was the first Jewish girl who had ever won . . . and I'm trying to think of the name of the man . . . I believe he was an anti-Semite . . . he came down for the Pageant . . . and, uh, he didn't want Bess to win the award, he didn't want Bess to be Miss America. Was there a Powers? . . . He had a modeling agency. He didn't want a Jewish girl to win. He wanted one of *his* girls to win."

Ginger Harteveldt Gomprecht, a daughter-in-law to the Harteveldts, recalled, "Those times were full of hatred because of the Jewish problem," she said. "But Mom and Dad Harteveldt were very tough. Mom said to the Pageant people, 'When one person wins on every level, you can't not give it to her. If she's won, she's won!' Mom threatened to go to the press and create a scandal if Bess was thrown over. There was a lot of discussion pro and con about it. Powers was not in favor of a Jewish girl. But he didn't want his name appearing in the papers in any story like that. The Pageant people were really frightened. They were actually *scared* into giving Bess her rightful crown."

So there it was. The system had conquered the personalities.

On Saturday night, September 8, 1945, the fifteen finalists went through their paces once again. The five top girls were selected. Then the judges decided in what order they should be ranked. MC Bob Russell had to vamp and crack jokes and wait for what seemed to be an eternity before the balloting was finished. The hall was packed. Ernie Sardo and Jimmy Wilson and their roommates had been brought to the Warner Theatre by their photographer friend Sam Belasco, who made sure they had front-row places. Well after midnight, the results finally came in. Russell began to announce the winners.

"Arlene Anderson of Minnesota is the fourth runner-up," he said. (Helen stood in the back of the hall, praying.) "Jeni Freeland of Florida is the third runner-up." (Sylvia sat immobilized, her mind a blank.) "Frances Dorn, Miss Birmingham, is the second runner-up." ("My God, she's going to win!" Helen thought.) "Phyllis Mathis of San Diego is the first runner-up." (Sylvia began to cry.) "Bess Myerson is Miss America."

Ernie and Jimmy were brought up onstage with other wounded

soldiers to share the glory. The Jews in the audience went wild, hugging each other, cheering, crying out, *"Mazel tov!"*

"Don't let anybody kid you," Bess said. "It was one hell of a terrific moment."

CHAPTER 8

████

One Title
Among
Many Managers

I expected the earth to move. Nothing less.

I was so excited at that moment of victory, so overcome with giddy joy, that I felt I could see every single face in the Warner Theatre, I felt that I could hear every single cheering voice. It seemed to me that everyone in America was there that night. I felt accepted. Appreciated. Loved.

In all honesty, I did not think immediately of my mother. My heart flew out to Sylvia.

It was she who thought of Mom.

She has told me that at the moment she knew I had won, she thought, "Well, give the Devil his due. All the pressures, the study, the practice were justified. Mom has produced a Miss America."

When I came offstage, everyone was hugging me. Lenora's controlled, studied smile had disappeared. She grinned unabashedly from ear to ear. She made me feel as though I were precisely the Miss America she and the Pageant had always wanted. Not until forty-two years later did I have any real evidence that the backstage drama surrounding my selection amounted to anything more than a paranoid suspicion on my part.

Lenora took me by the arm and steered me through the crowds. I was so intent on following her direction, I was so tightly in her grip that I could not find my sisters.

It was Lenora's inspirational rhetoric that shaped the moment for me. She made me feel that I was going to be a real queen presiding over the onset of postwar prosperity. She seemed certain that great corporations would be fighting for the chance to have Miss America promote their products.

I assumed the Pageant office would book me into advertising campaigns and endorsements, that I would work constantly. I imagined thousands of dollars accumulating in the bank. Immediately after winning, I began to daydream about moving my family into a spacious apartment in a building with an elevator, buying a grand piano with wall-to-wall carpeting beneath it, hiring a housekeeper for Sylvia, purchasing a new car for Dad, and having Mom fitted for new teeth. I thought I would go to graduate school, buy Helen a new violin and a new flute for myself. I peered into the windows of stores and imagined buying all the pretty dresses on display there.

Most of all, I believed that now that I was Miss America, everybody would like me and want to be my friend.

ON SEPTEMBER 9, BESS AND THE RUNNERS-UP IN THE PAGEANT made two appearances at the Steel Pier in Atlantic City. With the hundred-dollar fee in her pocket, she returned home and spent a few delightful days lapping up the love of her ecstatic family and regaling friends like Ruth Singer and Lenore Miller with tales of stretched Catalinas and musical judges. She basked in the spurt of fame her victory had brought her, even in cynical New York.

Then she was whisked away on a four-week tour of vaudeville houses in Newark, New York, Detroit, and Hartford, four shows a day almost every day between September 14 and October 4. The vaudeville tour carried the incredible salary of a thousand dollars a week. Even after you deducted William

Morris's 10 percent and expenses for living on the road, this was more money than Bess Myerson had ever dreamed of earning.

The William Morris Agency arranged for Bess to appear on *Stars in the Afternoon* September 16, with a promised fee of five hundred dollars. This prestigious CBS program originated in Carnegie Hall; Artur Rodzinski conducted. The booking agent for the Minneapolis Symphony asked her to appear as a soloist. He also offered a fee plus expenses. Her daydreams of big-time earning power seemed to be coming true.

Although the New York newspapers remarked only briefly on Bess's victory, the Atlantic City and Philadelphia papers, *Life* magazine, and the Marine magazine *Leatherneck* carried big stories on the doings in Atlantic City. The Jewish press swelled with pride that one of its daughters had walked off with such traditionally *goyish* honors.

The Sholom Aleichem apartments celebrated. Everyone who was there remembers the parties, the toasts, the boost to communal self-esteem. Cries of *"Mazel tov,* Bella!" followed Mrs. Myerson everywhere she went. She and Louis became the most honored guests in the cafeteria. Boys who knew Bess back home had parties in her honor in the Philippines, in London and Berlin. The head of the Sholom Aleichem houses wrote her a formal letter commending her on her achievement. A Jewish state assemblyman wrote reminding her that celebrities of good social conscience often did great things for the public with their fame.

However, the earth did not move. Perhaps just because Bess's victory seemed so unusual for a girl of her background, that blue haze of irony typical of Jewish jokes settled over her victory from Day One.

"I wouldn't say Bess is bad-looking," remarked her father to the *New York Post,* "but maybe if I was the judge I would have chosen one of the other girls." (Gee thanks, Dad.) Added Bella, who feared the beauty contest would give her daughter a bad reputation, "She's pretty and she's a nice girl and so she won. She's not one of those runaround girls, that's why we're proud of her."

Sophie Smith laughed and said, "Every woman in the building was secretly saying to herself, 'If Bessie Myerson could win this beauty contest, why not my Shirley? Why not my Rita?' "

In the press, Bess was described as "a raven-haired, hazel-eyed Oriental beauty." ("Oriental" was then an accepted euphemism for "Semitic.") Her measurements followed in the clinical detail so typical of Pageant tradition. "Five-foot-10, 136 pounds, 35 ½-inch bust, 25-inch waist, 35-inch hips, 20-inch thigh, 14 ½-inch calf, 8 ½-inch ankle, 13 ½-inch neck, 9 ½-inch upper arm, 5 ¾-inch wrist." As for her talent, Paul Whiteman— the famous bandleader—said she was the most talented amateur he had ever seen.

Columnist Earl Wilson asked Bess if she liked Sinatra ("I can take him or leave him."), if she wore falsies ("No!"), and if anything funny had happened in Atlantic City ("Yes," she said, "I won."). He described her father the house painter as a "decorator," deeply offending the *macho*-proletarian sensibilities of the lifelong socialist.[1] ("A decorator?!" Louis exclaimed. "They don't know anything about paint colors or how to mix them! They can't do their job without me to help!")

Bess's brother-in-law Bill now assumed he would be her manager. J. C. Pape assumed he would be her manager. So did Don Rich of WJZ. Sam DuBoff, the patriarchal head of Birchwood Camp, declared that he would be available for advice if Bess should need it, and he assumed she would need it.

Harry Kalcheim of William Morris figured he *was* her agent because he had made a written agreement with Lenora to that effect before the Pageant.

Sylvia might have enjoyed continuing in her management role after the exhilarating Atlantic City week. However, she now had to return to her two little girls and the domestic life. She wanted to make sure that someone from the family would protect and guide Bess in the year to come. She chose her husband, Bill. As the only authoritative, American-born male in the Myerson clan, he seemed the logical alternative.

No sooner did Bess leave town for vaudeville than Bill Grace

---

[1] Earl Wilson, "It Happened One Night," *New York Post,* (September 10, 1945).

and Harry Kalcheim fell into the first of what would be a long string of management disputes for control of Miss America.

After some careful research, Bill decided that Bess's fee for radio appearances should be $500 a shot. Lenora concurred. She turned down a radio gig that offered Bess only $250.

Mall Dodson advised Lenora that radio was free publicity for the Miss America Pageant, which the Pageant should grab no matter how small the honorarium. Lenora immediately changed here policy. Bill Grace stuck to his guns.

When Harry Kalcheim secured another radio appearance for Bess at a lower fee, Bill turned it down. An annoyed Kalcheim sternly reminded Lenora that *he* was representing the Pageant and the title, and Bess Myerson as the body with the title attached would have to go where the title's agent dictated.

Lenora now backed Kalcheim.

An annoyed Bill remined Lenora that Bess was a person, not a title, and that she had not personally signed any deal with William Morris.

"I didn't want to cross Lenora," Bess explained. "I didn't want to cross Bill. More than anything, I didn't want to take responsibility for the decision myself."

Kalcheim instructed Lenora to make it clear to Bess that William Morris, not Bill, was to run her life.

"I received a letter from her that is a classic," Bess said with a laugh.[2] "It was three pages, single-spaced, typewritten.

"First she was sweet. You've done so well in your radio appearances so far, she began, why a lady in a beauty parlor told me your inspiring words made her cry, and then the coach of this football team said you were terrific and these people wrote from Utah . . . and on and on.

"Then she would sidle up to the point. Now Bess, she would say, the William Morris Agency has your very best interest at heart, honey, and I am very cross with your brother-in-law for standing in their way and I told him I have the reputation for getting the most for the title and I am not going to work with anybody but Mr. Kalcheim.

"Then she would unleash veiled threats of doom. Unless I lis-

[2] Letter from Lenora Slaughter to Bess Myerson (October 3, 1945).

tened to her, great American corporations would not give me work. I would plummet into oblivion. She cited the example of my immediate predecessor, Venus Ramey. If I didn't want to blow the biggest opportunity of my entire life, I had better tell my brother-in-law Bill to butt out.

"And then there was the pitch, the gorgeous rhetoric that filled me with purpose. She didn't want to see me suffer because my brother-in-law thought that money was more important than success. Money was important only if it contributed to my happiness, and my happiness was the single most important thing in her mind. Harry Kalcheim would give me more attention, she said, than any of the other 'stars' he had ever handled. She pleaded with me to be guided by him. Even if I didn't make a fortune on the Miss America Pageant now, it would surely lead me to a greater fortune later on.

"And finally there was the intimacy. 'I think I understand the real Bess Myerson,' she wrote, 'the girl fate sent me to prove to the world that Miss America meant more than a flash in the night.'

"In that one long letter, Lenora moved me from pride to fear to hope. That was her genius. She capitalized her glorious abstractions — 'Success!' 'Happiness!' I never read between the lines. I never wondered if 'getting the most for the title' would actually mean getting the most for me. I had no inkling that this brilliant woman was whetting my appetite for fame and fortune while at the same time profoundly limiting my independence in seeking it.

"In fact, I wanted to be limited.

"I feared independence."

"You really told her off!" Harry Kalcheim wrote appreciatively to Lenora when she sent him a copy of her October 3 letter. He noted that he would soon meet with Bess to discuss a screen test with Twentieth Century-Fox, which could lead to a contract at the palatial salary of $350 a week.[3]

He did not realize that Bess would be in no shape for any further show business when she returned from her tour of vaudeville.

---

[3] Letter from Harry Kalcheim to Lenora Slaughter (October 4, 1945).

LENORA SLAUGHTER AND THE MISS AMERICA PAGEANT HAD precommitted the girls to vaudeville long before they arrived in Atlantic City. On August 21, Lenora had signed an agreement engaging Harry Kalcheim to act as sole and exclusive agent "in negotiating contracts for engagements in the Variety field for an act, unit, or show . . . composed of Miss America and finalists of the Atlantic City beauty contest of 1945."

With Lenora naming their "act" the "American Beauty Review," the girls began their tour on September 14. It was an eye-opener.

"I was used to the spotless concert stages where Dorothea LaFollette held her recitals," Bess said. "I had just come from the Warner Theatre in Atlantic City, where the girls were on their best behavior and never left a mess backstage. Now here we were in vaudeville, where the dressing rooms stank of urine and the mess hadn't been cleaned up in years."

There were raucous chorus girls with falsies and painted faces. Over-the-hill ventriloquists with foul-mouthed dummies. Warbling Irish tenors. The Riders of the Purple Sage ("Coooool, cleeear waaahter . . ."). Terrible comedians who told terrible jokes. And one great young comic, Jan Murray, whose imminent rise to fame was heralded by his election as Man of the Year for the Gagwriters Protective Association.

"There were *animal acts!*" Bess exclaimed. "The dogs would escape from their trainers and run around backstage and poop in the women's dressing room!"

Arlene Anderson of Minnesota sang and played her marimba-phone. At one theater, the management had the bad judgment to put her on the same bill with the Marimba Co-eds, seriously overvibing the *Variety* critic who panned the whole show. Frances Dorn of Alabama, who roomed with Bess throughout the tour, did her sprightly, upbeat tap dances. At least *her* act was somewhat in keeping with the expectations of the beery, raucous music hall audiences. Jeni Freeland of Florida sang

. . . and remembers with a nose still greatly out of joint that one of the host comedians treated her "like an idiot" just because she had a southern accent.

By her own testimony Bess was a colossal bomb.

"Imagine a mostly male audience," she said. "Now imagine that a lot of them have been drinking. I appeared onstage in one of my elegant, high-necked Kass evening gowns and played 'The Fire Dance' or 'Malaguena' on the piano as well as a flute solo. Now imagine the disappointment.

"I could hear the fellows in the first couple of rows complaining and muttering, 'What is this, a concert?! Who needs this broad in the long dress? Where's the bathing suit?' In the finale, when we all came out in our bathing suits, the boys would cheer.

"I lost twelve pounds on the road in vaudeville. I began counting the hours until the nightmare would be over."

By all rights, the first runner-up, Phyllis Mathis of San Diego, should have come along for the tour. "Oh, she was sent home," Arlene recalled. "She was very pretty but she had no talent. . . . She couldn't find anything to do onstage."

In all likelihood, that was what Arlene was *told* at the time. The girls seem often to have heard stories that turned out to be covers for deeper truths. Actually, Lenora was furious with Mathis's promoters because they had circulated the tale on the eve of the Pageant that she had recovered from polio. The polio story had, Lenora felt, made the judges exceedingly sympathetic to Mathis, which was why, Lenora was sure, they had voted her the second-place slot. When the story proved untrue, Lenora concluded that Mathis had won her first-runner-up title by duplicity.[4]

To make matters worse, Don Rich of WJZ told Lenora he had bumped into a guy in England General who said that he, the veteran, had previously been *married* to Mathis! And now they were *divorced*!

Lenora ultimately concluded that the veteran was "a patho-

[4] Letter from Lenora Slaughter to George Elliot of Catalina Knitting Mills (February 8, 1946).

logical liar" and laid the matter to rest. By that time, however, Phyllis had missed out on most of the vaudeville tour.

She had been substituted for variously by Miss Detroit and Miss South Carolina. Also substituting was the pert Miss Tennessee, Lee Henson, who had been one of the favorites to win in Atlantic City. She had not even placed among the final five, and many people—especially the soldiers angrily booing her exclusion—wondered why. For forty-two years, Bess Myerson has wondered why.

One of her classmates now corroborates what Jeni suspected: Lee Henson was sixteen, two years too young for the Pageant, and had been disqualified for that reason.[5]

In the wilds of vaudeville, with sleazy guys in the alleys outside the stage door offering deals and bonanzas, Bess learned that wise girls carry their armor on their backs. She envied her friends who had their parents along for protection and counsel.

"Bess thought my father was terrific," Arlene recalled with pride. "When we went into Loew's State, he said, 'Arlene won't go on the stage unless you pay her double what you're paying the other girls.' Because I was singing *and* playing. I think if Dad had pressured them, they probably would have paid me even more. . . .

"My mother was with me all the time. She stayed in the hotel with me. Thank goodness. There were a lot of stage-door Johnnies, all these men coming backstage, wanting dates. As soon as they saw my mother with me, they evaporated. I was young, naïve, and having Mother there was a lifesaver.

"Vaudeville was just exhausting. We had four shows a day. We were so tired from the contest, plus all the shows, we didn't talk, we didn't meet anybody. We were just onstage and went to the hotel and slept and went back to the rat race. It was no fun at all. I got so thin, I think I would have faded straight away if the tour hadn't ended when it did."

Jeni Freeland's attitude toward vaudeville reads much more positively than Arlene's by hindsight. "The tour was pleasant because we girls were friends," she said. "We enjoyed doing it; we had a good time at the Adams in Newark.

[5] Letter from Charles Turner to Susan Dworkin (March 27, 1987).

"When we came to Newark, John Boles was the headliner. He sang Sigmund Romberg songs, he was the idol of all the ladies. There was a big, heavyset woman who followed him everywhere he went, always hanging around backstage. One day we were getting ready to go on, and Frances Dorn was in her tap dancing costume, and this big fat girl walked up behind her and said, 'Oh, there's something on your back!' and with her fingernail she ripped this mole off Frances's back.

"Well, it started to bleed, it bled profusely. My mother got ice and a towel and stopped the bleeding. We didn't think anything of it at the time, but I guess it was the first indication that Frances had cancer. It was the cancer that killed her . . . later on, in the 1960s. She was so young. . . ."

Rooming with Frances Dorn on the vaudeville tour gave Bess her first opportunity to share her feelings with another survivor of the Miss America Pageant week. Both unchaperoned, the girls sat up late after the tedious, tawdry shows and talked for hours.

"From Frances I learned something I had never understood before, which was how scared some of the losers were, especially the girls from the smaller cities and the more rural states. In New York, few people cared who was Miss America, much less Miss New York City. However, when the less cosmopolitan contestants left home, the high-school band came out to play, the Chamber of Commerce called a merchants' holiday. How does one return a loser after all that? Does one say, 'I came in third?' 'I came in fifth?' Is the high-school band going to be satisfied with third or fifth?

"For just those reasons, Franny was reluctant to go back home. She came to New York, took an apartment on Gramercy Park, and went to work. I don't think she really settled down again in the South until she was married.

"She was such a kind, responsive, warm girl. She understood when I told her that I adored my father but wished for someone more like Arlene's father to run my affairs and help me along. I understood when she told me about wanting to get out of the Deep South, wanting to dance and be even a little famous, to see the world. It was wonderful to have somebody to talk to who was so different from me, yet so similar.

"Franny Dorn used to laugh at how Lenora Slaughter, who had taken such great pains to keep us sheltered and pristine on the Boardwalk, had now blithely sent us off to Slime City.

"As our tour progressed, we spent more and more time discussing how marvelous it would be to settle down and get married, to leave this creepy, exploitive situation. To be loved and protected by a nice, safe man in a nice safe home."

By the time Bess left Detroit, she had come to the end of her strength. Her exorbitant expectations for the vaudeville tour had come to a dismal end. The drunks in the audience, the dogs in the dressing rooms, the bleak hotels had driven her to desperation. One afternoon between shows, she summoned all her courage and called Harry Kalcheim. "I was crying," she recalled. "I said, 'Mr. Kalcheim, please, I can't stand any more of this, I don't mean to be a snob, but I tell you, it's beneath me, it's beneath all of us to do vaudeville. Help, please, let me go home!'

"He said, 'Don't worry, Bess. The tour is coming to an end. The prices go down after this and it won't be worth our while to send you out on the road anymore. Come see me when you're back in New York and we'll talk about your future in the movies.'

"I was incredulous. This man whom Lenora had taught me to fear turned out to be a sweetheart. . . ."

Jeni Freeland remembers that she was told that the tour was ending because Bess wanted to go on by herself without the other girls.

Bess wanted nothing of the kind.

Bess wanted out.

An ebullient Lenora Slaughter leading me out of the Warner Theatre after I won.

Posing for photographers the day after with the four finalists, left to right: Arlene Anderson, Margaret Neeley, Frances Dorn, and Jeni Freeland.

LOEW'S STATE · ON STAGE

ATLANTIC CITY BATHING BEAUTY WINNERS
starring IN PERSON

MISS AMERICA OF 1945
FROM THE BRONX

BESS MYERSON
...PLUS

The Four Finalists of the famous Atlantic City Beauty Pageant

MISS MINNESOTA.... Arlene Anderson
MISS BIRMINGHAM....Frances Lanell Dorn
MISS FLORIDA ... Virginia (Jeni) Freeland
MISS SO. CAROLINA.... Margaret Neeley

The most beautiful and talented girls in America ....
THEY SING .....THEY DANCE .....THEY ENTERTAIN .....

TOMMY HANLON JR.	*Fun in the Woods with*
America's Youngest Humorist	GEORGE PRENTICE
THE KEMMYS	*From Northwestern University*
Hats a Problem	The MARIMBA CO-EDS
	Modern Rhythm

Extra! JERRY COOPER
Star of Stage, Screen & Radio

*The posters anouncing Miss America & Company on their
six week vaudeville tour.*

Selling victory bonds.

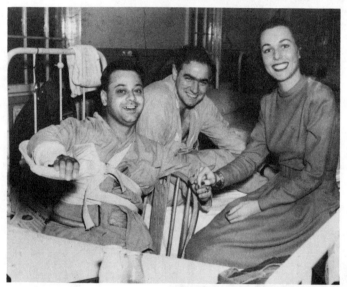

Visiting wounded veterans at Lovell General Hospital.

With the WACS—and my wild fur—in Wilmington.

Left: W. Ralph MacIntyre, head of Joseph Bancroft & Sons, with Frances Burke (Miss America, 1940), me, and Jean Bartel (Miss America, 1943). Below: some Everglaze fashions.

Students Vote 6 to 1 Against I

'You Can't Be Beautiful and Hate'

il. INQUIRERS 4-9-46

Beauty vs. the Beast—Hate

If men of all creeds and races can die together in war, why can't they live together in peace?

That question was put to students of two Milwaukee High Schools yesterday by tall, striking Bess Myerson, the reigning Miss America.

Speaking under sponsorship of Appreciate America, the beauty queen told her audiences at Girls' Trade and Technical High School

and Washington that hatred deterio physically.

"If you have fri religion or race, y shows in face and ma lose beauty of toleration priceless thing," she ad

Selected Miss Ameri last September at Atl Miss Myerson will con tour of high schools unti

---

BEAUTY QUEEN URGES TOLERANCE

Here under auspices of Youth Builders, Inc., to promote inter-racial understanding, Bess Myerson, Miss America of 1945, yesterday visited Stoddart Junior School to advocate tolerance. Shown with her of 118 N. Mole st. (left), and Jean

---

Chic. Herald AMERICAN 2-25-46

Miss America Warns of Hate

Miss America of 1945, glamazon Bess Myerson of New York City, today gave her recipe for beauty to 1,000 students at Von Steuben High School.

At two special assemblies, stressing brotherly love among all races and creeds, the statuesque Miss Myerson declared:

"You can't be beautiful and hate. Hate is a disease which affects your looks and personality.

"Some girls and fellows are born handsome, but their personalities and features are distorted because they question a person's color and religion before they decide to like him."

URGES UNDERSTANDING.

Miss Myerson urged young Americans to "co-operate and try understand each other." Her eyes sparkling, she said:

It's up to us to keep this a good America. Will you enter the war against hatred?" Project 36," Miss Myerson was delightedly at the whistles greeted her appearance on the school stage. She wore a smart red two-piece dress, with gold braid—her wavy shoulder-length. To admiring students her measurements as:

feet 10 inches; 136 pounds; bust, 36; waist, 25½; and hips, 36."

CREDITS EXERCISE.

Miss Myerson attributes much of her health and beauty to "lots of outdoor exercise and Summer camping."

Popularity is assured if a young girl makes herself "part of the party," can dance, engage in sports and talk intelligently," Miss Myerson advised the teen-age girls.

She recently turned down a screen test in favor of further dramatic study in New York, but said:

"I'm interested in a career in marriage, too, but all my plans are long range."

was crowned "Miss America" in Atlantic City last Sep-

OXERS HEAR A BEAUTY IN THE KN

2-25-46 PAGE I

Miss America to Speak On Racial Tolerance For Assembly Today

Miss Bess Myerson, Miss America of 1945, will address Emphites in the double assemblies Friday, March 1.

Miss Myerson has participated in the Youth Builder's programs in New York City. Bess is a beautiful girl who, through her own conscientious work, secured her own education. She earned her degree from Hunter college by teaching at summer camps and giving piano lessons in New York City in the winter. Hollywood has offered her many opportunities, all of which she has refused because of her great desire to teach music.

On March 21, Langston Hughes, internationally known Negro poet, will speak to the English and International Relations classes here.

Mr. Hughes has published eight books and has written many articles, stories, and poems, which have appeared in the leading magazines all over the country.

Bess Myerson (in suit), Miss America of 1945, gives some helpful hints to Von Steuben High School bobby soxers (left to right) Barbara Joss, Geraldine Fiebrick, Dorothy Friedman, Phylis Padden, Pearl Makofsky, Joyce Citron and Charlotte Obermanke, after lecturing the school's student body on racial tolerance.

[Daily News photo]

Miss America's Brainy, Too

Miss America of 1945—Bess Myerson of the Bronx—today asked the beautiful-but-theory into a cocked hat.

Von Stuben High statuesque brunette students for more than while she pleaded the racial tolerance and of man.

ING a scarlet suit

trimmed in gold, Miss Myerson rescribed the annual Atlantic City beauty contest as "real democracy in action."

"The girls who competed with me came from every section of the country, represented" every religion and creed," Miss Myerson said. "Nobody cared if you spoke with an accent."

She said she was enriched by her experience.

FOR THE benefit of the girls in her audience, Miss America pointed out that "you are all potential beauty contest winners.

"I'm just an ordinary girl," she said. "I didn't 'know the guy that knew some guy' when I went to Atlantic City. I represent all you girls."

Von Steuben's female element sighed.

Speaking to high school students and visiting housing projects during the Brotherhood Campaign.

Rehearsing for the Carnegie Hall concert at the end of my "reign."

The Boardwalk Parade, September 1946.

With Marilyn Buferd,
Miss America 1946.

My last walk down the
runway, with Vicki Gold
holding my train.

Lenora among her "creations."

As the Lady in Mink on "The Big Payoff."

The Myerson girls' trio reunited on "I've Got a Secret."

Allan Wayne and I are married.

Our daughter, Barra, as a baby.

Our family in the fifties. Left to right, top row: Me, Allan Wayne, Bill Grace, and Sylvia Grace, middle row: Michelle Grace, Barra, and Francine Grace, front row: Avram Weiss, and my sister Helen. Bella and Louis are seated at right, holding Lesley Weiss.

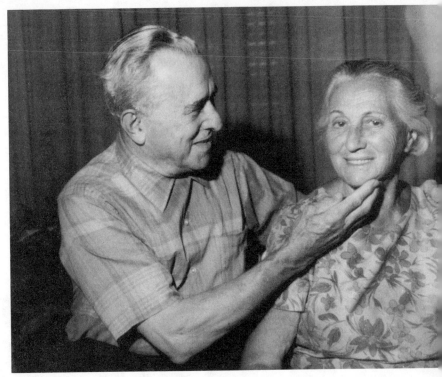

Bella and Louis Myerson were together for more than 65 years.

Bess Myerson in 1986.

KALCHEIM'S HOLLYWOOD PLANS FOR BESS CAME TO NOTHING. She studied for a screen test with director Marcella Cisney. However, she never took it.

"I was too tall to be an actress," she said. "I knew that. I had no talent for the movies. I had never studied acting, nor was I interested in it. I certainly couldn't play the piano onscreen. I didn't want to be ogled anymore or propositioned anymore by strangers who felt sure any girl who would compete in a beauty contest would welcome their attentions. I was fed up with being a sex object (although, of course, that phrase had not yet entered our vocabulary). All I wanted was to regain my dignity. To make it clear that I was not what the Miss America title had made me seem to be."

Eager for a strong hand to lead her out of this mess, she responded to the offers of advice from her old camp director Samuel DuBoff.

A New York lawyer during his winters, DuBoff had been offering her his guidance, but between Bill Grace and William Morris Bess thought she would not need it. Now she felt differently. DuBoff was irritated with the Pageant for sending his gifted music counselor into a gig that he felt disgraced her. He was irritated with Bess for *going*. He advised her to disengage herself from William Morris, which was glad to release her.[6]

The forceful DuBoff now took over Bess's career with swift authority. You will do [such and so] . . . he would write to her. You will sign the enclosed and return immediately. . . . Keep your head on your shoulders and don't make any more mistakes.

"Sam signed his letters to me 'Your Daddy,' Bess said. "I really felt that way about him. I felt that he was a surrogate father at that time."

DuBoff signed Bess with a new agent, Claire Wolff, who was supposed to engender the commercial endorsements that had so far eluded the new Miss America.

[6] Letter from Harry Kalscheim to Lenora Slaughter (November 15, 1945).

"I was impressed with her office," Bess said with a laugh. "I was impressed with everybody's office. I was impressed with people who took me to lunch to talk business.

"I needed the comfort of having a strong parent figure. I loved being directed—pushed around, even. Told in no uncertain terms exactly what I should do. I wanted that from Lenora. I thought she would give me sound advice. By November I suspected that her advice was really a lot of colorful bluffery to mask her own inexperience. Lenora sent me these long, newsy letters full of adjectives and superlatives.

"Bradshaw Crandall is going to do your picture, she would say, and you're going to be on the cover of *Cosmopolitan* magazine which is the best possible publicity that any girl can have!

"Here are five pictures of you in your crown and robe, which you must autograph for the sponsors, she would say, and she would tell me what I should write on the pictures . . . Thank you, Mr. Catalina, Mr. Sandy Valley Grocery, you're wonderful, I'm so grateful. Lenora kept explaining things to me. You realize that no matter how important a businessman may become, he is still proud as a little boy when his good deeds are recognized, she would say. I believed her and trusted her. I would do whatever she wanted me to, waiting, expecting, anticipating. Waiting for this shower of gold to fall on me. . . ."

Bess was receiving many invitations. Somehow they never carried a price tag. The Soviet-American Friendship League wanted her to be their guest at a luncheon. David O. Selznick wanted to interview her. Columbia University wanted her as the guest of honor at its Fall Festival Dance. She became the darling of the Jewish War Veterans.

In early November, Joseph Bancroft & Sons, one of the Pageant sponsors, brought her to Wilmington, Delaware, for a large Victory Bond rally, a tour of their fabric finishing plant, and a motorcade through town. Sam DuBoff acted as her chaperon. A Seventh Avenue firm lent her a black fur coat with the hides of some unfortunate silver animals flapping at the cuffs. It would have been more suitable for Mrs. Roosevelt, but Bess was grateful. She could not afford to turn up her nose at gift wraps, because she was running out of money. With her vaudeville earnings, she had bought her father a new yellow station wagon. On any free day, she would take a lesson from Mrs. LaFollette. She had to go to the beauty parlor regularly now and sometimes take cabs instead of subways. Although she asked Lenora for an advance on the scholarship award, Lenora refused, declaring that the award could not be made until the year ended and Bess had enrolled in a proper graduate school.

"The Joseph Bancroft people used me in a tour of department stores. The Fitch Shampoo people used me in advertising layouts in magazines. However, these companies had already paid me by supporting the scholarship. They didn't owe me another penny for my time.

"I kept hoping that Lenora or Claire Wolff would find me paid assignments. I did not have the slightest idea that they might be trying to get me jobs, but without success."

Bess made an appearance for the Victory Bond drive in Washington and visited the Senate. Senator (later Vice-President) Alben Barkley asked her to take a bow from her spot in the gallery.

She presented an award to the young lady who had sold the most bonds of any civil servant. She visited the White House; Mrs. Truman shook her hand. She visited the wounded at Fort Belvoir, at Bethesda Naval Hospital. Secretary of the Treasury Fred Vinson issued her a certificate of merit for her work on the campaign.

"Victory Bonds are very important to our wounded fighters," she said from the steps of the Treasury Building. "These heroes need us now as we once needed them. They fulfilled our faith in them. Now we must fulfill their faith in us. It is our Victory Bond money that will enable our government to reduce the Armed Forces as quickly as possible. And it is our Victory Bond money that will help veterans get jobs or go into their own businesses upon their discharge. . . . The best way we can show our gratitude is by buying—every single one of us—all the Victory Bonds we possibly can."

Sporadically, through the fall of 1945, Bess traveled, spoke, and posed for pictures, autographing them endlessly. Young men she met at bond rallies and during visits to veterans hospitals would take her to dinner, and women from all over the country were writing to her for beauty advice. She became the bedside companion of thousands of veterans laid up in a dozen hospitals. At the Marine Corps Air Station in Cherry Hill, North Carolina, they whistled and cheered. One of them told the press, "She put her Bess foot forward." Another yet more colorful soldier commented, "She can boil her stockings in my coffee any day." The chief of police in Mount Vernon was so pleased with her appearances there that he sent her some perfume with a card that read, "To a Lovely Young Lady who is Etching Herself Deeply and Gracefully on the American Heart."

But when Bess went south, she saw signs over the rest rooms that she had never seen in New York: "White Only" and "Colored." She walked onstage to greet the crowd in theaters where the white people sat in the orchestra and the blacks were consigned to the balcony. She heard repeated reports of the desecration of synagogues in her own city.

She began to consider the other, more base feelings that seemed to be deeply etched on the American heart.

And when a reporter from a newspaper at Camp Kilmer, New Jersey, asked her who she had in mind for "Mr. America," Bess said that he had to be a six-foot-tall, normally attractive veteran who was intelligent, athletic, possessed a good sense of humor, and *voted as a political liberal.*

At charitable affairs for Yugoslav Relief and Russian Relief, at one bond rally after another, she rubbed elbows with the likes of Libby Holman; Nannette Fabray, then starring in *Bloomer Girl;* the newly elected congressman from Harlem, Adam Clayton Powell; Leonard Bernstein; Lord Halifax; and opera star Mimi Benzell. Everyone found her charming. Newspaper reporters could always count on her for a good quote. She never failed to thank the Miss America Pageant for the wonderful scholarship. She was "a good girl," like her mother said.

In those weeks after the vaudeville tour ended, when I was going out to the bond rallies, speaking at hospitals, performing at meetings, I really thought I was achieving something. At twenty-one I had not yet learned that fame is not the same thing as impact.

Earl Wilson was writing columns about me. Everybody was quoting me. My picture appeared everywhere. I was having what psychiatrists call a "narcissistic high." Loving every minute of the attention and the adulation. Gaining a dangerous confidence in the irresistibility of my charms. Believing what people told me, and worse, believing that they believed what they told me.

It was like quicksand to be out there being praised, and I was sinking into it. My father saw that, and he saved me from it.

Right before I left home for the vaudeville tour, he said to me, "Now, Besseleh, don't forget who you are out there."

He was not saying, "Don't forget you're a Myerson." Not my father. He did not have that kind of vanity. He was saying, "Don't forget you're a Jew. Whatever you do will be laid at the feet of your people."

The immediate effect of his warning was to make me all the more afraid of every decision, and all the more docile and dependent with my managers. If I was criticized—as in Wilmington, where some people thought my unglamorous, borrowed fur too dowdy for Miss America—I was filled with anxiety that the local Jews might have been embarrassed by me.

The long-term effect was to protect me against the ravages of my own vanity. To keep my head above the quicksand. To commit my year to something more than my own glory.

At the moment I won, I looked out at the crowd in the Warner Theatre and saw all the Jewish people hugging each other, congratulating each other, as though they had won. I wanted to call out to them, "Hey, folks! Look at me! Look at ME! Am I not the victor here?"

My ego trip was shortchanged. On the other hand, I felt thrilled to have made so many strangers so happy. I didn't want to be their beauty queen. But if I was—and I surely was—I didn't want to disappoint them.

CHAPTER 9

Travel,
the
Great Teacher

In Bess Myerson's relationship with the Miss America Pageant, no one played a more paradoxical role than the sponsors. As far as Lenora was concerned, they had to be accommodated, sweet-talked, cajoled, and cuddled. She primed her new Miss America to work for the sponsors, promote their products, and for their support of her scholarship and those to come, thank them graciously at every turn. Unfortunately, now that she had a Miss America who was ready to work and promote and be gracious, three out of the five sponsors had little or no interest in using her.

The Harvel Watch Company used Bess on a radio program during which an able MC, the innocent victim of a careless script, repeatedly referred to Bess as "Betty." Pictures of Bess looking lovingly at her Harvel "Miss Victory Watch" appeared in *The Harvel Newsdial,* an in-house publication for Harvel dealers across the country.

And that was it.

Harvel didn't do much magazine advertising, certainly required no department store appearances by Bess. The dignified, charitable Harteveldts took her to the theater, liked to have her stay over at their home, encouraged her growing friendship with their daughter Ellen. However, the relationship was much more *personal* than professional.

"Mom and Dad Harteveldt adored Bess," Ginger Harteveldt

Gomprecht recalled, "and to her they represented a connection to the broader world of business, philanthropy, and gracious living which she was just entering, in which her own parents could not guide her."

Like the DuBoffs, the Harteveldts became another set of surrogate parents cast in Bess's unending search for stability and security. When she was in Detroit, they made sure that friends of theirs invited her for a home-cooked meal. Bess would have done anything for the Harvel Watch Company precisely because of her fond feelings for the Harteveldt family. Probably for the same reason, the Harteveldts did not dream of exploiting her.

Most important, in November 1945, events far beyond the scope of the Miss America Pageant made a business relationship between Bess and the Harvel Watch Company quite impossible. Harteveldt's watch business had been stymied by a long and bitter dispute with organized labor that typified dozens of economic crises during 1945–48.[1]

Millions of men had come home from the war demanding jobs and rates of pay every bit as high as those their wives and home-front buddies had earned while they were off fighting. The unions went on the march, especially against businesses relying on imports, and Harvel's mainstay was a watch manufactured in Switzerland.

". . . Every watch imported into the United States deprives an American worker of twelve hours' employment," said Walter W. Cenerazzo, president of the American Watchmakers' Union. "Twenty-five million watches have been imported since Pearl Harbor. This is fourteen years' employment for eight thousand American watchmakers."[2]

Watchmakers wanted quotas placed on the importation of Swiss timing mechanisms. The American Watch Assemblers' Association, five hundred Swiss watch importers, wanted to keep imports high.

While this battle raged, the industry slowed to a crawl.

Ginger Harteveldt Gomprecht remembered that between the

[1] Letter from Henry Harteveldt to Lenora Slaughter (October 9, 1945).
[2] *The New York Times* (December 6, 1945).

union disputes and the cessation of Harvel's large military watch orders from the U.S. Army, the company found it necessary to concentrate much more heavily on the manufacture of fine jewelry. With this major reorganization of priorities in the works, Harvel's advertising director regretfully withdrew financial support from the Miss America Pageant for the foreseeable future.[3]

Bess assumed that the California-based Catalina Swimsuit Company would use her to promote their line of pretty beach scanties. They never got in touch with her. To this day, she does not know why.

That left the Fitch Shampoo Company; the Sandy Valley Grocery Company; and Joseph Bancroft & Sons, the large fabric finishing concern based in Wilmington.

Fred W. Fitch, founder of the Fitch Shampoo Company of Des Moines, Iowa, had been a natural for the Miss America Pageant.[4] When Lenora latched on to him in 1944, his son Gail was serving as president of the large firm, but old F. W. remained in control, and his tastes and preferences still prevailed. Like Madame C. J. Walker and Helena Rubinstein, Fitch was one of those wildly creative American entrepreneurs who turned ordinary hygiene into over-the-counter "medicine." With a great flair for hyperbole, he sold oils and antidandruff shampoos and advocated the elevation of barbering into a branch of dermatology whose practitioners would be called "dermaticians."

In the 1920s, Fitch had put out a magazine for barbers called *Square Deal*, which promoted Fitch products, touted scientific hair care, and carried titillating covers on which Glorious Gilda Grey dreamily fondled her flower-covered breasts and adorable Alice Doll hiked her skirt up to her thighs, threw it over the ironing board, and pressed.

In the 1930s, Fitch allowed himself to be convinced by E. G.

---

[3] Letter from A. W. Lewin to Lenora Slaughter (November 26, 1945).
[4] Denny Rehder, *The Shampoo King: F. W. Fitch and His Company* (Des Moines, Iowa: Waukon and Mississippi Press and the Fitch Investment Company, 1981). For a privately published, family-authorized biography, this is an unusually forthright account of the life of an extraordinary personality in American business history.

"Jit" Naeckle of L. W. Ramsey Advertising in Davenport that he should sponsor a radio show called *The Bandwagon*. It wound up in the seven-thirty slot between Jack Benny at seven and Edgar Bergen and Charlie McCarthy at eight Sunday nights on NBC, one of the most popular family listening times on American radio.

Like Lenora, F. W. felt keenly his lack of higher education. The idea of promoting a scholarship appealed to him.

"As I recall, Lenora called F. W. Fitch one day and gave him a selling right then over the telephone," said Bill Henderson, a Ramsey account executive. "He got all excited about it.

"The Miss America thing made pretty good sense at the time. He was interested in promoting Fitch shampoo to the beauty trade. He asked us [Ramsey] for advice, but he had already made up his mind. He admired Lenora. If there is anything one salesman can admire, it's another salesman. You couldn't be around Lenora for five minutes before she'd either sell you something or get you to say 'yes' to something.

"We put pictures of Miss America on the product. We promoted it through the beauty shops. We had a schedule of advertising running in *True Confessions* and about twenty-five real strong beauty magazines that were sold in drugstores and dime stores. We milked it for about a year, from one year to the next. . . ."

It was too bad that Bess never met Fred W. Fitch, the hard-drinking, dapper old exaggerator with the moustache and the cane and the flower in his lapel. He probably would have fascinated her as much as Lenora did. As it was, the Ramsey Advertising bunch and Bess Myerson exchanged little more than deep disinterest.

She didn't like having greasy hair. They would have preferred a blonde. She was so cool to them that they thought she had no sense of humor. They were so cold to her that she thought they had it in for Jews. Bess was delighted to appear on *The Fitch Bandwagon Show* ("This is, of course, part of the scholarship contract," Lenora reminded her, lest she expect to be paid.) She was not so delighted to find that her face appeared in an ad for "Saponified Coconut Oil Shampoo" in *True Confessions*.

"The Fitch experience deepened the distrust of Lenora and the Pageant that I had started harboring in vaudeville," Bess said. "The whole Pageant was set up to convince us that we had to behave like ladies. It was like a coming-out party, a debutante ball, with a sorority installation at the end. Then when you had finally become one of the debutantes, what did they want? They wanted you to smile and wink and pull your skirt higher and sell hair tonic for them in the 1940s in the same manner that Glorious Gilda Grey sold it for them in the 1920s.

"Well, I wasn't built for it. I was too narrow in the hips, too wide in the smile, and any account executive would have given me low scores on sex appeal. I also wasn't suited for it emotionally.

"However, when sponsors like Catalina didn't want me to model their bathing suits, I felt like a failure. On the other hand, when Fitch put my name in *True Confessions,* I felt embarrassed. If they whistled at me on a stage in Newark, I felt degraded.

"I was caught between my ego and my ego, an impossible place. I wanted to be wanted, but only on my own terms. My family could not help me handle my ambivalence. In fact, my family was just as ambivalent as I was."

By Thanksgiving Helen was sick to death of being called "Miss America's kid sister." Sylvia had been exposed to a power role. Now she was so deeply enmeshed in domestic life that she was beginning to wonder if she had ever visited Atlantic City.

Bella Myerson loved being Miss America's mother. She did not so much enjoy the tasks involved in living at Miss America's published address.

"I returned home from a trip to visit veterans at Lovell General Hospital, in Massachusetts," Bess said, "and asked my mother for the mail and the phone messages. She informed me that she had stopped answering the phone because it rang constantly; it was too difficult for her to write down all those messages. I later learned that my Cousin Sidney thought there had been a death in the family. As for the letters, Helen had read Mom some of them. A few were quite obscene. So Mom had started throwing out the mail. Hundreds and hundreds of letters. Gone.

"Who knows? Maybe Ed Stewart of Catalina really did write

repeatedly and ask me to come to California to model his new line for the summer of 1946 and I just never received his letters because my mother threw them away. . . ."

ODDLY ENOUGH, IT WAS THE FIRM CLOSEST TO LENORA AND most supportive of the Pageant—Joseph Bancroft & Sons— that provided Bess with some of the most crucial skills she needed to begin to seize control of her own year as Miss America and break away from the iron embrace of Lenora Slaughter.

William Ralph MacIntyre, director and general manager of Joseph Bancroft & Sons,[5] could not have been more different from Fred W. Fitch. A Quaker who maintained a home in Stone Harbor and hobnobbed with many members of the Pageant board, MacIntyre addressed Lenora as "Respected Friend" whenever he wrote to her and served as her counselor and adviser whenever the Pageant encountered deep trouble.

For example, when the Fitch Shampoo people became outraged because Bess had made reference to a castile soap in a Whelan Drugs ad, it was MacIntyre who explained to Fitch that Bess was referring to castile soap *generically,* not to Castile Shampoo, a Fitch competitor.

"MacIntyre was firm, decisive," Bess recalled. "When he ended a conversation, it was *over.* He never raised his voice. If MacIntyre explained, Fitch was ready to calm down and forgive and forget. If *I* had tried to explain, they probably would have drowned me in hair oil."

Ralph MacIntyre had risen to the top of a highly technologi-

---

[5] MacIntyre became president of the company in 1947. Shortly before his retirement in 1963 he had overseen the acquisition of Bancroft by Indian Head Mills of New York, in September 1961.

cal field—fabric finishing—and in the postwar era mastered the new arts of worldwide licensing and merchandising of patented processes and registered trademarks such as Everglaze and Banlon. In 1945 Bancroft was producing shiny chintz fabrics for upholstery and clothing (the Everglaze line, which John Gilbert Craig Advertising would make famous using magazine layouts and department store promotions featuring Bess Myerson) as well as book cloth, window-shade fabrics, and industrial fabrics of many weights and uses.

Like Henry Harteveldt, MacIntyre possessed a highly developed social conscience. He thought Lenora's scholarship idea most admirable and in 1946 would raise his contribution from one thousand dollars to ten thousand dollars. He encouraged his company to pioneer in day care for the preschool children of its female employees. He served on the Delaware State Board of Education and chaired a state committee on the rehabilitation of the disabled.

John Gilbert Craig's son, John II, recalls that "Lenora Slaughter was always saying, 'The Pageant is too much of a skin show!' and this fellow Stewart, from Catalina, and she were always arguing about that, but MacIntyre *liked* the way Lenora was taking the Pageant. It was consistent with what he believed. . . . He *wanted* a tonier vehicle for the Bancroft line."

Bess started modeling chintz clothes for Bancroft in the Everglaze ad series in October. Her mentor on that project was an efficient, stylish woman named Lola Martin, who supervised MacIntyre's relationship with the Miss America Pageant.

Lola led Bess through complex photo shoots for the Craig advertising company; took her through department stores where she modeled Bancroft clothes; made sure her microphones worked and that the pianos she was given to play on were properly tuned. "Lola was always a real diplomat," Bess recalled with admiration. "If Lenora became furious with me about something—and Lenora could become furious, she had a terrible temper that would flair up like a tornado—Lola would say, 'Oh, don't pay any attention, it'll blow over. . . .' It always did."

Realizing that Bess was running out of money and had no

expectation of earning any, Lola Martin prevailed upon MacIntyre to *give* his lovely model the chintz clothes she was promoting.

"In those glossy, flowered dresses, I probably looked like I was impersonating a living-room sofa," Bess laughed. "But they got me through a lot of evening appearances."

Not only did Bancroft's people provide Bess with the protective chaperone she so desired, they also taught her the fine points of public presentation: how to stand, how to walk, which angle best suited a fashion photo, which small talk best suited a businessmen's reception. It was not lost on her that John Gilbert Craig, Bancroft's advertising executive, had received the coveted Merrill Kremer Copy Award for the best piece of ad copy written between June 1944 and May 1945.

On October 15, Lola Martin arranged for Bess to model a Bancroft magazine layout at the Benedict Frenkel Studio in New York. "We are going to use a bathing suit and a white housecoat," she wrote. "Would you please bring your gold sandals along? I thought them very becoming."[6]

Three months later, in January 1946, the layout appeared in print.

The shock waves in California might well have been recorded on the upper end of the Richter scale.

"Lenora wrote me the Catalina people were furious. She reminded me that I had signed a contract not to endorse or allow my picture to be used by any other bathing suit company. Now I had appeared in the Bancroft Everglaze ad in a bathing suit manufactured by a direct competitor of Catalina! Because of my terrible mistake, Lenora said, the Catalina people had become the brunt of jokes in the swimsuit industry, and now she was going to have to beg Mr. MacIntyre to pacify Mr. Stewart so he wouldn't pull out of the Pageant and withdraw support for the expanded scholarship program for 1946![7]

"Imagine how her letter upset me! Lenora had my number. She knew there was no better way to yank the chain of a Jewish girl than with a well-placed guilt trip. If Catalina pulled out of the Pageant, it would be my fault! If other deserving girls didn't

---

[6] Letter from Lola Martin to Bess Myerson (October 11, 1945).

[7] Letter from Lenora Slaughter to Bess Myerson (January 23, 1946).

get a scholarship and weren't able to become doctors and lawyers, it would be my fault!

"I was sleepless with remorse. What could I do to make
amends?! Who did I have to say 'I'm sorry' to?

"Lola Martin told me to stay cool, it wasn't my fault. John
Gilbert Craig told me not to worry, it wasn't my fault. Mr.
MacIntyre told me it would be handled. And it was."

Craig wrote a tough letter to Lenora intended to prove to her
that the rock in Delaware was no less hard than the hard place
in California.

"According to our contract, we are permitted to use photographs of Miss America any way we see fit . . . if there is a
contract of any other kind, such as you say Miss America has
with you or with Catalina, which affects our contract, we feel
we should have been properly notified by you. This, of course,
has not been done. . . ."[8]

MacIntyre's response to Lenora was much more openly threatening. "Frankly, I cannot blame Bess Myerson for this matter,
or as a matter of fact, blame anybody else but the Atlantic City
Pageant . . . ," he wrote. ". . . We have endeavored to give
Miss America good publicity and I think that we have done just
that and it should not be difficult for us to change our plans and
program toward the end of using a professional model rather
than whoever is Miss America; as a matter of fact, it would work
out in the end a much cheaper proposition. . . ."[9]

Bess observed all the players in this little drama with dawning
appreciation. Apparently Lenora needed MacIntyre to handle
things for her with Stewart just as Bess needed MacIntyre to
handle things for her with Fitch. Apparently these businessmen
were not "just like little boys" when it came to "their" Miss
America. Although Bess had been primed to think of all five
sponsors as philanthropists contributing out of the goodness of
their hearts to the cause of higher education for women, it was
now clear that the Pageant must mean more to them than a
notation in the goodwill columns.

W. Ralph MacIntyre might seem jolly and round, but be-

---

[8] Letter from John Gilbert Craig to Lenora Slaughter (January 25, 1946).
[9] Letter from Ralph MacIntyre to Lenora Slaughter (January 26, 1946).

neath the pleasant exterior lay a sleeping giant, and one ought to take a lesson from the ruined Japanese and not wake it if at all possible. Ed Stewart, who for reasons of his own did not want Bess in Catalina's swimsuits, would raise hell if she dared to appear in anyone else's. If these two powerful men were ready to fight over what she wore and what she said, *then it must be important to be Miss America, it must be profiting somebody.*

Lenora billed Bess as a do-gooder to the sponsors, just as she billed them as do-gooders to Bess.

In mid-November she assured Karl Vogel at the Sandy Valley Grocery Company that he could depend on Bess for a visit to Kentucky as soon as her work with the Victory Bond drive had ended. "She has given up theater appearances to work for Washington instead and her publicity is terrific," Lenora wrote.

"She isn't interested in money, so she will come to Kentucky for expenses alone if you want her. . . ."[10]

FRANK DEFORD, AUTHOR OF THE PREEMINENT ANECDOTAL history of the Pageant, loves to knock the New York/national press for being insufficiently attentive to hinterland personalities. However, even he dismissed Henry Harrison Wheeler's business New Yorkishly as "something called the Sandy Valley Grocery."[11] The fact is that by the mid-1930s, the firm had fifteen wholesale grocery companies in thirteen cities in Kentucky, West Virginia, and Ohio, owned a milling company and a coffee company, and sold the SV brand in its own outlets covering sixty-five thousand square miles in six states.

H. H. Wheeler had taken over the company in 1925. Ac-

[10] Letter from Lenora Slaughter to Karl Vogel (November 14, 1945).
[11] Frank Deford, *There She Is: The Life and Times of Miss America* (New York: Viking, 1971), p. 159.

cording to Robert L. Marsh's history of the neighborhood, "the wholesale grocery business was never to be the same again in the Big Sandy Valley or in Eastern Kentucky."[12]

Wheeler was a brilliant promoter who swam successfully in the muddy waters of mountain politics, and he expanded his little company into a local colossus by displaying a flare for public relations and a generosity during and after the Depression that endeared him to the Waltons-like families of the Kentucky hills.

"In the 1930s, most everybody else's business was going down," said his son David. "But my Dad's business was doing fine. Once he sponsored a train—a whole train, now mind you—to go to Chicago during the World's Fair in 1933. The train—it had five or six cars, maybe more—started up the Big Sandy River in the hills of Eastern Kentucky near the Pikesville area and went down through the mountain counties, picking up people who wanted to go, and then wound up in Ashland and picked up the Ashland High School Band and took them for free, and went on into Chicago. The mayor of the city greeted the train and he and my dad took a walk together through Chicago, oh, that was a big thing for Dad. . . ."

During the 1950s, Wheeler's business would be ruined by antimonopoly legislation and the growth of the huge supermarket chains. "Between the years of 1950 and 1965," David said, "when I was ten to twenty-five, I never really saw him smile that much. . . . But I hear from people that before that time, he enjoyed life . . . a lot. . . ."

The scrapbooks of former Miss Americas are filled with pictures of H. H. Wheeler enjoying life. He loved to go North and party. He took pride in importing national figures to mingle with the folk of Ashland. As far as H. H. was concerned, Miss America was a national figure. Starting with Bette Cooper, he imported them and employed them for promotions.

"Oh, it was pretty silly," remarked Marilyn Meseke Rogers, Miss America 1938. "We went down there and we stood by the stove in the cooking school and I believe we signed cakes of

[12] Robert L. Marsh, *And That's a Fact!* Vol. One (Paintsville, Ky., 1982), p. 33.

soap." She remembered Wheeler as a dignified southern gentleman albeit with a keen eye for the ladies. "I'll bet he didn't like Bess Myerson. Sure, she was too independent for that crowd. She wasn't docile like the rest of us."

"I looked forward to my Kentucky trip," Bess recalled. "Although I had no chaperone, I was not concerned. Since Washington and Wilmington, I had begun to feel more secure with the public.

"I was taken on a tour of the cooking school, the grocery stores, and the head office. I met the management and the employees. Then Mr. Wheeler invited me to see his private train. I was seated next to him in a parlor car. He asked me about my experiences as Miss America. Suddenly he stretched out on the train seat and put his head right in my lap.

"I was shocked. I jumped up. 'Please don't do that!' I exclaimed.

"It was embarrassing for both of us. I was unnerved. I felt I had handled this small incident without finesse, that I would now never be invited to work for this sponsor. I was right. Sandy Valley never used me. And whatever explanations they gave encouraged the Pageant to believe that I had been unacceptable in their locality because I was Jewish."

Some weeks later, Wheeler got Bess's phone number from Lenora and called to apologize. Glad for the opportunity to smooth over the bad feeling between them, she accepted his invitation to be his guest at a canners' convention in Atlantic City. Forty-two years later, Lola Martin would recall what she knew of Bess's experience in Kentucky with great distaste. Lenora Slaughter would dismiss the Sandy Valley Grocery Company, which never participated in the Pageant again, as "a local firm," much too small and provincial to be part of her widening scholarship program.

For Bess Myerson at the time, the incident served to teach the same lesson Jean Bartel had learned two years earlier: If Miss America wanted respect, she would probably have to do something extraordinary to earn it.

DURING THE COURSE OF HER YEAR AS MISS AMERICA, BESS
Myerson made another trip to the South. She is sure she had a
chaperone for this one; in fact, she thinks Lenora herself was
there, although Lenora cannot remember the occasion.

Bess has never forgotten it.

"We were doing a promotion for the Pageant," she explained,
"because Lenora was trying hard to increase her scholarship
kitty to twenty-five thousand dollars so all the runners-up as well
as the winner could receive awards in 1946.

"I was supposed to go to the local country club in the evening,
to make a short speech and play the piano. We were driven to a
gorgeous antebellum mansion to change clothes. It had a wind-
ing staircase, crystal chandeliers, servants in livery. I had brought
along a ball gown designed by one of the students at the
Traphagan school. A breathtaking dress. Romantic.

"I was escorted to a spacious bedroom with a canopied four-
poster and eyelet-trimmed throw pillows on the silk-upholstered
chairs. I put on the dress, and when I looked at myself in the
mirror, I must admit, I felt like Scarlett O'Hara.

"I started down the staircase, then stopped short. At the
bottom, our hostess was telling the members of my party that
there had been a terrible mistake, the country club was restricted, and no Jewish person could possibly be welcomed there.

"As I sit here, I remember the pain of that moment. I felt as
though I had walked into a stone wall.

"I went upstairs, took off the ball gown, and stopped pretending to be Scarlett O'Hara. Someone drove me to the train
station. I went home.

"I remember the railroad station, the long, bleak railroad
station. I remember not knowing when the next train to New
York was going to come, but being determined not to stay in
that place one more minute. Maybe it was Wilmington again
. . . I think I had to change in Washington . . . maybe it was

Kentucky or North Carolina. . . . I remember sitting on the train and crying. It was a desolate journey for me."

The rejection at the country club, the noninterest of Catalina, and the paucity of bookings and invitations coming her way all served to underscore Bess's new awareness that she was somehow not as desirable as some other Miss America might have been. She had successively blamed her lack of physical sexiness, her inexperience in handling delicate situations like that which had arisen in Kentucky. Now she realized that her ethnic origins, too, posed a problem.

The one bright spot was the veterans. Somehow they made Bess feel meaningful in her role as Miss America. She would visit them, sit at their bedsides, kid around, feed them, play the flute and piano for them. She felt welcome in the wards and inspired herself by the hopefulness and good cheer of the men.

"Visiting the veterans really counted on an emotional level. After a couple of months of posing and smiling and making speeches that counted for nothing, I wanted to *count* more than anything.

"I remember there was an affair at the Waldorf-Astoria in New York to benefit the March of Dimes and the victims of infantile paralysis. I went to Atlantic City and personally invited Jimmy Wilson and Ernie Sardo to come with me.

"Do you know that Jimmy *drove* to New York? He *drove!* With those prosthetic hooks. In a regular car, not even a special car. All the way from Atlantic City, with Ernie in the passenger seat. It was incredible! A shot of sunlight in this darkening winter.

"All the veterans were Ernie and Jimmy to me. I believed that if those fellows could recover from that much suffering, the whole world could recover, from war, from hate, from polio, from every dreadful affliction.

"So I went to another veterans hospital. . . . I don't know where it was . . . it doesn't matter. The doctor said, 'Listen, Bess, I want you to pay a special visit to the boy in this room because he's been very badly wounded, and he may never get out of here and he wants to see you.'

"Of course I headed for the room. Suddenly the boy's mother appeared and stood right in front of the door.

" 'My boy doesn't want to see you,' she said. 'I don't want you near him. Because of the Jews, we got into this war. Because of the damn Jews, my boy was maimed. We would have been better off if Hitler had killed every last one of you people. Don't you dare come near my boy!'

"Oh, God . . .

"Do you think I blamed her? I didn't have it in my heart to blame her. If I wept because this woman insulted me, I blamed myself for weeping because my grief at being insulted by her was so much less than her grief at having her son destroyed. . . . I had all this *feeling,* for the poor boys, for the poor Jews, for the poor, for the blacks in the balcony, in livery, all this dammed-up *feeling* that wanted to pour out and *do* something. Anything. Just not to be helpless. Just not to stand there helpless and speechless while this woman wished me and my sisters dead."

From time to time during the course of the year, Lenora would bring Bess to Atlantic City for the sake of the Pageant. She requested her presence at conventions and meetings. She sent her to local Pageants to talk up the scholarship program.

On one occasion, Bess was sitting at the head table at a gathering of businessmen. There was a dance band. Although many wives had come, several of the men found themselves without dance partners and invited Bess for a turn around the floor. By now acutely aware of the impact of her behavior and striving to restore some dignity to her role as Miss America, she repeatedly declined. "No, thank you, I'm not dancing tonight," she said with her warmest smile.

"Then Lenora came over. She had had quite a bit to drink. She had a businessman in tow, undoubtedly someone on whom she was prevailing for a contribution to the scholarship fund. She said, 'I want you to dance with this man, Bess.'

"I protested that I couldn't, that it wouldn't look right because I had been refusing everyone else.

"Lenora insisted. I held firm.

"She became very angry. She lit into me with a fury I had not seen. She called me every name in the book. I got up and left.

"It was the first time I had defied Lenora outright. I had

always leaned toward strong people, but I no longer believed that she was one of them. She had made an embarrassing, vulgar scene with me. I realized that just like the people in the vaudeville audience, she really had no idea who I was. She wanted me to be dignified when it suited her, but not when it suited me.

"Well, it didn't suit *me* to do what she wanted that night. I wasn't her Miss America anymore. Whatever Miss America I was going to be, I wasn't going to be *hers.*"

In barely three months, Bess Myerson's year had gone flat. Expectations failed. Hopes paled. The conflict built into the foundation of all beauty contests, between the self-esteem of the woman and her public role as a sex object, flared up like a toxic residue, barely buried, hot and potentially explosive.

Lenora had a problem. Long after Bess Myerson had made her personal peace with the Pageant and the title, she would still have the problem, and her successors would have it, too. It was the problem of the beauty contest genre. The problem of a form that cannot stand up to substance.

By the winter of 1945 I knew I had created real difficulty for Lenora, for the Pageant, and for the sponsors. They had wanted me because I was a lady, educated, well spoken. That fit in with the new image of Miss America. However, some of the people I had begun to meet didn't want me because I was a Jewish lady.

I don't believe there was anything personal in Lenora's feelings about me as a Jew. I believe that she would have equally disliked having any difficulty at all with her winner.

She disliked having the problem of Venus Ramey, my predecessor as Miss America in 1944. Venus had gone public with her complaints about the Pageant when she gave an interview to Fannie Hurst at the American Weekly. *I remember how Lenora* pursued me, how she set Vincent Trotta pursuing me, to convince me to write an answer defending the Pageant. I was not in any hurry to do it—although I did eventually—because by then I rather sympathized with Venus.

I realized that Lenora had no bookings for me and wouldn't have any, that from here on in, it was going to be bond rallies and veterans hospitals where they barely paid your expenses and nothing more. When Sam Duboff enlisted Claire Wolff as my agent, I expected that things would change. They didn't. I stopped expecting them to.

There were a couple of great moments. Lola Martin and I had a wonderful trip to Chattanooga. I judged the Miss Tennessee contest. We went for a ride on a riverboat, we laughed and met scores of friendly people. The Jewish store owners were irate because I hadn't been booked with them. With her flair for diplomacy, Lola immediately made amends and arranged for me to appear in the Jewish community.

I learned from the sponsors during the course of the year. I watched Ralph MacIntyre pleasantly, politely, irresistibly get his own way. I watched Henry Harteveldt stand like a rock through all those labor troubles. I watched Ed Stewart of Catalina pursue his own interests on the swimsuit issue to a final parting of the ways with Lenora. When Yolande Betbeze refused to be crowned while wearing a swimsuit in 1951, he summarily abandoned the Miss America Pageant and started the Miss Universe contest. These men were tough. Watching them was like getting the better part of an M.B.A. What they taught me by their example stood me in great good stead during my career.

I learned a lot from Lenora. I was always impressed by her ability to sell. Those she couldn't convince, she charmed; those she couldn't charm, she simply outlasted. I watched her feed her "dreams and ideals" pitch to hundreds and hundreds of people and make them believe it as I believed it. Truthfully, I have never stopped believing it. In all these years, I have never stopped believing that great good could be achieved through the instrument of the Miss America Pageant.

However, the more I learned from Lenora, the more I knew I couldn't let her go on trying to run my life.

If the Pageant had any special difficulty with me, it was not

so much that I was Jewish but that I had a Jewish social conscience, instilled in me by my father and the Sholom Aleichem
houses, nurtured by the IWO rallies in Union Square and
Mayor LaGuardia and the ideals of the High School of Music
and Art. I was determined to do something with my year, to
make it mean something, to give the crown some real weight.

So when my sister Helen's friend Harold Flender asked if I
would like to meet some of his associates from the Anti-
Defamation League of B'nai B'rith, I said, "Yes, that is exactly
who I would like to meet."

CHAPTER 10

The Brotherhood Campaigns

I⊦ BESS MYERSON FELT A SENSE OF SOCIAL URGENCY IN THE midst of her flagging schedule as Miss America, that came from the air she was breathing in the winter of 1945. The reality of Hiroshima and Nagasaki—populations incinerated where they stood—would not be accepted for many years to come, if it is yet. However, the horrific news of the Nazi death machines had begun to filter into America's postwar euphoria. The truth had begun to come out. And it was not just the truth of Europe. It was also the truth of a world that had been, with pitifully few exceptions, unanimous in its disregard for the slaughter of the European Jews. It was the truth that would dominate Bess's life and those of her coreligionists until the end of their generation— that being Americans, they were the random survivors of the greatest cruelty ever wreaked on a single people, that they had been saved by the merest geographical accident and would never understand why.

The smarting slap of anti-Semitic rejection that Bess had felt in her own small travels around the country was part of an overall upsurge in bigotry toward all minorities that had accompanied a war supposedly fought to end racism.

In 1942, only two months after the Japanese attack on American forces at Pearl Harbor, 110,000 Nisei, Japanese Americans, were herded into internment camps. Congress supported this move; the U. S. Supreme Court upheld it; appalled liberals like

Governor Herbert Lehman of New York had to accept the cold comfort of President Roosevelt that no similar action was planned against Americans of German and Italian heritage.

During 1943, the infamous "zoot suit" riots broke out against Mexican Americans in Los Angeles. Twenty-five blacks and nine whites were killed in a race riot in Detroit that left scores more wounded.

In a South Harlem hotel, a white policeman and a black soldier got into a fight about a girl. The black soldier ended up with a bullet in his shoulder. Within minutes, the news reached the street that he had been shot in the back and murdered in cold blood. A major race riot was only averted because LaGuardia, Police Commissioner Valentine, Walter White (then head of the National Association for the Advancement of Colored People (NAACP), and other black leaders in the city toured the area all night in sound trucks, scotching the escalating rumors, telling people to be calm.

In Boston and New York, Jewish kids were beaten bloody by anti-Semitic gangs from Catholic neighborhoods; in Washington Heights, where some German Jews who had managed to escape were settling, every single synagogue was desecrated during 1944–45.

Wrote one analyst: "American anti-Semitism . . . reached its historic peak in 1944. . . . [In 1945] public-opinion expert Elmo Roper warned, 'anti-Semitism has spread all over the nation and is particularly virulent in urban centers.' "[1]

On V-J Day in one Texas town, a busload of war workers, both black and white, were sitting together on their way home when they heard someone shout, "The war is over!" The bus driver stopped his vehicle, turned around in his seat, and said, "Okay, you niggers, you've had your day. Get to the back of the bus."

Senator Theodore "The Man" Bilbo of Georgia, a Klan member who was famous for answering critics' letters with the salutation "Dear Kike" or "Dear Nigger," made racist speeches on the floor of Congress. During the 1944 presidential cam-

---

[1] David S. Wyman, *The Abandonment of the Jews: America and the Holocaust, 1941–1945* (New York: Pantheon, 1984), p. 9.

paign, Sidney Hillman of the Congress of Industrial Organizations (CIO) became the focus of racist attacks from "those who did not wish to see any major American union involved with minorities which might start voting and throwing their weight around."[2]

The minority most feared by reactionaries in the immediate postwar era were the blacks, who had finally begun to organize themselves into a great power block in the northern cities. The black population of Detroit increased by 30 percent between 1940 and 1944. Chicago's black population had increased by sixty-five thousand during World War I and now by another seventy-five thousand during World War II. Although these newcomers had jobs, they had no place to live. Ninety thousand souls now crowded into housing projects meant for thirty-five thousand. Bigotry added to the misery. Out of twenty-two hospitals in Los Angeles, only one would accept black patients.

"Migrating Negroes have had to make their homes in shacks and hovels abandoned by former owners as unfit for human habitation," wrote Ernest A. Gray, Jr., in the monthly *Harper's*. "The results: exorbitant rents, bad sanitation, inadequate schools and other services, a shortage of recreation facilities. Naturally many Negroes want to move elsewhere and some whites object to their doing so . . . while the chances of bitter feeling are much intensified by a general housing shortage everywhere."[3]

As black families spilled into white neighborhoods in the early 1940s, rioting broke out in Chicago, Dallas, Miami, Detroit, Los Angeles, Cleveland, Indianapolis, and Kansas City. However, black numbers inevitably added up to black power. A flashy and eloquent minister from Harlem, Adam Clayton Powell, now represented his people in Congress. The black leadership demanded that the black veteran be given equal preference under the GI Bill of Rights and that the Armed Services cease

[2] Morton Keller, "Jews and the Character of American Life Since 1930" in Charles Herbert Stember et al., *Jews in the Mind of America* (New York: Basic Books, 1966), p. 265.
[3] Ernest A. Gray, Jr., "Race Riots Can Be Prevented," *Harper's* (December 1945).

maintaining segregated units. A. Philip Randolph had led the black community into loyal participation in the war, but he wanted something in exchange: equal opportunity in federal employment. When Randolph threatened a huge protest march on Washington in 1941, Roosevelt responded with Executive Order 8802, requiring unions and employers "full and equitable participation of all workers in defense industries, without discrimination because of race, creed, or color or national origins." The Fair Employment Practices Committee, which was established to oversee the order, tried hard, but had little luck enforcing the provisions where management was racist and unions were weak.

It was clear that blacks who had served in the war or who had moved North to work in the war plants would now become dominant in many a blue-collar union. That Sidney Hillman, the son of a Lithuanian rabbi, and his CIO associates welcomed these black workers and helped them to organize *politically* convinced the bigots that the Jews and the Negroes were linked in an unholy alliance to undo corporate power in white America.

For their part, the Jews felt a lot less militant than the blacks in 1945. The Jews were in a daze of grief; they had not found the strength of their anger. Understanding eluded them. How could it have happened? What was the source of this interminable hatred?

"If *they* were born with the disease of bigotry, why were *we* the ones who grew up suffering from it?" Bess asked.

It was a rhetorical question. In 1987 she still did not have the answer.

During the war, a conference on anti-Semitism sought to prove what seemed to be apparent at that time, that anti-Semitism was a subfunction of totalitarianism and the antidemocratic personality. After the war, Laura Hobson in her 1947 best seller, *Gentlemen's Agreement,* sought to show that ordinary people who considered themselves quite nice went along with anti-Semitism. In 1944 the great Swedish social thinker Gunnar Myrdal, published *An American Dilemma,* which pointed out that Americans who proclaimed ideals of democracy and equality abroad while condoning de facto apartheid at home placed themselves in a moral crisis that could destroy the nation.

Among liberals, the idea took hold that bigotry (in dictatorship and democracy alike) was thoughtlessly spread from parents to children until so many people had it that they couldn't see they had it. They decided that a progressive gentle campaign to influence the minds of children might be the only way to break the cycle.

In 1945 Bess Myerson was an idol among American children, and she was ready for a campaign.

"As winter approached, I had begun to feel deeply frustrated," she recalled. I was overqualified for everything they were giving me to do, and they weren't giving me much. I could not complain of poor management because now I knew full well that no manager could have made me a palatable Miss America in an America that rejected Jews. Whenever I didn't get a job, I was told that the local people wouldn't accept me, or the potential corporate employer couldn't afford to be associated with my slightly famous Jewish name. I was expected to understand. Expected to be grateful for what I had been able to get. Expected to remain sweet and dignified and calm.

"Outwardly that is exactly what I did. Inwardly I felt a rage that has never left me. There seemed to be no way to fight back. I was trapped in the disguise I myself had agreed to wear. The only way to break out of the trap was somehow to cross over into the serious world of social, political, and financial endeavor, which had been introduced to me by men like Henry Harteveldt and Ralph MacIntyre. That's what the people of the Anti-Defamation League did for me. They opened the door to that serious world and the serious task of fighting bigotry, and they invited me in."

THE ANTI-DEFAMATION LEAGUE OF B'NAI B'RITH HAD BEEN founded in 1913 to protect the Jews against anti-Semitism, to refute demagogues, to prevent the circulation of smear propaganda like the horribly effective "Protocols of the Elders of Zion," and to fight for justice for the Jewish people in America. In 1913 there was no justice for the Jewish people in America. The ADL grew up in direct response to the sad case of Leo Frank versus the state of Georgia.

In July 1913 Leo Frank, a young married man who ran his uncle's pencil factory and served as president of the Atlanta B'nai B'rith Lodge, was charged with the murder of a fourteen-year-old girl. He was innocent. The governor knew he was innocent. So did the attorney for a man being tried as an accessory to the crime. So did an eyewitness who did not come forward to speak for half a century. But the vitriol and hatred of a man named Tom Watson, who would later be elected a U.S. senator, churned the crowd and the town against Frank. "Hang the Jew or we'll hang you!" was what the judge and the jury heard from the mob that roiled outside the courtroom. The sentence was death.

The racist Watson offered Governor John M. Slaton a seat in the U.S. Senate if he would let Frank hang. Slaton couldn't do it. "Two thousand years ago, another governor washed his hands of the mob and turned a Jew over to it," he said. "For two thousand years that governor's name has been a curse. If today, another Jew were lying in the grave because I had failed in my duty, I would all my life find his blood on my hands and must consider myself an assassin through cowardice."[4]

Slaton commuted Frank's death sentence to life imprisonment, which was just enough to destroy Slaton's political career and save his conscience, but not enough to save Frank. In jail,

[4] Nathan C. Belth, *A Promise to Keep* (New York: Times Books, 1979), pp. 59–68.

a convict inflamed by Watson's rhetoric tried to slash Frank to death. Four days later, Leo Frank was dragged out of prison and lynched by the local citizenry. Said Tom Watson, "A vigilante committee redeems Georgia and carries out the sentence of the law. . . . Jew libertines take notice."

Spurred by this sickening incident, the Anti-Defamation League did everything in its power to spot the bigots and blunt their impact. It attracted tough young lawyers, counterpropagandists, many of them raised in the small, embattled Jewish communities outside of New York. The ADL knew the hinterland. No group could have been better qualified to chaperone Bess Myerson through a thicket of bigots.

In 1945 the ADL, the NAACP, and the Urban League worked tirelessly together for common goals. Their executives were friends, their bond with each other apparently unbreakable. They were always looking for someone who could touch the conscience of audiences, and in the wake of the war, they were especially interested in *young* audiences. They had seen Hitler Youth on the march. They believed the current thinking that antidemocratic *values* engendered racism, and they sought access through the schools and youth fellowships of churches to young people whose sensibilities could be turned away from hatred at an early age.

An ADL activist named Irving Bebow, who had kept track of events in Atlantic City, wanted to call this Jewish Miss America and enlist her help on the high-school circuit. One of his colleagues didn't agree.

"We have discussed your cheesecake suggestion of Bess Myerson around the office," he wrote to Bebow, "and it makes very interesting discussion. Of course, you are aware that the coverage on the beauty contest has been excellent and the consensus of opinion is that we might be putting our foot in it to exploit Miss Myerson in conjunction with the Jewish problem. The name itself is ample evidence of her Jewish ancestry. Besides, it might constitute special pleading if we tried to make out a case for the Jews by using Miss Myerson in any special promotion. We feel that it is against all the laws of discretion and dignity to exploit Miss Myerson as Jewish.

"As for her telephone number, even if we knew it and we don't, I would be one of the last guys to share it, you wolf!"[5]

This standoffishness about Bess lasted only as long as it took for Harold Flender, a young writer who was dating Helen, to mention her name to his cousin-by-marriage, ADL Counsel Arnold Forster. "Clearly the man who wrote that memo was an idiot," Forster said. "That's why no one here can recall who he might have been."

A fifty-year veteran of the war to end racism in America, Arnold Forster could, better than anyone, put the marriage of the Anti-Defamation League and Bess Myerson into some historical perspective.

"Before the war, we had come through a period in which there were many organizations on the American scene of an anti-British, pro-German, anti-Soviet character . . . some of which counted millions of members," Forster said.

"The Christian Front, for example, was not an actual organization but an umbrella group representing Father Coughlin's organization. It was situated in a small town just outside of Detroit and it had five million supporters. The Ku Klux Klan and the German-American Bund counted many hundreds of thousands of members. In addition, you had an assorted three or four dozen organizations that had memberships from twenty-five roughnecks or street goons up to five or ten thousand. . . .

"This panoply of organizations was also antiblack. They had stimulated violence on the streets of New York, Chicago, Detroit, and other metropolitan areas where there were large numbers of blacks.

"With the onset of the war, what had been pro-Nazi but legal suddenly became treason. So some of these organizations disbanded, but most of them went underground and became silent but remained in existence.

"They had created a mood of anti-Semitism in this country that had the Jews terribly worried. Elements in the Catholic community were then the heart and soul of the Christian Front. They believed that the Soviet Union was crossing the entire world successfully and would eventually destroy Rome,

---

[5] Memo to Irving Bebow, ADL files (October 2, 1945).

the Vatican, and Catholicism, that the Jews and Mr. Roosevelt were part of that international Communist conspiracy.

"The Jews saw the Soviet Union from a different bridge. They saw a Soviet Union, which had become the first country in history to outlaw anti-Semitism, and they assumed, many of them, that the Soviet Union was a friend. Most of the Jewish community did not fall into that trap. But you did have some loudmouths who became active in the Communist Party and this gave fodder to the claims of the rabid, far right wing.

"When the war was on, the cardinal in Chicago made a public announcement that Father Coughlin did not represent the Catholic community. Within months after the declaration of war, Coughlin folded his entire enterprise because of pressure from the hierarchy of the American Catholic Church.

"In the meantime, however, the divisions that had been created placed the blacks in one community, the Jews in another, the Protestants in another, the Catholics in still another. That was the situation in 1945.

"The ADL, which had been concentrating on finding and exposing the anti-Semites and pro-Nazis, then sat back and said to itself, now where are we?

"First of all, we said, the world has now learned the evil and the stupidity of war; maybe in five hundred years we'll have another. This is how simple and primitive and foolish and unknowing we were in those days. Having seen many of our kids killed in the service—and the blacks had seen the same thing—we, all of us agencies in this field, sat down and decided now was the time for a massive educational drive to repair the damage.

"The blacks were bitter because they had served in second-class positions, even in the military. In the Navy, which was a lily-white organization, the blacks got as far as swabbing decks, cleaning toilets, or washing dishes. With an exception here or there, they couldn't get themselves beyond the lowest grade, and this was endemic in the military establishment, despite which many thousands of blacks went to their deaths defending the United States.

"So the blacks and the Jews decided they were going to close ranks, to change the thought processes, the mind-sets, the antagonisms, to rebuild the bridges that had been torn down in the United States during this ten-year aberration of Hitler. We were looking to use radio, veterans organizations, labor organizations, we reached out to the then budding television stations, we put out books to show who were the American heroes—as if to say to the American people: Look, how can you treat as second-class citizens this kind of Jewish community, this kind of black community that gave so much blood and made such sacrifices to defend democracy?

"It was a position that I think we would not work from today. We long ago decided that we don't come to the American people hat in hand and we don't plead for tolerance any longer. But it was a matter of habit then. If you asked me to sum up ADL programming the day the war started, I would say we were pleading for tolerance.

"Looking at it today, it's outrageous to think that we begged the American people to tolerate Jews!

"But you see you were in a period of time when the Jews accepted that the only thing you could do about anti-Semitism was to 'go sue city hall.' They accepted that they couldn't get into colleges or graduate schools because of 'Jewish quotas,' that they couldn't live in the Bronxvilles of America because they were Jews, that they couldn't work in insurance companies and public utilities and certain banks because they were Jews.

"In creating an educational campaign, we wanted most of all to change the *institutions* of prejudice. Now, how do you do that? You do that from the ground up. You reach out to the American from the day he is able to think in kindergarten to promote tolerance and brotherhood, and acceptance of those who are different.

"When Harold Flender brought Bess Myerson into this office and said to me and to Ben Epstein that she was ready and willing and able to work, we recognized in her a woman who had just had a fantastic front-page publicity, who was obviously intelligent, consciously Jewish, aware of what we had all just lived through. We recognized that wherever we might send her, she had the skills and the ability to seize the platform."

The proletarian nature of Bess's fame made her even more attractive to Forster and Epstein. The Jews always suffered from a sense of isolation at the top of the academic and intellectual worlds. It was bitter indeed to realize that many Americans believed Hitler's anti-Jewish extermination policies were bad mostly because they *almost* got Albert Einstein—for if Hitler had sent Einstein up the chimney, how in the world would we have invented the bomb and obliterated the Japanese?

As the liquid-eyed hero of Lena Wertmuller's *Seven Beauties* would observe, gazing down on Auschwitz, intellectual prowess had not saved one Jewish soul in Europe. The great yeshivas of Vilna, the "Jerusalem of the West," lay in ashes now, like their brilliant students. And a great yearning for "normalcy"—for ancestral turf with ancestors buried in it, for standing armies and baseball players and beauty queens—seized the benighted survivors.

When Bess had visited the Senate in November, the Yiddish columnist S. Margoshes wrote in *The Day*, "If a traveling salesman you happen to meet in a club gets particularly philosemitic after the third highball, all he is apt to recall as the glory of Israel . . . is the glory of Einstein. To him, as to most Americans, we are divided into two categories—Jews with money and Jews with atoms. He has not begun to realize that Jews, like most Americans, have been active in all departments of American life, including sports and beauty and what-not. As long as the Senate takes time out to grab a look at a Jewess who is a beauty queen, we need not worry over much. The common touch of humanity which is the chief and abiding trait of the American people can still be depended upon to see us through and save us from the hate-mongers. . . ."[6]

It was that "common touch of humanity" that Arnold Forster and Ben Epstein hoped to stimulate with the magnetic person of Bess Myerson.

"They made me feel as though I could finally do something worthwhile," Bess remembered. "I did not have to prove to them that I was smart as well as pretty.

"Arnie Forster was the radicalized voice, passionate, clear. He was the one who could stand up and read off the most horrifying statistics and the most disturbing examples. Ben Ep-

[6] S. Margoshes, "News and Views," *The Day* (November 12, 1945).

stein was more moderate, more businesslike. He didn't have Arnie's *Sturm und Drang*, but he, too, had tremendous impact, helping to end anti-Jewish quotas. As a one-two combination, they were unbeatable. The minute I met them, I knew I was home."

Epstein and Forster wanted Bess to lecture in high schools all across the country. They had invented a pleasant-sounding front, the American Lecture Bureau, to book speakers for them and for the black defense organizations, with Rotary groups, schools, Kiwanis clubs, and women's groups. The American Lecture Bureau provided speakers who would attack fascism *and* racism, communism *and* racism. She recalled that they offered her twenty-five dollars per appearance.

Bess made speeches for the ADL for at least two weeks out of every month for the rest of her year as Miss America. It was the most nourishing experience of her life.

"Arnie wrote a speech for me," Bess recalled, "and then every time I went to a new place, I would expand on it and tailor it to the group I was addressing. But the theme was always the same.

" 'You can't be beautiful and hate,' I would say.

" 'Because hate is a corroding disease and affects the way you look.

" 'Do you know the girl who wants to be Miss America of 1946—or 1950—or 1956? Well, here's one *must* to remember . . . and this is firsthand.

" 'Miss America represents all America. It makes no difference who she is, or who her parents are. Side by side, Catholic, Protestant, and Jew stand together . . . and we would have it no other way.

" 'For prejudice is a dangerous thing. It has a kickback worse than a bazooka. It makes you hate—and once you start hating, you're finished.

" 'You can't hide it—ever. It shows in your eyes. It warps your expression. It affects your character, your personality.

" 'And all those things are important in Alantic City—or anywhere else where real Americans take your measure and pass judgment.

" 'In veterans hospitals I have seen white and Negro, Jew and Gentile, Yank and Dixie sharing the same ward, sharing their thoughts and hopes and plans as they shared hardship and struggle on the battlefield.

" 'If you have any prejudice against any race or religion, they would tell you—beg you—to forget it.

" 'For there is no happiness in hate. No one ever succeeded by it. Nothing good was ever built by it. No nation was ever permanently unified by it.

" 'And if we want a strong, united America pushing on toward its unlimited horizons, there can be no place for prejudice in our nation . . . or in our hearts.'

"That was my first speech for the ADL.

"That was the first meaningful and important thing I said when I was Miss America.

"I still believe every word of it."

━━━━━━

SHE STARTED IN CHICAGO. HENRY POHLY, CHIEF OF THE AMERican Lecture Bureau and another ADL offshoot called Youth Builders, Inc., took her under his wing and introduced her to ranks of smart, funny ADL men who would kibitz her through their deadly serious endeavors and keep her laughing.

Harold Sachs, then director of the Chicago operation, recalled, "If Bess was an insecure refugee from the Bronx, she sure didn't give that impression when we met her. She was poised, smart, fun to be with. Julius Kahn, one of our assistants, just loved the idea of traipsing around Chicago with Bess. It was the best job we had to give out that year."

To honor her celebrity, Sachs threw a little luncheon for Bess in Chicago, just for the ADL professionals and lay leadership. "Delicatessen," he said. "Nothing fancy. My father, who lived in Council Bluffs, Iowa, was in town that week and so I brought him to the luncheon. He couldn't get over it. He had never seen a real live Miss America, and here she was in the flesh, and she turned out to be a Jewish girl with a name like

Myerson! I tell you, that luncheon added ten years to my father's life."

It fell to Herbert Lizt to warn Bess of the darker, more sinister aspects of her tour through fifteen cities.

"Try to learn as much of your prepared text as possible since you might not have the benefit of a podium," he wrote to Bess. "After all, you're going to Paterson, New Jersey, and there may not be a podium in the entire city."

The Chicago ADL men introduced Bess to the first new girlfriend she had made since vaudeville—Martha Glazer, public-relations consultant for the Chicago Mayor's Commission on Human Rights. The Mayor's Commission was sponsoring Bess's appearances in the Chicago area, part of an effort to forestall the racial troubles that had been brewing since the beginning of the war. "Martha was a short, sunny girl with a warm, embracing quality. She made me feel instantly comfortable and at home."

Bess made her speech at two assemblies at Von Steuben High School; went off to Milwaukee, where she appeared at three high schools, then went to Hartford to do a joint meeting of the Rotary, Exchange, Civitan, Kiwanis, and Lions clubs for the Red Cross and appear at two high schools and one junior high. In Springfield, Massachusetts, she spoke at two technical high schools. The National Conference of Christians and Jews, then a young organization, wanted her to come back in a month and talk to the grown-ups.

"I have just returned from a thrilling four-day tour through Hartford with Bess Myerson," Herb Lizt wrote to Ben Epstein. "The cops like her, the newsmen and photographers like her, the kids are crazy about her. She tells our story—and with what an appeal! . . . The high schools which were selected for her to speak in were all located in troubled areas . . . and the enthusiasm with which she was received there was tremendously heartwarming. . . . Crowds gathered around her almost every place she went. Children would swarm around her in the streets with that look of worship and adoration. . . . Every speech she has delivered so far has carried a freshness and vigor so important in sustaining audience attention. She's doing a grand job and we have cause to be mighty proud of her."[7]

[7] Memo from Herb Lizt to Ben Epstein (March 26, 1946).

Bess's image had begun to change. Her association with the tolerance campaign was finally bringing her the credibility and respect she had never enjoyed before as Miss America. Nobody seemed to care if she never appeared in a bathing suit again, and if anyone dared to suggest it, her agents at Claire Wolff's office scoffed and said, "Bess Myerson? Crusader for tolerance and brotherhood?! In a *bathing suit?* Not on your life!"

In April Bess went to Nashua, New Hampshire, and then stopped in Boston to have breakfast with sixty-five high-school editors and address the Massachusetts Independent Voters Association. The Jewish Community Center in Quincy grabbed her for its Civic Youth Forum, comprising kids of all faiths.

Then she returned home and went to Brooklyn to lecture at Eastern District High School.

There happened to be an English teacher in Eastern District High at that time named Mrs. Gertrude Ellis, a Protestant, who found herself mightily impressed with Bess and the various programs the ADL placed in the school over the succeeding years.

In January 1956, ten years after Bess appeared at Eastern District High, Gertrude Ellis died.

"Her will was opened by her lawyers," Arnold Forster wrote to Bess, "and we received notice that five charities have received $1000 legacies, and *the balance of her estate goes to the Anti-Defamation League for educational purposes.* The balance turns out to be something over $100,000(!) plus a house in Queens."[8]

Bess could not have dreamed that her tour would reap such extraordinary results for its sponsors. In Buffalo she made nine appearances in two days at everything from the youth assembly of the Urban League, to the Girl Reserves of the YWCA, to the Young Peoples Club at Temple B'nai Zion. Missing the ebullient Martha Glazer, Bess convinced her old Hunter classmate Lenore Miller to accompany her to Philadelphia for the better part of a week.

At the Quaker City Lodge of B'nai B'rith, she appeared on a panel together with Miss Sepia America, Dolores Fairfax, a sophomore at Temple. It would take many years before the

---

[8] Letter from Arnold Forster to Bess Myerson Wayne (February 9, 1956).

weird classifications of color would be dropped from the vocabulary of beauty pageants. (Was Bess white? She sure didn't feel white. Was Dolores sepia? What the hell is sepia, anyway?) Beatrice Harrison, the district director of the ADL Women's Division, wrote to Bella that "no single youngster could commit an act of unfriendliness after hearing . . . your very lovely daughter."[9]

At every high school there were crowds of kids at the door when she left, and a couple of them would always hang back and ask her quietly, "Miss Myerson, could you tell us, are you Jewish?" And she would say "Yes." And they would squeal and say, "I knew it! I knew it! Oh, my mother is going to be absolutely just so excited when I tell her it's true, you're really one of us!"

Bess enjoyed meeting the kids. But lest she forget the origins and stimulus for this wonderful trip, she got a letter from Germany.

"As a Jewish chaplain now stationed here where the destructive results of hate and prejudice so tangibly meet the eye everywhere and whose victims are countless men, women, and children broken in body and soul, I found it rather difficult to suppress the feeling of profound admiration you have evoked. Best wishes for success in the sacred task in which you are engaged."[10]

To the chaplain with his long, hard view from the vantage of Europe, the work seemed sacred; to Bess and her colleagues it was highly pragmatic. It spoke to real troubles in high schools that had been boiling over ever since she won the Pageant.

In the early days of October, a brawl between black students and white students at a basketball game at Benjamin Franklin High School in East Harlem quickly escalated into a riot. Children needed police escorts to make it safely to the subway. Cops confiscated knives, razors, ice picks, and homemade guns from fifteen-year-old kids of both races.

In Gary, Indiana, crosses had already been burned on the

---

[9] Letter from Beatrice Harrison to Bella Myerson (April 15, 1946).

[10] Letter from Albert N. Troy, captain, U.S. Army, to Bess Myerson (April 30, 1946).

lawns of liberals. White students went on strike at Foerbel High School, demanding resegregation of their school. Their parents held a mass meeting to support them.

On Chicago's South Side, twenty-five hundred white students went on strike, demanding that black students be removed from the school. The mayor, Edward J. Kelly, attributed the trouble to "a childish prank," but he was worried, and he instructed Martha Glazer's committee to plan a week of consciousness raising for brotherhood that would bring the effective Bess Myerson back to Chicago in June.

By this time, Bess was a pro. Her little speech had been expanded to twenty minutes. The impact of her appearances had been incalculably enhanced by a linkup with Harold Russell, the handless veteran who had starred in the definitive film of postwar American life, *The Best Years of Our Lives.*

In his own memoirs, Russell remembered sitting around with Bess and hearing her stories of being insulted and snubbed on the Miss America tour. "I thought it was a shame that disabled American vets like me had sacrificed in World War II only to find this still going on back home, and I stayed on the B'nai B'rith tour much longer than planned. . . . It was something I obviously didn't do for the money. . . . I was certain doing what I felt was right for myself was worth more than any financial killings."[11]

"Nothing could top Harold," Bess recalled with undimmed admiration. "He would hold those steel hooks aloft in front of the children and cry out, 'Did I lose my hands so you keep some black kid off the Student Council?! Did I lose my hands so that you can keep some Jewish kid out of your lily-white neighborhood?!' Most of the time I was his curtain raiser. I don't think that any other single person could have been more effective as a crusader for tolerance than he was."

The tours and speeches of Bess and Harold Russell were only a small part of the nationwide movement to stop the tide of prejudice, which now engrossed the liberal community. Frank Sinatra's short "The House I Live In" played everywhere. A

[11] Harold Russell with Dan Ferullo, *The Best Years of My Life* (Middlebury, Vt.: Paul S. Eriksson, Publisher, 1981), p. 53.

popular children's book with the same theme of brotherhood, *Henry's Back Yard,* was brought home to thousands of kids. *Gentlemen's Agreement* was in the making. *South Pacific* was about to go on Broadway, and with it the theme song of the whole postwar tolerance movement: "You've Got to Be Carefully Taught [to Hate]."

"In vaudeville I had been introduced by my measurements. On the ADL tour I was introduced as a Hunter graduate by a principal who treated me with respect. I learned to wait and vamp through the first few minutes of every speech, to allow time for the buzzing and squirming to stop. Then the children would grow attentive and thoughtful; I could see their faces; make eye contact. Afterward some of them would come backstage and make a pledge—to themselves, to me—that they would try to get along with the other children in the school.

"I found acceptance at the PTA meetings, too, even though I wasn't a parent myself. If one person in the entire room was moved, I felt I had helped to undo the hate of centuries."

———

FROM THE PAGEANT OFFICE ITSELF, REACTIONS WERE MIXED.

Elizabeth Murray, an accountant who would send Bess reimbursement checks for expenses or bits of scholarship money to pay for the piano lessons she took when she was in New York, congratulated her on all the publicity she was getting and the fine work she was doing. But, according to Bess, Lenora Slaughter was not so happy. She was having a premature attack of the 1950s.

"When I saw Lenora," Bess recalled, "she was angry and full of recrimination. She accused me of squandering the good name of the Miss America Pageant by making highly publicized appearances at political events I had not even cleared through her. She told me that in her opinion I had fallen into the clutches of the Jewish Communist garment manufacturers from the city of New York and declared that I was betraying the people who had given me the scholarship by allowing myself to become a tool of the racial minorities!

"I thought she had lost her mind.

"I felt she should have been proud of me. A year later, twenty years later, forty years later, she said she was. In the spring of 1946, however, the people in Atlantic City who had not wanted me as Miss America in the first place were convinced that their dire predictions had come true. In their view I was a runaway who had to be caught and stopped.

"I remember receiving a letter about one incident in a restaurant in Atlantic City. A racially mixed group of people had gone out to dinner after a union convention. The waitress wouldn't seat them. They picketed outside the restaurant. *They* were the ones who were arrested and fined. Lenora was telling me that I was dishonoring the Pageant, and right there in Atlantic City, under the nose of the Pageant, these incredible un-American abuses of the rights of citizens were taking place and dishonoring the whole community!

"There was no way she was going to convince me to agree with her. I simply wasn't afraid of her anymore. I brought the Pageant more and better publicity than it had ever received before, but they saw me as a renegade, sullying my title with political activism.

"*They* could have utilized me, you know. It could have been them, not the ADL. They could have said, 'You speak well; let's find something good and useful for you to speak about. There are themes and causes we can develop together to give you the kind of year we will all be proud of.'

"They did nothing of the sort. The only one there with any vision was Lenora, and her vision stopped with the scholarship fund. It was a lot. But it wasn't enough for me."

In June, Bess returned to her port of embarkation—Chicago.

She attended a luncheon for community leaders, an interfaith youth dance sponsored by the Commission on Community Interrelations. The Junior Chamber of Commerce threw a party for her. She dedicated the new union headquarters of the United Transport Service Employees of America, which represented the Pullman porters, one of the few unions in the country dominated by blacks. She went to Farragut High, Cregier High, Flower Technical, McKinley, Gage Park High, Roosevelt High, and Crane Technical. The Michigan Boulevard Gardens Project staged an outdoor pageant in her honor, at which a new ballet was performed with the upbeat title *The Spirit of American Youth.* She addressed the tenants councils at the Altgeld and Cabrini housing projects. The Minority Relations Committee of the Mayor's Commission on Human Rights arranged for her to tour veterans hospitals. She appeared on Elizabeth Hart's radio show and Don McNeill's *Breakfast Club.*

Chicago citizens who heard her sent her letters that she keeps to this day.

"If your efforts may seem for naught, take a personal satisfaction in knowing that at least you tried . . ." they said.

"I congratulate you on your stand against intolerance. It gives a person a grand feeling to know that we have wonderful people to take up the fight on behalf of the little people and the minorities . . ." they said.

"Tell that nice lady that spoke over the radio . . . to get in touch with Mrs. Roosevelt in Hyde Park or wherever she is to stop them publishing dirty stuff inciting race riots and causing mountains of trouble for the colored folks . . ." they said.

To her boss, Mayor Kelly, Martha Glazer reported that Bess had been on twenty-nine programs in June plus three radio shows and had been interviewed by four different newspapers. She had appeared in the flesh before thirty thousand Chicagoans, young and old, and brought her message to hundreds of thousands more by the print media and over the airways.

Martha got a pat on the back and a successful future as a publicist.

Bess got a new kind of attention from the racist press.

Wrote the *Gentile News* of Oak Park, Illinois, "A rather personable Jewish lass by the name of Bess Myerson won a bathing beauty contest and now is being 'sent' around the country to state in effect: 'If you have hate in your heart, your good looks will disappear.'

"Now if 25% or over 30,000,000 people in the United States hate the Jews there must be a reason for the hatred.

"What millions of Americans are thinking . . . is that we millions of Gentiles might develop crestfallen, homely countenances because (1) we've been 'gyped' not once but many times; (2) we've got Communists in our hair trying to destroy our own Christian churches and form of government . . . ;, (3) shady politicians; (4) high taxes (5) can't find a place to live. . . . Why should Bess Myerson and her Jewish race be alarmed at how homely we're becoming? Maybe she and some of her friends on the inside aren't troubled with the aforementioned list of causes for developing sour pusses."[12]

"Congratulations," Herb Lizt wrote to Bess. "When the bigots begin to attack you, you *know* you've arrived."

Bess also received this letter from Germany:

"I was reading over one GI's shoulder the other day in *Stars and Stripes* about you speaking for Racial and Religious Tolerance," wrote the soldier, "when out of the blue sky this GI says: 'I can see by the paper that Miss America is a nigger lover, she's got a helluva nerve using her title for that crap.'

"Well I got rather sore, and I laced it into him for a few torrid minutes. I'm writing to sort of encourage you in the work you're doing, for you may have heard from other people who think as he does. The title is yours to speak under. And you are speaking as a true Miss America. So keep it up, and speak out damn loud."[13]

———

The brotherhood campaigns were the high point of my year as Miss America. They gave me stature in my own eyes—at last. They also gave me a career I had never imagined, because a man named Walt Framer saw me at an ADL meeting, and

[12] *Gentile News*, Oak Park, Ill. (June 1946), p. 4.

[13] Letter from Jack Edelstein, U.S. Army, to Bess Myerson (April 30, 1946).

years later, when he was producing The Big Payoff, *he looked me up. He said that we need people with different kinds of ethnic backgrounds on television to support the variety and diversity of America. That's what I represented to him, because of the "hate and beauty tour." When he put me on his show, my television career took off.*

I grieve now for those wonderful alliances we had, the blacks and the Jews, the churches and labor. Racial tolerance has been neglected as a mission. Isn't there still a need? Look what happened in Howard Beach in New York in 1987! Community leaders had to create brotherhood programs out of thin air in five minutes because there were so few programs in place. They had been dismantled—obsolete, out of date, like the old liberals.

People have such short memories. They can't see beyond their own little lives. They feel they owe nothing to the sentiments and precedents of history.

If they could know what I know, they would see: History is one of the great comforts in this life. Being part of history is like being part of a good orchestra. It helps you forget your troubles. It helps you live beyond yourself. It gives you a context and a meaning, so you never feel alone.

There's a Jewish word for what I got from my ADL work: koved, pronounced like "covet." It means stature in the community.

Becoming famous doesn't bring koved. Investing your strength and substance and love in a good cause does. I knew if I brought koved to the family, I would make my father happy and maybe even more important, I would make my mother happy. The koved my father got from his work as a house painter came in the letters of appreciation that said that he was a craftsman, that made him feel honored, and that brought a little glory to his name.

My mother loved it when I toured for the ADL.

The Miss America letters she had thrown away.

But the letters she received from people like Mrs. Harrison in Philadelphia, who said my speech there had helped youngsters to overcome bigotry, those letters she carried around for years.

I have always been happiest when I am involved with something larger than I am. For better or worse, the ticket to "larger" was being Miss America. Over the years, whenever I felt help-less or hopeless, I would go on a show, make a speech, fight for a cause—the United Jewish Appeal, Another Mother for Peace; I would get dressed and look in the mirror at this spiffy woman, I would see what other people saw in me, and I would try to become that, to become . . . important.

The need for koved was one of my most serious weaknesses. It was also my greatest strength.

CHAPTER 11

The End
of the
Beginning

IN MAY 1946, WHEN ONLY THREE MONTHS REMAINED TO HER as Miss America, Bess was asked to play the piano as a soloist with the New York Philharmonic at a concert in Carnegie Hall.

She took the honor seriously, studying with Dorothea LaFollette every day that she was free. At home, she practiced constantly: Rachmaninoff's Second Piano Concerto.

"I remember my parents' excitement and Lenora's excitement with those magic words, 'Carnegie Hall.' The newspaper ads for the concert announced proudly that the audience would have the comfort of one of our postwar wonders: air conditioning."

Bess's newspaper interviews were more candid now, without the kind of kibitzing she had done with Earl Wilson back in the fall.

"If I'm supposed to be representative of the American girl," she told the *Brooklyn Eagle,* "I want to make constructive use of that fact. In the tolerance talks I've been making, it's a great draw. Last week in a Brooklyn school I got 100 percent attendance—six thousand girls, all there on time. Of course, most of them came to see what I looked like. But they stayed to listen.

"With the music, it works the other way around. Being Miss America becomes a natural barrier. And I have to work twice as hard. People expect me to play concerts in a bathing suit."[1]

[1] *Brooklyn Eagle* (June 1, 1946).

When the Carnegie Hall concert was scheduled, Lenora released Bess's scholarship award. Bess had been requesting it for some time; however, the Pageant's working principle in that first scholarship year was that a winner should be enrolled in school before she received her award. The initial plan was for Bess to attend Juilliard. However, subsequent events precluded that, and she ultimately used the scholarship for graduate courses at Columbia, among other things.

"I bought a fabulous Steinway grand piano and a beautiful new Haynes flute. I bought the complete *Grove's Dictionary of Music and Musicians* and dozens of orchestral scores and symphonic records, and a new Victrola for my father. Although I never pursued advanced studies in conducting as I had once thought of doing, I continued with my music at Columbia and also took courses there in the new fascination of the country: television.

"I always believed that the reason Lenora withheld the money for so long was that she disapproved of the brotherhood speaking tour and felt I might do something political that would force the Pageant to disassociate itself from me. Of course, it had turned out that all the publicity I was getting had helped the image of the Pageant. Lenora's attitude toward me grew calmer, cooler, more professional and respectful."

Before the Carnegie Hall performance, Lenora wrote to Bess:

"I am proud as can be of your scheduled appearance as the guest star of the Philharmonic Orchestra at Carnegie Hall this week. You certainly make the top spots, and everyone associated with the Pageant will agree with me that the reigning Miss America is just about the finest and most accomplished person in the world. Good luck to you.

"With kindest regards, I am

"Most cordially yours . . ."[2]

Amid the applause of the concert, a young girl reached up from the orchestra pit and handed Bess a bouquet of long-stemmed red roses. Mixed in with the "Bravos!" came anonymous cries of *"Mazel tov!"* Music critics likely to wait eagerly

[2] Letter from Lenora Slaughter to Bess Myerson (May 31, 1946).

for Miss America to fall on her face admitted unanimously that Bess had done a fine job.

"My mother hadn't changed," she said with a laugh. "Mrs. LaFollette came up to her after the performance and said, 'Bess was wonderful, Mrs. Myerson.' And my mother answered, 'I don't know why. She never practices.'"

But Bess herself had changed enormously.

The joys of fulfilling her youthful fantasy and playing at Carnegie were now tempered by self-knowledge. She knew this was a one-shot appearance, that she would never be a concert artist, despite Dorothea's dreams for her. Her younger sister, Helen, had already appeared at Carnegie Hall with the National Symphony Orchestra, albeit not as a soloist. Bess had the high and the hall in perspective.

She had touched politics; social action. She had learned to be out among people. Like many a young woman maturing in the war years, she had weathered loneliness, paid her own way, tasted independence, and acquired a sense of what it could mean to take control of her own life. "Of course, that was the very last thing I wanted to do," she laughed.

What she wanted to do was get married.

The American government itself had made a substantial investment in convincing Bess and the women of her generation that marriage must be the obvious, logical, patriotic next step after the war. Having employed brilliant propagandists to convince women to leave home and go to work during the fight, our leaders now felt compelled to undo their success. Washington economic planners took very seriously the commonly held opinion, voiced by *Newsweek* magazine, that "keeping women in the home following the war may prove as difficult as keeping the boys down on the farm after they'd seen Paree." So government-sponsored films and newsreels were issued throughout the mid-1940s to urge women, for the sake of culture, country, and personal happiness, to give up their jobs to homecoming veterans and go back to tending the family love nest.

Why should Miss America be any different? The times required that she operate just like the heroines of the 1940s radio serials, which occupied four and five hours of airtime every day in 1946. "The woman at the center of the serial is a strong character," wrote critic Gilbert Seldes, "but if she were permitted to function in strength, the plot would blow up in a few days; she has to be harried and chivvied and above all prevented from taking action."[3]

Bess's personal daydreams had always centered on a cozy home with an all-providing man to make her decisions and solve her problems. Although Bella's pushing and shoving had geared her to withstand, even enjoy pressure, she *imagined* that she longed for what she *imagined* would be the stressless life of the cared-for wife and mother. At the pinnacles of her year of fame, she had drunk at the cup of celebrity with an immediate loneliness chaser. Almost all her friends had married. Many were already pregnant. She wanted to be like them.

She reacted to success not with self-confidence and pride but with plain fear, an illogical synapse achieved by centuries of female conditioning, one that many women would one day recognize and call their own. To Bess in the spring of 1946, the only safe harbor seemed to be a man.

———

Allan Wayne and I met in May 1946 in Atlantic City. I was there at Lenora's command to sign autographs and have my picture taken with some of the manufacturers at a toy convention. Allan's father, Gus, who was in the toy business, had purchased exhibit space. Allan was keeping him company.

Allan had just returned from four years in the Pacific and was still wearing his captain's uniform. Not only was he handsome, he was also taller than I was. He introduced himself, told me he lived in New York City, and said that he had heard about my winning the title when he was still overseas. A Jew himself, he

[3] Quoted in Joseph C. Goulden, *The Best Years: 1945–1950* (New York: Atheneum, 1976), p. 150.

was very proud that a Jewish girl had won; he had never dreamed that he would actually meet her.

I found his ardor wonderfully appealing. He wasn't intimidated by my title. He sent me flowers, gifts, started to accompany me on some of my appearances, and was always gracious and helpful. I felt comfortable with him—and less lonely.

I knew that when my year ended in September, I'd be home in the Sholom Aleichem with my parents. Who was going to look for me there? How was I going to meet somebody? I began to think that if I didn't marry Allan, there wouldn't be anybody else suitable to care for me.

One night when Allan was escorting me home from dinner, we found a soldier leaning against the wall in the entrance hall of my building.

"Does Bess Myerson live here?" the soldier asked.

"No," I said, "you've made a mistake."

"You're Bess Myerson," he insisted. "Don't you remember me? You visited me in the hospital in Italy. I found your address in the Yank Bulletin. I came all the way from my hometown in Iowa to find you."

It wasn't the first time that a soldier with delusions had come looking for me. I was so frightened by these incidents, so tired of being exposed and vulnerable.

Allan sent me upstairs, took the soldier to Grand Central, and put him on a train to Trenton, where he had an Army buddy he could visit. But the soldier came back several times and finally Allan arranged for the man to go to a veterans center near his home, where he could get help.

The experience unnerved me and my family. We all wanted to recapture my anonymity. I needed to feel safe again. Who could better provide safety than Allan Wayne?

Mom loved him. Up to that time, no one had been good enough for me. Allan charmed her and changed her mind. For the first time since I had started playing the piano, I had come up with something that put a smile on her face.

Allan's family life was very seductive to me. The Waynes—who had shortened the family name from Wayneschenker—lived in an elegant West End Avenue apartment. Gus Wayne was *jolly and loving and prosperous; he always wore a hat in the house. Katherine Wayne was a chain-smoking, dignified, well-read woman who rustled with silk and aspired to quality. The first time I had dinner at their home, I started to stack the dishes at the meal's end, but Katherine touched me gently on the arm and said, "You don't have to do that, dear. The maid will clear."*

September came and my reign ended. I relinquished the crown to Marilyn Buferd. I went home relieved to be free of it but wondering what it would be like to be alone again, not knowing what I was going to do. I asked Sylvia. She thought I should marry Allan.

You must understand, the women of our generation were never taught to be alone. We were raised to equate the unmarried state with a kind of death. When I have made speeches around the country, I have met many women my age who have told me that no matter how much they achieved, they could not bear to be alone with no one to do for or care for except themselves, they could not bear the silence in the night.

It's so strange. You struggle for a room of your own, and you finally get it, and then you discover that you don't want to be alone in it. You cannot stop looking for love.

Maybe the war did that to us. Or maybe it was all those soap operas. . . .

When Allan and I were married, letters of congratulation poured in from people I had met during my year, from the sponsors and the managers, from Arnold Forster and Ben Epstein, from Herb Lizt and Julius Kahn. I received a lovely note from Lenora. She put up a good front, but I knew she was disappointed. She didn't want to see her Miss America as a housewife dabbling in scattered courses. She wanted me to get a Master's degree. She couldn't understand why I would give it all up to get married.

Apartments were difficult to come by after the war, so Allan and I moved in with his parents. A year later, our daughter, Barra, was born. Gus adored her, his only grandchild. He would stack up toys for her in the foyer so that when she entered the front door, she would literally tumble into the furry arms of stuffed pandas and floppy-eared puppies. The bigger she grew, the bigger the pile of toys in the foyer grew.

Allan was working in his father's business. I was being a wife and mother. It wasn't enough for me, not after what I had experienced. I started giving piano lessons again. One day a student said to me, "How come you're doing this, Mrs. Wayne? You were Miss America. Shouldn't you be doing something more?"

That young child had read my mind.

I started doing some television—an appearance here and there, then a regular spot on a weekly network show. In 1951, when Walt Framer asked me to be on The Big Payoff, my career suddenly expanded. Allan was pleased. He took a more active role in my work, supervising business matters, handling speaking engagements, controlling the checkbook. I had everything I wanted: a busy career and a man to run it.

Then Allan's father, Gus, died.

It was a terrible loss for all of us. But for Allan, it was catastrophic. He was inconsolable. He had adored Gus. Now he refused to leave the funeral parlor or allow the coffin to be closed. He kept taking off things of his own—his watch, his tie clasp, a ring—and putting them in with the body. We boarded a train and took Gus's body back to his hometown, Baltimore, for burial. Allan rode in the car with the coffin. He refused to eat. During the last days of Gus's illness, he had started drinking. He never stopped.

He couldn't get his life back together after that. His overwhelming grief triggered memories of the war so terrifying that they gave him nightmares. He would wake in the night trembling, drenched in sweat.

He changed radically. He stayed out all night. His drinking made him impotent. He blamed me. My success had once pleased him; now it angered him. He threatened to storm into the television studio and disrupt the show. He became physically abusive, and his rages were terrifying to me and Barra. Our family life was disintegrating, and nothing could stop it— not psychiatrists, not anyone. I felt helpless. My safe harbor was no longer safe.

When I went to tell my parents that I was leaving Allan, my

dear father said, *"You don't leave a marriage. No matter what, you don't leave. Go back and make it better."*

My mother, who had so carefully trained us to be financially independent enough to survive even a bad marriage, now shook her head as my father spoke and tried to be philosophical. *"How can you leave Allan?"* she said. *"You just bought new living-room drapes."*

Why is it that almost every story I tell about my mother makes me laugh and then makes me want to cry?

When I finally found the courage to declare that it was all over between us, Allan sued for custody of Barra. During the litigation, it came to light how badly he had managed our finances. What he really needed and wanted was not custody, but money. His lawyer informed mine that Allan would give me the divorce and sole custody if I gave him all the money.

I had been working for ten years and done extremely well. Now, however, I was faced with being the sole support of my child. I was working in a business that regularly replaced on-camera people like me. During the early 1950s, dozens of my colleagues had been whisked into oblivion for holding political opinions not far different from those I had been raised on. My wonderful career could vanish like a shooting star; I knew that. Hard times could return. I was scared to give up my money.

In desperate need of advice, I went to visit the man who had become Allan's employer, Mr. Schrank, who was in the hospital recovering from an illness.

"Look, Bess," he said, *"your marriage isn't working, Allan's drinking is getting worse, and you must get on with your life and take care of your little girl. Start thinking like a man. When a man's business fails, he cuts his losses and walks away and tries to start over. That's what you should do. Give him the money, take Barra, and walk away."*

And that's what I did.

When I look back, it seems ironic indeed that the day I gave up my two greatest sources of imagined security—my money and my marriage—I experienced my first taste of freedom.

The divorce wounded me deeply, but I couldn't afford the luxury of self-pity. I had to provide a livelihood and a decent *home life for myself and my child. I had to move on and take risks both in my personal life and in the more visible worlds of television and public service.*

There have been accomplishments and disappointments. There have been wise moves and there have been serious mistakes, with their price tags of great pain. Through all of it, something has always kept me going—something inside me that is not so much ambition as a will to survive, to prevail, to please, to shine. It was ingrained in me in my childhood and tested during my year as Miss America. Even though some powerful people wanted me to lose in Atlantic City that year, I had won the title. And once it was mine, I wanted to do something meaningful with it. The truth is, the title didn't just stick to me. I stuck by the title. Whenever it proved a little snug, tight-fitting, I tried to stretch it—just as Sylvia had stretched the small white bathing suit—until it would fit a television star or a public official.

What would my life have been like if I hadn't been Miss America? Would I have chosen other husbands, other friends, a less public life? I don't speculate about that anymore. It happened. I was. I am, and the title and the moment were, for me, a high point, a training ground, an indelible experience.

───────

AS BESS PREPARED TO RETURN TO ATLANTIC CITY FOR THE ceremonies marking the end of her year, the Miss America Pageant was already trying hard to learn from the mistakes that had been made with Bess Myerson.

A new contract governing the relationship of the winners to the sponsors was written to prevent precisely the kind of disorganization that had so plagued (and assisted) Bess. There would be no more inbuilt conflicts among the sponsors, as there had been between Catalina and Bancroft, no more feuds among managers. Lenora was determined to consolidate control.

"In the event I am selected Miss America 1946," the contract read, ". . . I hereby appoint the Miss America Pageant as my sole, exclusive, and only agent and attorney for the period commencing with my selection . . . and ending September 15, 1947."[4] Henceforth, Miss America would be all tied up.

"Jit" Naeckle from the L. W. Ramsey Advertising Agency made it clear to Lenora that F. W. Fitch Shampoo would participate another year only under certain conditions:

"We want it understood that the winner will pose with a beauty operator washing her hair and also in a picture showing her giving herself a shampoo. These two poses would be in addition, of course, to straight hair pictures. We would also like to use her gratis for more than one radio show. We would like to use her for two and possibly three shows. . . . If you can give us assurances as outlined in this letter, it is possible we may be able to get together."[5]

A special operations subcommittee of the Pageant executive sent in a list of recommendations to guard the next winner's activities so that no one would be able to wander off into the wilds of politics as Bess had done.[6]

Miss America, they said, should have a business manager directly accountable to the Pageant.

She should have a chaperone, provided by the Pageant, to go with her on all tours.

A budget of ten thousand dollars should be set up to manage Miss America in 1946, which amount would be paid to a female assistant for Lenora.

In keeping with Lenora's aspirations to get "the legmen" out of the judges' box, the warmhearted Mall Dodson came up with some creative suggestions concerning the judges.[7]

---

[4] Contract for the National Finals, Miss America Health, Beauty, and Talent Pageant for the Selection of Miss America, 1946.

[5] Letter from E. G. Naeckle to Lenora Slaughter (February 2, 1945).

[6] Letter from Kenneth B. Walton to Park Haverstick (August 19, 1946).

"From my contacts with the public and the press," he wrote, "the one glaring fault in the past has been the judging. Maybe not so much the judging as the judges, and it is popular opinion that the time is right to use judges who will spend more serious thought on the contestants than on the round-the-clock social calendar they have to maintain. To this end may I suggest an all-woman jury based on the fact that woman artists, stage directors, dance directors, college presidents, etc., will judge a girl on her talent, her demeanor, and her beauty with a more expert eye than a male, who, it must be admitted, will probably 'go' for some one or more of the girls and thus be prejudiced."

Mall's plan worked—a little. In addition to Lois Wilson, Prunella Wood, and Vyvyan Donner, the Board of Judges in 1946 included Mrs. Henry G. Doyle, president of the Washington, D.C., Board of Education and a director of the National Symphony Orchestra; and Jean Bartel, Miss America of 1943, who had just finished a stint on Broadway in *The Desert Song.* But with threatening phone calls long forgotten, Conover, Arthur William Brown, Vincent Trotta, Conrad Thibault, and Dean Cornwell were all back, and to that number were added Russell Patterson and another illustrator, Hap Hadley. A thirteenth judge (presumably a tie-breaker), Dr. Edward M. Gwathmey, president of Converse College in Spartanburg, South Carolina, represented the academic community.

The illustrators, sick and tired of Lenora's rhetoric, were turned off by the presence of so many women on the panel. As far as they were concerned, Miss America of 1945 had been a scholar and a lady, and that was quite enough. "It was the year they brought out the rubberized bathing suit," Russell Patterson said, "and we voted for the girl with the best of everything showing."[8]

Marilyn Buferd won. She went to Hollywood, then to Europe. According to Frank Deford, Roberto Rossellini threw over Anna Magnani for Buferd and give her a role in a movie called

[7] Letter from Mall Dodson to Park Haverstick (February 18, 1946).
[8] Frank Deford, *There She Is: The Life and Times of Miss America* (New York: Viking, 1971), p. 164.

The Machine That Kills Evil-Doers. Then he left Buferd for Ingrid Bergman. In 1948 Lenora was still begging Buferd to enroll in a university, even a language school.[9]

It was the high-water mark of the illustrators. By the next year, their past power over the Pageant slipped into history. Barbara Walker became Miss America in 1947 and she was, finally, what Lenora wanted: a Sunday school teacher. Alas, like Bess Myerson, she got married much too soon for Lenora's big plans and dreams.

When Bess returned to the Pageant in 1946, she told the show's MC, Bob Russell, that it had been the most wonderful year of her life, and she thanked all the people she had met all over America who had taught her so much. Then she walked one last time down the runway.

A little girl named Vicki Gold, daughter of Al Gold, Frank Haven's predecessor as chief photographer of Atlantic City, held her long train. Six years old and a bit nervous, Vicki tripped and almost fell. Bess turned and gave her a bright smile of encouragement.

"She was so beautiful," Vicki said. "She looked so calm and so self-assured, like she would never have a doubt in the world."

BESS MYERSON started her TV career as Mistress of Ceremonies for "The Big Payoff" on CBS-TV from 1951 to 1959. During that period, she also regularly substituted for Dave Garroway as host of NBC's "Today" show, and served as commercial hostess of "The Jackie Gleason Show" and "Philco Playhouse." She was a regular panelist on CBS's "I've Got a Secret" from 1958 to 1967. Together with John Daly, Walter Cronkite, and Douglas Edwards, and as a solo hostess, she was commentator for the Miss America Pageant television shows from 1954 to 1968. Two documentary series—"A Woman Is" and "In The Public Interest"—which she hosted between 1975 and 1977 were nominated for Emmies.

From 1969 to 1973, she served under Mayor John Lindsay as Commissioner of Consumer Affairs of New York City, and was architect of the most far-reaching consumer protection legislation in the country at that time. She then went to work in the private sector, as consumer consultant for both Bristol Myers and Citibank (1973–1980) and as a contributing editor of *Redbook Magazine*. She wrote a nationally syndicated consumer column ("Listen Bess") for seven years, and also covered the Sadat–Begin peace initiative as a reporter for the New York *Daily News*. Her book *The Complete Consumer* (1979) became a basic volume in the library of consumer protection, and in 1982 *The I Love New York Diet*, co-authored with Bill Adler, reached *The New York Times Book Review* "Best Sellers" list.

From 1983 to 1987, she served under Mayor Ed Koch as Commissioner of Cultural Affairs of New York City. During these four years she substantially broadened financial support for the city's arts community, so that more funds were made available, and more groups became eligible for funding, than ever before.

Her presidential appointments include Lyndon Johnson's White House Conference on Violence and Crime; Gerald Ford's Commission on the National Center for Productivity and Quality of Working Life; and Jimmy Carter's Commissions on Mental Health and on World Hunger.

Her political activities include service on the Alliance to Save Energy (1976–1980); the Commission on Critical Choices established by Vice President Nelson Rockefeller (1973–1975); the Ad Hoc Group Counseling the House Ways and Means Committee on Tax Legislation (1973–1979); and the Carter-Mondale Task Force On Consumer Affairs (1976). She was a speaker at the Democratic National Convention in 1976. She held positions in political campaigns on a city, state, and national level, including the campaigns of Senator Daniel Patrick Moynihan and Governor Hugh Carey.

She has served on the boards of the New York State Council on the Arts, the International Rescue Committee, The America-Israel Cultural Foundation, The Committee to Advance the Goal of Higher Education for the Disabled in the City University of New York, The Consumers Union, The Eleanor Roosevelt Memorial Fund, Another Mother For Peace, The National Academy of Television Arts and Sciences, and many other groups. She has been honored by the Girl Scout Council of New York, The National Conference of Christians and Jews, the New School for Social Research, and the Columbia School of Journalism.

Today she lectures frequently nationwide. Through the Anti-Defamation League of B'nai B'rith, she sponsors a national annual "Bess Myerson Journalism Award," open to college newspapers and journalists, for the promotion of intergroup harmony on campus. An ovarian cancer survivor, she sponsors ovarian cancer support groups. Hunter College, Keuka College, Long Island University, and Seton Hall have presented her with honorary doctorates in law and public health. She is a board member of "A Living Memorial to the Holocaust, The Museum of Jewish Heritage in New York," where she has established an archive of holocaust films and films of Jewish life.

SELECTED BIBLIOGRAPHY

BLUM, JOHN MORTON. *V Was for Victory: Politics and American Culture During World War II*. New York: Harcourt Brace Jovanovich, 1976.

Bronx Museum of the Arts. *Building a Borough: Architecture and Planning in the Bronx, 1890–1940*. New York: Bronx Museum of the Arts, 1986.

CONOVER, CAROLE. *Cover Girls: The Story of Harry Conover*. Englewood Cliffs, N.J.: Prentice-Hall, 1978.

DEFORD, FRANK. *There She Is: The Life and Times of Miss America*. New York: Viking, 1971.

GALLO, MAX. *The Poster in History*. New York: McGraw-Hill, 1974.

GOULDEN, JOSEPH C. *The Best Years: 1945–1950*. New York: Atheneum, 1976.

HOWE, IRVING. *World of Our Fathers*. New York: Simon & Schuster, 1976.

LEVI, VICKI GOLD, and EISENBERG, LEE. *Atlantic City: 125 Years of Ocean Madness*. New York: Clarkson N. Potter, 1979.

LEVINE, SUZANNE, and DWORKIN, SUSAN. *She's Nobody's Baby*. New York: Simon and Schuster, 1983.

Selected Bibliography

MEIER, AUGUST, and RUDWICK, ELIOTT M. *From Plantation to Ghetto.* New York: Hill & Wang, 1966.

MILLER, ALICE. *The Drama of the Gifted Child.* New York: Basic Books, 1981.

MORRIS, JAN. *Manhattan '45.* New York: Oxford University Press, 1987.

O'NEILL, WILLIAM L. *American High: The Years of Confidence, 1945–1960.* New York: The Free Press, 1986.

PERRETT, GEOFFREY. *A Dream of Greatness: The American People 1945–1963.* New York: Coward, McCann & Geoghegan, 1979.

RHODES, RICHARD. *The Making of the Atomic Bomb.* New York: Simon & Schuster, 1986.

SCHERMAN, DAVID. E. (ed.). *Life Goes to the Movies.* New York: Time-Life Books, 1975.

STEIGMAN, BENJAMIN M. *Accent on Talent: New York's High School of Music and Art.* Detroit: Wayne State University Press, 1964.

STEMBER, CHARLES HERBERT, et al. *Jews in the Mind of America.* New York: Basic Books, 1966.

WYMAN, DAVID S. *The Abandonment of the Jews: America and the Holocaust, 1941–1945.* New York: Pantheon, 1984.

LINGEMAN, RICHARD R. *Don't You Know There's a War On?: The American Home Front, 1941–1945.* New York: G. P. Putnam's Sons, 1970.

REED, WALT and ROGER. *The Illustrator in America, 1880–1980.* New York: Madison Square Press, 1984.

INDEX